HEROES & HISTORY

Voices from the NHL's past!

STAN & SHIRLEY FISCHLER

McGraw-Hill Ryerson
Toronto   Montreal

First published in 1994 by
McGraw-Hill Ryerson Ltd.
300 Water Street
Whitby, Ontario, Canada
L1N 9B6

1 2 3 4 5 6 7 8 9 0 Q P 3 2 10 9 8 7 6 5 4

Canadian Cataloguing in Publication Data

Fischler, Stan, 1932-
   Heroes & history : voices from NHL's past

ISBN 0-07-551639-X

1. Hockey players — Interviews.   2. Hockey —
History.   3. National Hockey League — History.
I. Fischler, Shirley.   II. Title.

GV848.5.AIF5 1993   796.962′092′2   C93-095394-0

Cover photographs used by permission of The Hockey Hall
of Fame.

Inside photographs used by permission of The Hockey Hall of
Fame, Toronto, Canada

Publisher: Donald S. Broad
Cover design: Dave Hader/Studio Conceptions

Editorial services provided by Word Guild, Toronto

Printed and bound in Canada

CONTENTS

ABOUT THE AUTHORS **iv**
INTRODUCTION **v**

I

THE GREATS WHO ARE GONE 1

Chapter   1/   CYCLONE TAYLOR 3
Chapter   2/   EDOUARD "NEWSY" LALONDE 9
Chapter   3/   BILL DURNAN 15
Chapter   4/   COOPER SMEATON 29
Chapter   5/   BOBBY HEWITSON 37
Chapter   6/   JOE PRIMEAU 45
Chapter   7/   JOHNNY GAGNON 57
Chapter   8/   EBBIE GOODFELLOW 69
Chapter   9/   BABE PRATT 81
Chapter 10/   FRANK FREDERICKSON 91
Chapter 11/   FRANK BOUCHER 101

II

THEY CAN STILL LACE 'EM UP 111

Chapter 12/   ED SANDFORD 113
Chapter 13/   ROD GILBERT 121
Chapter 14/   EDDIE MIO 131
Chapter 15/   BOB NYSTROM 137
Chapter 16/   JOHN DAVIDSON 141
Chapter 17/   REG FLEMING 157
Chapter 18/   MAURICE RICHARD 165
Chapter 19/   BILL CHADWICK 175
Chapter 20/   ULF NILSSON 187

STAN AND SHIRLEY FISCHLER have authored the highly-acclaimed *Hockey Encyclopedia* which is universally regarded as the bible of the sport. A professional journalist since 1954, Fischler has written for *Sports Illustrated, The New York Times, Inside Sports, Maclean's* and *Sport* magazines. He has authored a syndicated column "Inside Sports" for the *Toronto Star* Syndicate — now in its 20th year. Fischler also writes two weekly columns for *The Hockey News* and also appears regularly in *Hockey Digest* and *Inside Hockey* magazines. He is regarded as the dean of North American hockey authors. Stan and Shirley live in Manhattan with their family.

INTRODUCTION

In 1954, when I started my first full-time hockey job as a publicist for the New York Rangers, I began interviewing players. Some of the interviews were done in a formal manner; others were on a casual basis.

It was quite common for all manner of hockey people to drift into the Rangers' press office. Sometimes the visitors were out-of-town newspapermen and, on other occasions, hockey executives, coaches and managers. Even the legendary Howard Cosell would drop in for a chat. Naturally, hockey stories flowed as freely as the Hudson River, which the Garden overlooked from its West-side location. Such rollicking characters as Rangers' coach Frank Boucher, referee Bill Chadwick and legendary newspapermen like James "Thirsty Jim" Burchard delighted us with their stories. It was during that time that I originally got the idea of collecting hockey stories and writing an oral history. At the time, it was merely an idea and not backed by so essential a piece of modern technology — a workable tape recorder.

In time — after I became a full-time hockey journalist — I took this challenge more seriously and started saving most of my interviews. In 1968, after getting married, I began a formal pursuit of the oral history project. During a trip to the Northwest, my wife, Shirley, and I arranged a series of interviews with legendary hockey characters.

The quest to obtain these historic interviews took us to many diverse venues. For instance, on another trip, we dined with the legendary Maurice Richard in Old Montreal, and later savored the tales of Eddie Shore, Lorne Carr and Milt Schmidt. Over the years these interviews were collected and transcribed, and some made print years ago in Those Were the Days.

Since those early interviews, every one of the "oldtimers" has passed away, except for Richard and Chadwick.

Stan Fischler
New York, 1993

In February of 1968 Stan Fischler and I were married, and in April of that year my first hockey piece appeared — a full page on the women's section of the Toronto Daily Star — about hockey wives.

A quarter-century love affair with hockey had begun, and it had come about because I was a sucker for a good story.

A mere eight days after our wedding, the New York Rangers played their last game in the old Madison Square Garden. A week later, they opened in the New Garden, with much ceremony and fanfare. The ceremonies included the appearance of many former stars, particularly former Ranger stars. On that night I met Frank Boucher, the Cook Brothers, and several former Ranger captains such as Camille "The Eel" Henry and George "Red" Sullivan.

After the game, Stan and I went out with Boucher, Henry and a former Montreal Canadien, Aurel Joliat. All night I listened to the tales of some of the finest men who ever put stick to puck.

Joliat was actually present on that frigid night that the victorious Canadiens left the fabled Stanley Cup sitting by the side of the frozen Rideau Canal in Ottawa. Frank Boucher was a Ranger the night that Lester "The Silver Fox" Patrick, coach and GM of the Blueshirts, climbed between the pipes at age 42 and helped the Rangers to win a crucial game.

One reason why each fan loves a sport is because of the living history of the game. Every American kid who is a baseball fan loves the game not just because he can watch the pitching-batting duel on TV, or because Dad takes him to a real game — or even because he plays the sport. Part of the game is collecting cards, reading the stories and hearing the "oldtimers" talk about the good old days. For Canadian kids, there is the same rich history in hockey.

Here I was, soaking up the marvelous adventures of a bygone era in hockey, a rare opportunity for a young woman from the States who had only witnessed her first NHL game a few months before.

Hearing the tales and sagas were what attracted me to the game from the beginning: not simply the speed, beauty and finesse. Certainly I did get to enjoy those elements of hockey, despite the fact that it was the first season of expansion and experts were already shedding copious quantities of salt water over the "watering down of the game." But it was listening to oral histories of the sport and the people who had once played it that formed the bedrock of my love affair with hockey.

The summer between the 1967-68 and 1968-69 seasons gave us even greater opportunities to absorb the flavor and drama of hockey, through oral histories. Stan and I went to the West Coast to visit my family and, while there, arranged to do lengthy taped interviews with three living legends of the game: Frank "Cyclone" Taylor, Walter "Babe" Pratt and Frank Frederickson — Hall of Famers, all.

Over these subsequent 25 years, there have been hundreds more lengthy talks with the great men who have enriched the game of ice hockey, and the essence of some of those talks are presented in the following pages. We have attempted to make the narrative flow, in order to simply tell the tales, as they were told to us. If the details were forgotten, or misremembered, we have, wherever possible, done research to insert numbers or dates.

Shirley Fischler
New York, 1993

PART I

THE GREATS
WHO ARE GONE

Cyclone Taylor   **(Hockey Hall of Fame)**

Chapter 1

CYCLONE TAYLOR

Born on June 23, 1883, in Tara, Ontario, Fred Taylor was retired in the city of Vancouver, British Columbia, when we talked to him in September of 1968. The oldest living member of the Hockey Hall of Fame at that time, he was tiny and frail, but very alert. Taylor's ongoing interest in hockey was obvious by the several telephone calls he received from members of the B.C. Amateur Hockey Association during our visit.

Although he appeared several times to be on the verge of criticizing the modern game of hockey, Taylor opted instead for diplomacy, saying only, "I still love the game, and I'm glad to help the youngsters whenever I can."

Cyclone Taylor died on June 9, 1979, less than two weeks from his 96th birthday, a man who had watched the game of hockey move from the seven-man rover game of his youth, wearing little or no equipment — to the modern game of plastic, padding, slapshots and Wayne Gretzky.

I grew up in Listowel, Ontario, which was then a small town of about 2,500 souls, not far from Stratford, where they have that annual Shakespeare Festival. At that time Stratford was very small, but it was considered one of the best hockey towns in all of Canada. Remember Howie Morenz, called the "Stratford Streak"? . . . one of the best.

This was Stratford and the game of hockey as it was at the turn of the century, when the world was a far different place. Even the weather was different then; the whole world seemed to be frozen solid and snow-covered for more than five months of the year. In fact, I could skate from home to school nearly all winter, so that skating became as natural as walking to me.

There were outdoor rinks all over my hometown of Listowel, but I didn't really come into my own until I began to play for Stratford in 1902, at the age of 19. We played in a league with neighboring towns like Palmerston, Harrison, Mount Forest and Mitchell. People began to notice my style of play, and in 1904 I was invited to Portage-la-Prairie to play in the Manitoba Senior Amateur League.

Remember, the NHL didn't exist at this time and professional hockey of any kind was just beginning. Amateur hockey was supreme, and the Manitoba League was one of the most competitive on the continent. We played against the famous Rat Portage club, two teams from Winnipeg and a couple of others. At first I played left wing, but soon I switched to a position they don't have today, called "rover." At that time hockey was a seven-man game: a goaltender, two defensemen, three forwards and the rover. The extra man was out there to either help the defense, or move up and work with the forwards. In short, he roved, going wherever he was needed most. For that reason, he had to be one of the best men on the ice.

As I said, professional hockey was just starting up. Ironically, it was a league based mostly in the States that actually first called itself professional. The cities that had teams were Pittsburgh; Houghton, Calumet and Sault Ste. Marie, Michigan; and Sault Ste. Marie, Ontario. But the players were almost 100 per cent Canadian.

It was actually a couple of buddies of mine who spread the game of hockey in the States. They attended dental school in Detroit, then decided to stay in the U.S. and start a practice. They were both hockey lovers, so they picked Houghton to set up shop, and decided to organize a hockey team in addition to filling teeth. Houghton was really frigid in the winter, so they didn't need a rink with artificial ice — the natural thing was just fine. The new professional league would have done well, since hockey was already popular in all of those cities, except for the "depression" of 1907. Northern Michigan was copper country and for some reason the bottom fell out of the copper market that year, and stayed dead for more than a year. The whole area sank into a big economic pit and the hockey league had to suspend operations.

By that time there were teams in Montreal, Toronto, Ottawa and Quebec that were glad to take the better players who had been cast adrift with the folding of the league. These players ended up getting paid pretty good, too. Of course, their salaries wouldn't even pay the shoeshine bill for one of today's stars. Depending on the player, a salary would run from $1,200 to $2,500, and it wasn't just talent that determined the pay. Just like today, a player's ability to negotiate was almost as important as his performance, only now it's agents who do the negotiating.

By 1910 I had become a pro, too. I was playing for a team called the Renfrew [Ontario] Millionaires, for $5,260, the most ever paid a hockey player up until then. If I had been one of those good negotiators, I could've gotten $10,000 — a real fortune then, because they wanted me real bad.

There was a reason why I was in such demand then. I had already built a reputation for myself, and was lucky enough to have acquired the catchy nickname, "Cyclone."

This all came about in 1907, after I'd been invited to play for Ottawa in a fine new arena which was distinguished not only for its size — it held about 7,000 people — but also because the governor general of Canada, His Honour Earl Grey, and members of Parliament liked to attend games there. In fact, the governor general was at the opening of the rink in December 1907, when we played the Montreal Wanderers.

The place was packed that night, because the Wanderers were the Stanley Cup champions (remember, even though the NHL didn't exist yet, the Stanley Cup had been the emblem of hockey supremacy — first amateur, then professional for years already), and a big attraction. Also, there was the big fuss over the new arena, and over me.

For this particular game I was moved back to defense instead of playing rover or a forward position. The Ottawa coach felt I could play defense, and the results made him look good. We beat Montreal, 8-5, and I scored five goals on individual rushes, the way Bobby Orr did a half-century later.

One of the newspapermen covering that game was Malcolm Bryce, sports editor of the *Ottawa Free Press*. Hockey received big coverage in those days, and the *Free Press* devoted an entire page to the game, about which Bryce wrote: "I understand that this boy, Taylor, was nicknamed 'Tornado' when he played in Manitoba. And I further understand that when he moved into the International League they called him 'Whirlwind.' But starting today, based on his performance last night, I am re-christening him 'Cyclone' Taylor."

That wasn't the only nickname I got; it was just the one that stuck over the years. Once when we played an exhibition game in New York somebody called me "The Jim Jeffries of the Ice," after the boxer. Naturally this made me feel great, because I was young at the time and very impressionable. But "Cyclone" fit best.

The game truly was a completely different phenomenon back then. For one thing, we all played the entire 60 minutes without substitutes, and it didn't seem tiring. For another thing, we were highly motivated. Players were terrifically dedicated and there was a tendency to magnify the importance of the game, because no television, radio, few cars and very few picture shows existed then. We lived in the arenas in winter and the parks in summer.

One of the myths of how I came to be called "Cyclone" was that I once scored a goal while skating backwards, but that simply isn't true. Even though there were, for many years, a lot of elderly people in Ontario who would swear they saw it happen, it's just one of those stories that was blown up.

Shooting a puck was considerably different then, too. For one thing, there was no such thing as a slapshot. Our only shot was the basic wrist shot, pretty damaging and 10 times more accurate than the slapshot. But in those days, 90 per cent of the game was skating and 2 per cent stickhandling; the rest was courage and conditioning. That's my theory, anyway.

I don't think the modern player skates any faster than I did. Today's game just looks faster because of the passes and all that lateral movement. We'd hold onto the puck until we could give it to a teammate, or until the puck was taken away from us.

It was a rough game, and I played 18 years of it with the pros — 60 minutes a game — and I never lost a tooth or got a scar. My style was skating, and I always felt that once I passed an opponent, I didn't have to worry about him anymore. I made no attempt to be rough or dirty. I'd have been foolish to try, because I was too small and didn't have any enemies anyway — why would I want to make any?

But it was easy to have trouble when you were on the ice for the whole 60 minutes, getting hit after hit. The physical aspect would grow on you. Today, players hit each other one minute, but they're pulled off the ice the next, and they cool down. And it's not to say we didn't have some genuine tough ones back then. "Bad" Joe Hall was an excitable type. If he heard before a game that someone was out to get him on the ice, he'd get charged up and go after that person first thing.

The brothers, Lester and Frank Patrick, were really good players then. Lester was a classical player in every phase of the game, whereas Frank was mainly strong on defense. But even Frank could carry the puck from one end of the rink to the other if he had to, and he often did. There wasn't so much of a distinction between stay-at-home and rushing types as there is today. You'd think that Bobby Orr had invented the rushing defenseman style, but it was actually pretty common in the early days of hockey. In fact, I'd say that Orr had re-invented the rover position, and that would be more accurate — only now they call it the offensive defenseman.

But to get back to Lester and Frank Patrick, they inadvertently brought about the change in hockey from a seven-man game to a six-man game, as it is today. The family had moved to British Columbia and Lester, Frank and their father decided to build some rinks and start a league out on the West Coast. The only problem was, they couldn't get the Eastern owners to cooperate and yield up some players. So Frank went out and simply raided the East, getting 25 of the best players around. This shrank the talent pool out East so badly that they decided to play without a rover, and six-man hockey was born. Meanwhile, I went out West and we continued to play seven-man hockey for years, until 1925, in fact.

Every year the best teams from the two leagues would compete for the Stanley Cup. Regardless of which team held the Cup, it was to be played for in the West in odd years and in the East on even ones. My team, the Millionaires, now out of Vancouver, challenged Ottawa, and in 1915 the first Stanley Cup finals west of Winnipeg were played. One of our defensemen, Griffis, was injured, and the club owner, Frank Patrick, tried to sneak brother Lester — who had been an All-Star with the Victoria [B.C.] club — aboard as a substitute. Ottawa screamed bloody murder and Frank didn't make an issue out of it; he knew we had a really great club that year.

To give you an idea of how great the Vancouver Millionaires of 1915 were, I scored two goals in the first game (we won 6-2) and three goals in the second (we won 8-3), and I wasn't even the star of either game! Then, in the third and final game, they managed to hold me to only one point, my linemate Mickey Mackay got three, and teammate Barney Stanley took the day with four points. We massacred them, 12-3.

To put the game in perspective, each of us was awarded $300 for winning that Cup, while the Ottawa guys each got $200! I was the high scorer of the series with six goals (they hadn't started to award assists yet!), but there was no such thing as scoring bonuses or trophies.

We never won the Cup again, but I had some more good years with the Millionaires. Once I scored six goals in a game against Victoria (February 1, 1916), and in 1918, in a Cup series against Toronto, I scored seven goals in five games. I was getting kind of old by that time [35 in 1918], but it just seemed to get easier! Finally, after I missed almost half of the 1920-21 season, I decided to retire. I played one last game in 1923, when I was 40 years old, and I could just feel that I couldn't do some of the things I used to.

Most players supplemented their hockey income with side or off-season jobs. There were always people who owned stores and factories who'd help you earn a little money and would give you a job and allow you time off to play hockey. In fact, most of us used hockey as a stepping stone to other things.

Of course, there wasn't the chance to earn the really big money like NHL superstars do today. The first offer I ever had to endorse anything was from an underwear firm, but my wife, who was a hockey fan, didn't want me parading around half naked, so I dropped the idea. There just weren't the advertising opportunities. But players were recognized anyway, and many of them rose to become big-time business moguls or members of Parliament.

Today the game has more polish and definitely gets more coverage, but I don't think I'd like to play the game now. I was used to going on at the start of the game and playing to the finish. I think any man between the ages of 18 and 35 who can't play 60 minutes of hockey — well, he just doesn't want to play, that's all. They do it in soccer football in England, and that's a strenuous game, with all that running from one end of the field to the other, taking body checks along the way.

We had some great players in my day, and they'd have been stars in the NHL today, I'm sure. But, by the same token, today's super-stars would have been great when I was out there on the ice.

Chapter 2

EDOUARD "NEWSY" LALONDE

When one recounts the legend of the Canadiens, the name of Edouard Lalonde immediately comes to the fore because of his association with the original Montreal club and the excellence he brought to the game of hockey.

Nicknamed "Newsy" while he briefly held a job in a newsprint plant, Lalonde was an 18-year-old in Sault Ste. Marie, Ontario when he made his first impact in the ice wars.

Professional hockey was in its infancy when Lalonde was signed by Les Canadiens in 1910. By his second season in Montreal, Newsy had established himself as a star, leading the Habs in scoring with 16 goals in 16 games while the Canadiens finished second.

A fearsome performer, Lalonde was an intimidating personality during an era when hockey was played in a more frontier-like ambience than it is today. Newsy was not particular about his foes. He frequently clashed with Joe Hall, whose nickname was "Bad" — not because of his gentility.

During an especially rugged game with the Montreal Wanderers, Lalonde virtually compacted Odie Cleghorn into the boards with a vicious body check. Sprague Cleghorn, Odie's brother, was so disturbed by the action that he pursued Lalonde, smashed Newsy across the forehead with his stick and nearly took out one of Newsy's eyes.

Lalonde was a member of the Canadiens' early Stanley Cup-winning clubs, and played at a high level through the 1921-22 season. When his career appeared to be on the downside, club owner Leo Dandurand traded 36-year-old Newsy to the Saskatoon Sheiks for Aurel Joliat who would become one of the Habs' finest players.

Newsy Lalonde   **(Hockey Hall of Fame)**

As both coach and player for the Sheiks, Lalonde continued to excel, but finally hung up his skates to become coach of the New York Americans, the first NHL club in Manhattan. The move did not sit well with all the Amerks, some of whom remembered Lalonde as a mean critter. "He was," said Jakie Forbes of the Americans, "the dirtiest sonofabitch I ever played against."

One night Lalonde discovered his players partying after a loss and suitably scolded them. When Alex McKinnon shot back that Newsy was a bum coach, Lalonde kayoed him with one punch and then offered, "Anybody else?" There were no takers.

In 1932, Lalonde returned to Montreal where he coached the Canadiens through 1935, although the relationship between Newsy and the Habs was no more cordial than it had been in New York. Newsy was replaced as coach after 16 games of the 1934-35 season after which they had a disappointing 5-8-3 record.

Lalonde's name was frequently mentioned long after he left the NHL scene and always carried a romantic touch to it because of Newsy's long-time association with the game. In his travels across Canada, Stan Fischler sought an interview with Lalonde and finally located him in the summer of 1970 at a nursing home in Montreal.

The Hall of Famer, who was born in 1887 at Cornwall, Ontario, seemed lonely and somewhat hostile to the visitor he had never before met. At first he had difficulty recalling incidents that had taken place more than a half-century earlier, but would suddenly revive when he did recall pleasant moments. It was, however, the most difficult of any encounter Fischler had during the course of collecting the oral histories. On November 21, 1970, less than a half-year after the interview, Lalonde died.

If you think hockey is a tough game nowadays, son, you have no idea what toughness is all about. There were some real "beauts" back in the early days — Bad Joe Hall of Quebec, Sprague Cleghorn of the Canadiens, and Cully Wilson who played for lots of teams including Toronto, Seattle and Calgary.

When Wilson played for Calgary in 1925, he hit Dick Irvin so hard in the mouth that Dick's teeth were practically embedded in his tongue. Irvin was then a star with Regina and anyone who knew Dick realized that he wouldn't take that kind of guff from anyone.

After Wilson got five minutes for high-sticking, Irvin skated over to Cully at the penalty box and smashed him right over the head with his stick. Wilson was unconscious; out cold. Cully took enough stitches in him to weave an Indian blanket.

Life was a lot tougher for us than it is for the hockey players nowadays, and that explains why we behaved differently. My family came from Cornwall, Ontario, where I was born, and we didn't have much money. My father owned a small shoestore while my mother took care of the house. They were both French-Canadian, although I could speak a little English when I was young.

I didn't get my first pair of skates until my 13th birthday. We didn't have a rink in our neighborhood so we played wherever there was ice — the street, a pond, whatever. After a while I really started to get good at it and by the time I was 18 a couple of men asked me if I wanted to become a professional hockey player.

In those days the game wasn't organized the way it is today, but there was one outfit called the International Pro League that had quite a few good teams, and one of them was in Sault Ste. Marie, Ontario. I got an offer to play for them and accepted. My parents were quite willing to let me play; my mother occasionally would watch me play while my father wasn't much interested.

The team in the Soo offered me something like $50 a week to play for them which, in those times, just after the turn of the century, was pretty good money and a lot more than people were making where I came from. I gladly accepted, although I must admit that some of my friends warned me that I would be 'way over my head and would get myself killed in the pro league.

After listening to the warning, I bought myself a one-way train ticket to Sault Ste. Marie. We left Cornwall at night, rolled west all the way across Ontario and steamed into The Soo about 24 hours later. Since I didn't have much money to my name, I didn't indulge in a sleeping car berth. I got a coach seat and made the best of it, which meant that I didn't sleep a wink.

When I got to the rink and met the team I was one frightened young man. I was given a pair of rugby pants, a shirt that was too long, some stockings that looked a dozen years old and skates that would fit an elephant. The coach told me that I wouldn't get on the ice unless someone else on the team got hurt, because 'way back then everybody played the full 60 minutes.

The longer I stayed, the more I wanted to play; it didn't matter which position. I could play center, or rover — that's when they still had six skaters and a goaltender with the rover being the extra skater — and defense if necessary. The way hockey was played then, the rover was behind the center and he just stood there; he wasn't a scorer or a defenseman. Personally, I never felt there was much difference between being a center and a rover.

Finally, one of our players got hurt early in a game and I was sent in as a replacement. I scored two goals and we won the game, 3-1.

The hockey in that era was a whole lot different than it is today. At that time defensemen frequently would hoist the puck up in the air and hurl it down the rink instead of carrying it along the ice. Lester Patrick helped change that style of play, but there were still plenty of teams using the old throw-the-puck-in-the-air technique. Well, I figured I'd take advantage of it, and so I tried a little trick. When I saw a defenseman get ready for a lifter, I skated in front of him like a football player trying to block a kick and deflected the puck off my body.

That first time it worked; the puck bounced off me right near the net so all I had to do was turn around and flip it past the goalie. The second time was almost exactly the same; two deflections, two goals.

One night I scored nine goals during a game in Renfrew, Ontario. We were playing against Cobalt and beat them 17-2. I was playing center at the time and Cyclone Taylor was rover.

Over the years, many people have said that Cyclone once scored a goal skating backwards down the rink, but I don't know about that. I'm more inclined to think that he was looking the other way when he put it in. That's been done before; it's how I used to get a lot of my goals. I knew where I wanted to put the puck, but I never looked there.

Never, in my playing days, did I used the slapshot the way you see it used in the National Hockey League now, with the curved sticks and all. With us there was no other shot to use but the wrist shot. When a man makes a slapshot today it's more powerful than a wrist shot, but you can't place it in the same way. The modern player just shoots the puck in the general direction of the net and that's it. We knew where the puck was going and didn't have to look twice.

I can tell you a story about a guy who should have looked twice. It happened in the old International Pro League and we were making a trip to Calumet, Michigan, which then was quite a hockey center. I was nervous and some of my teammates were too, because Calumet was notorious for its rough fans.

Late in the game the score was tied, 3-3, and the other nervous kid and I started up the ice. I fed him a pass on right wing and the next thing I knew he turned on the steam and skated madly down his alley. The only trouble was that he seemed to be going too far on the right without much of an angle.

At the last second he got off a shot from a pretty bad spot and, of course, it missed. But he never looked at the net to see where the puck went. He just kept skating to the end boards, leaped over them, headed straight for the exit and disappeared. I figured he went to the dressing room, but when we got there after the game it was empty.

This got my curiosity going so I started looking all around the arena and finally came to the toilet. I had been shouting for the fellow and when I got there I noticed the door was shut so I called out again. This time the kid answered. He had run in figuring he'd be killed if he scored, and he was too afraid to even look back to see whether he had or not.

As I got more experience, I got less and less nervous and really began to enjoy professional hockey. The money was good and I was able to make some extra cash playing professional lacrosse. I played in Vancouver and got $6,000 for 12 games. That was in 1912. It came out to eight dollars a minute!

Hockey was the tougher game — much tougher. You'd think it was the other way around because of the swinging sticks in lacrosse, but nobody ever got hurt. In hockey it was different. One night Joe Hall nearly crushed my windpipe and I came back and almost broke his collarbone.

If you think that was bad, you should have seen Sprague Cleghorn in action. He said he once knocked out three players in one night in Ottawa. Then there was the time he got arrested in Toronto when he attacked me. But I went before the judge the next day and pleaded on his behalf. The judge let Sprague off with a small fine.

Sprague was as wild as they came. He once said that he had counted the number of stretcher-case fights he had been in and the grand total was 50. Imagine that! 50!

With all the fighting, though, my worst injury happened because of a simple accident. I was up with the Montreal Canadiens by this time and we were playing the Wanderers. A fellow named Stram was on his knees and I fell right on his skates.

When he stood up he tore my arch to pieces and also ripped the whole side of my leg with his skates. It was the worst I ever got; they had to sew up the artery first, then the arch. I don't think I played any more that year, and I still have a hole in my arch.

I'm not trying to say that there aren't tough guys in the modern game. After World War Two, I saw plenty of hockey and there were hitters like Ted Lindsay of the Red Wings and Bill Ezinicki of the Maple Leafs who could mix it up pretty good. One night, after Ezinicki got traded to the Bruins, they went at it in Detroit and Lindsay cut Eznincki for about 20-odd stitches. Looking back, I'd say the Dick Irvin-Cully Wilson brawl was a better one, but not by much.

What I'm saying is that I really liked the game in the early days and now it's so much different than it was when I played. I'll grant you that it's an entertaining game now; there's no question about it and I have no complaints. It's a lot faster because the players are changed more often. But I'll tell you, son, if I had the chance, I'd sure like to play this new kind of game and get the money they're getting today. I was a professional, you know.

Chapter 3

BILL DURNAN

In a way it's a pity that Bill Durnan played in the 1943-50 era rather than in the present-day video replay super-hype era where major media attention given to hockey.

Had Durnan played today, he might very well be hailed as the best goalie of all time.

A rare ambidextrous netminder, Durnan virtually owned the Vezina Trophy during his seven-year career in the National Hockey League. During that span Durnan annexed the Vezina no less than six times: 1944, 1945, 1946, 1947, 1949 and 1950. Likewise, Durnan also was named to the First All-Star team in each of those years.

Originally owned by the Maple Leafs, Durnan was buried in the Toronto system during some of the best years of his goaltending life. By the time the Canadiens rescued him, Durnan was all of 29 years old. Imagine if he had broken in at age 21!

But Durnan made the most of his relatively short career. The 6-foot-2, 200 pounder — oversized for his time — powered the Habs to first-place finishes four times and helped the Canadiens to Stanley Cup victories in 1944 and 1946.

Although the Montrealers were sprinkled with such impressive leaders as Maurice "Rocket" Richard and Emile "Butch" Bouchard, coach Dick Irvin thought so much of Durnan that he named him team captain.

During his time, Durnan played as flawlessly as a goaltender could in an era when netminders did not wear protective masks. Thanks to his ambidexterity, Bill was able to switch hands depending on the shot he was facing and so fool the shooter. (This was just before the blocker mitt was adopted by NHL goaltenders).

Through the late 1940s, Durnan retained his agility but experienced more and more tension before going on the ice until it reached the breaking point. During the 1949-50 playoff semi-final round, Durnan simply lost it

Bill Durnan   **(Imperial Oil—Turofsky Hockey Hall of Fame)**

and, after the third game, Bill pulled himself in favor of the younger Gerry McNeil. After the Canadiens were eliminated, Durnan retired.

Having watched Durnan play goal during his finest seasons, Stan Fischler was appalled at Bill's condition upon visiting him at his Toronto home in 1969. The once-peripatetic athlete was suffering from arthritis and could hardly move from one end of the apartment to another. Durnan was 53 years old at the time of the visit. Mrs. Durnan prepared a light meal while Fischler conducted the interview with Durnan.

Accommodating despite his affliction, Durnan was joined during the get-together by former Canadiens' teammate Murph Chamberlain. The result of the evening's dialogue is the following narrative.

Bill Durnan died in 1972.

Usually goaltenders wind up in the nets instead of on defense or as forwards because they were poor skaters as kids. That was partly the reason why I wound up as a goalie when I was nine years old. My mother had died four years before and my dad didn't have much money, but he worked hard, saved his pennies, and bought me a second-hand pair of skates for $1.50 which were about four sizes too big.

Our neighborhood team was the Westmoreland United Church in Toronto and I was a big kid when I tried out for them. Because they were grouping the players by weight and I was a big kid, they moved me into the nets. I guess they figured I couldn't keep up with the older boys who were good skaters and, since there was a lot of me to fill the net, it'd be hard for the opposition to score. Anyway, that's how I wound up as a goaltender and I've never regretted it.

My first lucky break was having a good coach, Steve Faulkner. He showed me how to switch my stick so I could play goal ambidextrously. He worked me by the hour until I had the technique down pat and we won five city championships in six years while I played for Westmoreland. I had more fun being a goaltender than most guys do as forwards; to me, stopping a puck seemed more satisfying than scoring goals.

Being a professional hockey player wasn't on my mind at the time. Those were the Dirty Thirties, and the big thing was making some money so you could eat. I know my father had been through hell after my mother died and the whole experience had made quite an impression on me. With my older brother and myself, Dad moved from boarding house to boarding house, and while he worked we went to school. When I came home I cooked for him, so I knew what hard times were all about.

I played for Steve Faulkner until I was 15 or 16 and learned something every game. His idea of switching the stick hand really impressed me when I played against better teams, since the goalie always keeps his catching hand out toward the big part of the net. In those days I had fingered gloves on each hand, so it was a lot easier to switch than it would be now. Of course, learning this style was pretty hard at first; I was a right-handed shot and I threw right. Normally, I'd hold my stick in my left hand as a goaltender — my right would be my catching hand. Steve would urge me to change as often as possible to get the feel of it. At first it felt as though I was transferring a telephone pole from one hand to the other, but after a while I'd hardly realize I was doing it. Soon I noticed the opposition was unaware that I was switching hands, and later on when I was in the NHL it often took years before the other guys knew I was ambidextrous.

After the Westmorelands, my next club was the North Toronto Juniors, a farm team of a farm team of the Toronto Maple Leafs. We were just a bunch of kids off the street who had made it to the first round of the playoffs and along the way had made an impression on a few people. One of them was Red Burnett, the hockey writer for *The Toronto Daily Star*. He recommended me to the coach of the Sudbury, Ontario, junior team who invited me up to play for them the following year.

I must've played well there, because the Leafs signed an agreement with me and I planned to go to their training camp that fall. I was 20 at the time, playing a lot of softball and feeling pretty good about life. But that summer I spent a weekend at Wasaga Beach and got into a wrestling match with a buddy; unfortunately, I wound up ripping my knee very badly. That's when I got hurt mentally as well as physically.

When the Leafs found out about my injury they dropped me and I vowed that even when I got better never would I play pro hockey. I was disillusioned and figured if that was the kind of treatment I was to get, then hell, I didn't want any part of it. Besides, there wasn't much money involved; in those days they weren't paying anywhere near the money to be had today. So, I quit altogether. Playing in the NHL was about as far from my mind as swimming on Mars.

The kid and his dreams were shot. When my knee got better I took a job at a gold mining mill in Kirkland Lake, a city of about 20,000 in northern Ontario which turned out to be a terrific hockey town. I played between shifts at the mill and our club — the Blue Devils — was really strong, strong enough to win the Allan Cup [senior championship of Canada] in 1940. That success was really something out of the blue because I had gone up there just to pass the winter and earn some money at the mine, but after we won the championship I moved down to Montreal. There I worked in the accounting department of Canadian Car and Foundry Company and played goal for the Montreal Royals in the Quebec Senior League, a pretty fast one in those days.

My boss was Len Peto, who was also a director with the Canadiens and a man who knew his hockey. I hadn't given the NHL a second thought; that incident with the Leafs was still sharp in my mind and I never wanted to go pro. Money wasn't a problem any more; I had a good job and was making a little extra from the Royals, so everything was just fine until Peto started pressuring me to sign with the Canadiens. This was in October 1943, when I was 29.

I wasn't ordered to sign, but there's no question that some stress was put on me, which I resisted at first. Somehow I managed to hold out until the day of the opening game and got the Canadiens' management to give into my wishes. I signed for the huge sum of $4,200 and found myself on a hockey team just beginning to jell.

Take Rocket Richard; he hadn't become the "Rocket" yet. As a matter of fact, at first he was a rather sickly looking guy whose position management couldn't decide upon. We had an exhibition game in Cornwall, Ontario, and coach Dick Irvin needed a right wing for Elmer Lach and Toe Blake. They placed the Rocket there and he scored three goals; he was never changed after that.

On defense we had big Butch Bouchard, all meat and muscle, who was an awkward, tough kid. And Mike McMahon, a rolypoly who would scare the hell out of me whenever he played the point; I always expected the other team to jab the puck away from him and come in on me all alone. Then there was Leo Lamoureux, a real character.

Leo was a worry wart: if something was going to happen, it would be to him. He was also always in and out of mischief, along with his pal Murph Chamberlain. They gave Irvin so many headaches between them that Dick actually missed them once they were gone. Irvin used to say: "Geez, if we could only get some guys on this team who could get in trouble like those two we'd be all right."

Once while we were on the road, Leo phoned the guys from his hotel room. From his window he could see a couple in a room across the courtyard; whatever they were doing, it was obviously a little on the warm side since they'd raise and lower the window blinds every so often.

We found out what room they were in, and as soon as the blinds would go down we'd give them a minute, then phone the room and say, "Is Mary there?" The guy would answer, "There's no Mary here!" We went through every girl's name imaginable and kept asking for them; that poor guy must have been going crazy. We also had the house dick up at least a dozen times. Finally, Leo took one of the floor lamps and flashed it over there through our open window; he damn near fell a nice four-storey flop while he was leaning out.

On the ice we were a little more serious. I was improving as we went along and so was the rest of the team. The guy who kept us all in line was Irvin. He considered coaching a real *profession*, and it showed through his actions; he lived it. Irvin was proud of what he did and refused to be known as just a guy who looked after a bunch of weekend revelers.

Dick was a tremendous psychologist. It always amazed me that he never swore — anybody associated with a bunch of dodos who'd go hairy now and then would have to curse once in a while. But Dick never drank and he never swore, but he could dress you down and make you crawl. He never played favorites either, and that went for the Rocket, too.

One night in Detroit he benched Richard for two periods, at a time when the Rocket was Mister Big. Dick sent everybody else out on the ice and we all knew the Rocket was fuming. Finally, in the third period he put Richard on the ice; it was like letting a hungry lion out of his cage. That Rocket hit everybody but me.

Irvin once got on me for gaining too much weight. He took me aside and said the difference between a goal and no goal was about four ounces. I'd had a bad training camp as I always did, but this time I really stunk. Dick came to my room and talked about my wife, two girls, and this, that, and the other thing. I sat there just wishing he'd swear at me or do something to get me mad.

He said only the truth and after 45 minutes alone with Irvin I could've walked right through the door for him. Some of the things he told me were hard to take, but I knew in my heart he was right and just couldn't argue with him.

Some guys reacted to Irvin a little more nervously than I did. One afternoon before a game Dick gave us a bit of a tongue-lashing and afterwards Toe Blake sidled over to me and said, "Wait for me after the game." When we got on the ice that night he came around again, "Don't forget; wait for me." Same thing after the second period and I said, "Yeah, yeah, I'll wait." By then I was getting a little mad about this but later realized that Blake was worried about me. He figured I was a rookie and would be upset about Irvin's reprimand.

So, after the game we went out to have a few beers and soon it was past 1 a.m., our curfew on this particular trip. Meanwhile, Toe kept drinking and drinking and I tried to get him back to our hotel in one piece. I finally hauled him up to the front of the hotel and leaned him against the building while I ran in to check the lobby to see if Irvin was there. I came back just in time to catch Blake before he fell forward. Then, I managed to sneak him up to his room without Irvin knowing about it. All this because Blake was worried over me, a rookie, going bonkers after the coach's tongue-lashing.

Irvin's whole point was the pride in being a professional. He believed that was the difference between a top star and a guy who isn't one. The player who doesn't look after himself isn't going to be as good. Rocket was the perfect example; he just wanted to be number one. The star — whether it was hockey or softball. His linemate Toe Blake was the same way. You could take Blake apart — shooting, skating, anything — and he'd be no better than the guy around the corner, but Toe led the league in scoring one year and helped set records for the Punch Line. It was all a result of his tremendous desire to be something.

I had to do a little overcoming myself because of that knee injury I had as a youngster. At first I tried moving to the spot where I thought the puck would go before the shot, but that soon hurt my game. I realized I had to steel myself to say, "I can go there or there or there when the guy shoots it." But in all the years I played, I never classified opposition shooters according to who gave me the most trouble and stuff like that. Everybody in the league could score on me if they shot for certain places, so I had to prepare myself for those shots. When you start anticipating, you lose.

Irvin gave me a little more responsibility than most goaltenders by naming me captain of the Canadiens. In those days a captain could complain more to referees than now. One of my duties was to report back to the coach as to what was happening on the ice when something went wrong. Well, I looked a little stupid if there was a bad call against us — me with all those pads and the big stick, chasing after the referee and then running to the bench to hear Irvin. I used to have a few run-ins with ref Bill Chadwick, but he had a knack of saying, "Hey, Bill, where are you going to eat after the game?" whenever I'd reacted my most heatedly. That would completely distract me and I'd wind up flabbergasted.

We all had our own ways of training. Every new season I swore I hadn't played the year before and had to learn everything all over again. I don't know why but I was never cocky; I wasn't ever really sure of myself. It just seemed that goaltending was a terribly hard job every fall come training time.

The Rocket would hang around with Larry Moquin, the professional wrestler, when he trained. Larry taught Rocket all the holds and things, then Rocket would try them out on us and at times he'd almost break your arm. Not intentionally, of course; he was just so strong. He sure put those lessons to good use on the ice when anybody got tough with him. The fight that really stands out happened sometime in March 1947 at Madison Square Garden; we had played a home-and-home set with the Rangers and were fighting them for a playoff berth.

It started when one of the Rangers clobbered our defenseman Kenny Reardon in the mouth with a stick. When Kenny went off the ice for repairs, somebody on the Ranger bench said something to him and then there was a fuss and suddenly both benches emptied onto the ice and everybody was swinging.

Normally, I stayed out of fights because goalies, as a rule, are neutral, but by this time everybody was in it including the New York goalie, Chuck Rayner. So I skated over to look for Bill Moe, the Rangers defenseman, since there was no love lost between us. I remember finally getting him over by the fence and not being able to swing. It seemed the two of us stood there for about three minutes threatening each other, and then he poked me once and our battle was over. Meanwhile, the main fight kept going on and on and nobody could break it up. It would seem to peter out five or six times and then bust out all over again. People were everywhere on the ice; there was even a cop who kept saying, "Break it up, break it up, the fans are coming down from the stands."

Sometimes we'd get into fights among ourselves. Once, on a trip home to Montreal from Detroit, the Rocket and Butch Bouchard got into an argument. It was a wild train ride since it was the end of the season. Every time the train stopped we took on more beer. Joe Carveth was with us at the time and he'd be at the door to take the suds since he was the guy who wired ahead for the stuff. After a while we were walking on beer and that's when the Rocket and Butch had their go.

Nobody was idolized in our club the way the Rocket was, especially among the French-Canadian fans in Quebec. I remember one incident that you wouldn't believe, but I was actually there and saw it happen. We were playing an exhibition game in Rimouski, which is somewhere up the St. Lawrence River. Before the game Richard, myself and a few other players took a walk through the town.

We hadn't gotten very far when a married woman and at least four other gals ran up the Rocket and began talking to him in French. I could understand quite a bit of the language and they were telling Rocket to come upstairs with them and they'd give him something to remember the town by. There was no blushing, giggling, or anything like that. I honestly think if he had said okay they'd have rushed upstairs with him and everybody else in town would be jealous of them.

Rocket was quite a man. On the ice he was all they ever said he was, and then some. He would get that puck at the blue line and go. Being a goaltender, I could hear the Forum crowd react to him better than the guys who were skating. Starting as a low hum — "m-m-m-m" — it would grow, and if Rocket scored a goal the roof came down.

One of the bum raps against him was that he'd just hang at the blue line and that's all. Actually, Rocket rarely scored a scrabbly goal. His were things of beauty, and in the last years of Blake and

Lach it was the Rocket who kept them in the league. Blake kept saying, "Geez, I hope Rocket keeps putting them in the net 'cause I'll be here 'til I'm 50."

I could see it all from the nets. Elmer would pass the puck to Blake and Toe wouldn't have it more than a second. He'd be looking all over: "Where's the Rocket? Where is he?" And he'd throw the Rocket a pass and watch him score. Then Toe would say, "Now, I get an assist."

Irvin appreciated Toe for his spirit and his stubborn streak. But he wouldn't spare Blake any more than he would the next fellow. There was a time when Toe was injured and the club wasn't going well; Toe could move around but wasn't able to play. What do you think Irvin did? He had Blake come all the way to New York with the team even though he knew Toe wouldn't be able to play. We had a game the night before and Dick was furious with the way he played. He wanted Blake along just so he could sit in on the pep talk in New York. Nothing else — just for that meeting!

Fans are fickle and funny. Nobody knows that better than me because I had my troubles with them in Montreal. I had played in the NHL for six seasons and won the Vezina Trophy in five of them, but the fans weren't always satisfied. I remember we ran into a slump in 1947 and the Forum people started chanting, "We want Bibeault! We want Bibeault!" They were asking for Paul Bibeault, who had played some goal for the Canadiens before me. They booed me and made me feel six inches high. I don't know whether you've ever heard 13,000 people all calling you the same bad name at the same time, but it sure makes a loud noise. In the dressing room after the game some newspapers quoted me as saying: "They can have Bibeault. I'm through. I'm quitting while I have my health and my nerves!"

I don't think I said the things they attributed to me — at least not in the sense they wound up printed. Nevertheless, I got my come-uppance, all right. Doug Smith, who was doing the Canadiens' play-by-play in those days, got on the air and started preaching; when I got home I put on the radio and heard him give it to me real good, he was so mad. I didn't quit and I did come back. Recalling the incident now, I realize that the fans pay their money and have a right to boo, but it was still hard for me to take.

When I got depressed Irvin would work on me. He was very influential and, like me, he loved his baseball, *really* loved it. Whenever we'd go on a road trip, Dick would make a point of visiting the ball park in whatever city we happened to play. He'd actually go out to see *the bloody empty field*, just for the chance to look at a major league ball park. Then he'd tell us about all the big-league ball players he'd met, like the Cooper Brothers, Mort and Walker, from the St. Louis Cardinals.

Dick would recall his conversations with them. "When you get a nine-run lead, do you ease up?" he'd ask Mort Cooper. The answer would be in the form of a pep talk. "No, sir," Cooper would say, "you just keep throwin' the ball, 'cause if you ease up and they get to you, you ain't gonna get started again. You just keep bearin' down."

Dick had a habit of staying out of our sight when we were carrying on, especially during the train trips when he knew we weren't bothering anyone but ourselves. On one of those long rides I can remember there was a big drinking thing going, and we were also indulging in little games like hiding clothes and maybe ripping a jacket or two. We had a big defenseman on the team named Roger Leger who didn't go for any of this stuff, so he went up to his berth and stayed there until he heard a lot of noise and got the notion they were tearing up his clothes.

He climbed out of his berth and started looking around until he found one of Butch Bouchard's expensive sport coats hanging in the smoker. Roger grabbed it by the two tails and tore it right up the middle. Then he went back to bed figuring he had evened things up. Actually, neither Butch — nor anybody else for that matter — had touched Roger's clothes. They were just hiding them.

Finally, Butch went back to the smoker and the first thing he saw was his jacket ripped up the middle. All Butch could say was: "Hey, that isn't fair. You gotta be *in it* to be ripped!"

Actually, Bouchard was a sweet guy. Even though he was French-Canadian he learned to speak English and had a habit of telling jokes to the English players that were God-awful. But Butch would always explain, "It just doesn't sound as good in English as it does in French."

After a while we developed the habit of ignoring Butch when he started to tell those lousy stories and, boy, did that get to him. If you wouldn't listen, he'd turn around, stand up against the wall, and mutter "B-b-b-b-b-b-b-b." One of the guys would then ask, "What are you doing, you big, dumb so-and-so?"

He'd smile and reply, "I often heard my mother say that when she was ignored she might as well talk to the wall."

We kidded Butch a lot in those days but, kidding aside, he was really one of our proud accomplishments. He's the only hockey player I know who's a self-made millionaire. I'm proud of that. At least I can say to these jerks who knock us for what happened to some hockey players after they quit that there was one guy who made himself a bundle, even though he couldn't tell a joke in English. But he worked at it as far back as the war days, since he was exempt from the draft because he was a bee farmer.

One day we went out to his farm and he pulled out a ledger to show us his eight-year profit-and-loss statement. In those eight years as a bee farmer in his worst year Butch still made a $3,000 profit. He actually made enough money from his bees to build an apartment house without putting in a downpayment.

I'll always remember the time we were riding on the train from Toronto to Montreal. Hearts was the card game on this particular day and I turned to Bouchard and said, "Butch, it's your play." He just sat there staring out the window. One of the other guys said, "The hell with him, let's go on with the game." But we all were fascinated with Butch and watched him for a good five minutes. He finally says, "Huh, huh, huh. What's up? What's up?"

I said, "It's your turn. What the hell are you looking out there for?" We were passing the shores of Lake Ontario at the time and he replied, "I was just thinking if I could have a beach like that in Montreal I'd make a million dollars." That's the way Butch's mind worked. Here we were in the middle of a hockey season and he's got sand on his mind!

Not that he wasn't a keen hockey player. They sure didn't come any better than Butch; nobody was more respected as a defenseman. Take it from a goaltender who knew what it was like. When Butch teamed up with Leo Lamoureux, poor Leo got all the work because the opposition just steered clear of Butch. When Butch was on the ice that was one time I didn't have to switch my stick hand. I'd just say to myself, "Well, Butch is on so they're going to come down Leo's side." Sure enough, that's where they came.

Kenny Reardon was another character on defense. He was a western Canadian from Winnipeg, like Irvin, and this was good for him. Anybody who was a Westerner often had an inside with Irvin, but not all the time. Reardon found that out one year when we were barnstorming.

There was a game in Edmonton, and for some unknown reason Irvin didn't start Reardon and Kenny was furious. Irvin used Leo and Roger Leger and kept them on for 15 minutes in the first period. Meanwhile, Reardon is screaming, "These are my people in the stands and he won't even play me." At last, Irvin put him out and Kenny was so excited he made a big dash up the ice. The second he got to the other blue line he fell, head first, and just looked like a fool. There was a whistle and Roger skated over to him and said, "Kenny, in Edmonton you have to be careful; they have high blue lines here!"

As a player Reardon had some strange ways about him. He had an awful phobia about anybody skating in on him one-on-one. If he teamed up with Bouchard, he'd plead with Butch not to do any rushing and say, "Please don't leave me!" Frankly, in those situations Reardon couldn't stop my daughter. When I say Kenny had a phobia about one-on-one I mean it. Twice in practices Irvin started one-on-one workouts; Reardon left the ice and got dressed. Can you imagine that? It was unheard of.

If Butch or I had done that it would have been an automatic $25 fine. But Reardon just shouted, "That's a helluva way to practice; that's a crazy way to do it." Say what you will about Irvin as a disciplinarian, this was the one time I had my doubts about him — Reardon got away without a fine or anything.

Overall, though, I couldn't argue with the way Irvin ran the team, but I certainly wasn't crazy about Tommy Gorman who was our manager for a while. He had been around hockey a long time and had this reputation for being a great guy, but he was just that way with newspapermen.

He could be cruel with the players because he didn't give a damn about them. Gorman liked to play up the French versus English nonsense when the Canadiens still owned Paul Bibeault. I had already won a couple of Vezina trophies and Bibeault was getting older, but the Canadiens still owned him and Gorman would use him to rile me. Once I had a bad cold and missed a practice, so Gorman got hold of the newspapermen and they made a big deal, "Durnan Won't Play", "Durnan Will Play." He was an old newspaperman himself and would write his own copy for these guys. We'd go weeks without losing and then we'd finally blow one and I'd get it from Gorman. I was "disillusioned", "disappointed" — anything to make copy.

Frank Selke followed Gorman. He had been Conn Smythe's assistant in Toronto and came over to Montreal after the war. Selke was a far more knowledgeable hockey man than Gorman, although I know when he got older he made himself a judge of people, a holier-than-thou type.

That personal stuff wasn't for me, really. I was interested in the game and except for a few bad periods I was enjoying myself with the Canadiens.

Hockey started to get rough for me at the end of the '40s. I began hurting and was going to be 35 years old in an era when goalies played a whole season without an alternate. And there were no such things as masks to protect you. I had broken my hand and after it mended it felt as if my arm was falling off whenever I'd catch the puck. The 1949-50 season was the turning point for me; the beginning of the end.

One of my main reasons for chucking it all was because the fun was going out of the game for me. A lot of my old pals were leaving — or had gone — and much of the camaraderie was missing. In the heyday of the team it was a common thing for us to get together in the smoker of the train and talk about the team, the games, the strategy, and all that. As far as I'm concerned the Canadiens' fortunes turned downward when the gang stopped gathering in that smoker.

In January 1950, I told Dick I'd be gone for good after the season. My reflexes had gotten a little slow and, besides, the money wasn't really that good. With all those Vezina trophies and all those write-ups that said I was the greatest goaltender of all time, the most I ever made with the Canadiens was $10,500. That was my top salary. I'll admit, if they were paying the kind of money goaltenders get today, they'd have had to shoot me to get me out of the game. But at the end of any given season when I was playing I never seemed to have more than $2,000 in the bank, so I wasn't really getting anywhere that way. And people kept telling me you're an old man after 40; I wasn't educated and I had two girls to raise. All this worried me a great deal — and I was also hurting. Everything came to a head in March 1950 when we went up against the Rangers in the first round of the playoffs.

We had finished second that year and the Rangers were fourth and, naturally, we were favored to beat them. But they took us 3-1 in the first game in New York, then came up to Montreal and beat us again 3-2. We then went back to New York and they won 4-1. We were down three games to none and, since I knew I'd be quitting after the season and was also aware that the Canadiens had a good young goalie in the farm system — Gerry McNeil — I told Irvin to let the kid finish the series. I was afraid I was blowing things. I really wasn't, I guess, but we hadn't won a game and I didn't want to be blamed for it. And I felt I wasn't playing as well as I did in the past.

The "nerves" and all the accompanying crap were built up. It was the culmination of a lot of thinking and I realized, "What the hell, I'm quitting and this is as good a time as any. If the kid goes in and wins — well, great, it's a terrific start for him."

A lot of people thought it was a nervous breakdown but it wasn't. To this day, people still won't believe me. Before the fourth game of the series Irvin asked me to go in and tell the team that it was my decision to quit, not his, and I did get a little emotional then. Gerry went out and won the game, but the Rangers came back in the next one to take the series. But that was it for Bill Durnan.

I'm glad I went out when I did. Okay, maybe things didn't work out for me the way I wanted them to as far as income, jobs and what-not are concerned, but I did the right thing from the viewpoint of playing hockey. A few more write-ups weren't going to interest the grocer that much.

I still watch hockey a little nowadays, but it's a changed game, no doubt about that. Now it's congested and half the time you don't know how the puck went into the net. They just don't have the plays we had; they simply shove the puck in the corner, then there's a wild scramble, with three or four guys behind the bloody net. The puck comes out and somebody bangs it in. At that point even the

announcers who are supposed to know what happened start guess-
ing, "We *think* it was Joe Doakes."

And the players have changed, especially their attitudes, though
at least until recently there were a few honest skaters left. John
Ferguson, who played for the Canadiens, is an example. I was at a
party with him a few years ago and somebody asked him why he
was such a stinker on the ice and a nice guy off of it. Ferguson
replied, "When I'm on the ice, I'm at work!"

Now that's the kind of answer we oldtimers would give.

Chapter 4

COOPER SMEATON

One of the most distinguished non-hockey playing members of the Hall of Fame was, in fact, a player of note before turning to officiating. Born in Carleton Place, Ontario on July 22, 1890, Cooper Smeaton was an All-Sports star for the Westmount Amateur Athletic Association in Montreal before joining the Canadian Armed Forces and serving overseas in World War I.

Prior to his enlistment, Smeaton had already established himself as a first-rate hockey player and could easily have turned pro, but instead he opted for an officiating career. In 1913, he was appointed to the refereeing corps of the National Hockey Association and officiated major games in Allan and Stanley Cup competition. After his World War I stint, Smeaton officiated in the NHL until taking on the managership of the new Philadelphia Quaker franchise in 1930. When the Quakers folded a year later, Smeaton was named head NHL referee and continued in that capacity for six years until his retirement as an official. In later years he was named an offical trustee of the Stanley Cup. Stan Fischler interviewed Smeaton at his Montreal apartment. He was a jovial, eloquent and gracious host who happily recounted his whistle-blowing experiences. The following narrative is based on that interview.

Cooper Smeaton died in 1978.

Although Ottawa was my birthplace, the family moved to Montreal when I was about three, and that's where I learned sports. As a child I played everything — baseball, football, hockey. When it came to hockey I played for the Westmount Amateur Athletic Association on defense, only in those days it was called "point."

We didn't win every championship, but we certainly won our share. This was just past the turn of the century when amateur hockey was a lot more prestigious than today. Getting a regular job was considered the most important thing in life at that time, and I got my first with the Dominion Steel and Coal Company in Montreal.

Cooper Smeaton   **(Hockey Hall of Fame)**

Then, in 1910, a strange thing happened. I got an offer to go down to New York City, of all places, to play hockey. I wasn't the only one; Sprague and Odie Cleghorn — a terrific pair of skaters — also were invited down by the New York Wanderers, and to this day I don't know who told those New Yorkers about us. Anyhow, the deal was an attractive one; in addition to playing hockey we were given jobs. I worked for the Spalding Sporting Goods Company, Odie was at a stock brokerage concern, and Sprague went with the telephone company.

We weren't professionals because our salaries were paid by the companies we worked for and we just played hockey at off-time. Lots of people think hockey was relatively new to New York, but actually it was booming back then in 1910. We played in a little rink up near Central Park, an old riding academy that had skating facilities on the second floor. There was a bar and restaurant downstairs, where the dressing room was, and the rink was one flight up.

New York had a regular hockey league. Besides our club, the Wanderers, there were the St. Nicholas Hockey Club, the New York Hockey Club and the Crescent Athletic Club which, I think, came from Brooklyn. Compared with Canada, the caliber of play was not bad at all.

I had fun in New York. At that time it was a good city. You could go places with five dollars in your pocket, which you can't do today, and for what it was, even my job wasn't bad. Actually, I might have stayed longer except I had to leave for family reasons and so I came back to Montreal, got another job, and soon found myself refereeing more than I was playing.

The new job was one reason I turned to refereeing. I liked work but it didn't give me the chance to play a full schedule of games. By refereeing, I could pick my spots, keep in shape at the same time, and also be with the boys, which was important.

I worked at the Sun Life Insurance Company as a clerk in the agency department, and while there I met my future wife through goaltender Riley Hern. Mrs. Hern and Mrs. Smeaton-to-be were friends, I was introduced to her, and we got married in 1913. That was also the first year I began refereeing professional games.

This was the old National Hockey Association, the predecessor of the NHL. They were having trouble with their referees at the time and it happened that the sports editor of *The Toronto Daily Star* had seen me work and had become a booster of mine. He kept telling Frank Calder, the secretary of the NHA, "Why don't you give Smeaton a chance?"

One day I got a call from Mr. Calder asking me to referee a game between the Canadiens and the Wanderers. I inquired who the other official was and learned that it would be Harvey Pulford, a big, strong fellow who was not afraid of anybody, and so I said, "Sure,

I'll go on." In those days there were two officials: the referee and a "judge of play." The referee — in this case, Pulford — had final say.

I'll never forget the first penalty I called in that game. It was against Newsy Lalonde, one of hockey's toughest players. Newsy was a center in those days of seven-man hockey, when a rover made up the extra skater. I faced off the puck and Newsy passed it back to the rover, then started skating. I noticed he was offside so I called him for it.

When Lalonde heard the call he wheeled around and came tearing back at me like he was going to knock my head off. Well, there I was, just a rookie with a better-than-passing knowledge of the rulebook, and I knew I had the right to fine him. So I said, "Two minutes and five dollars!"

Newsy nearly dropped dead when he heard that. He stopped in his tracks and said nothing. I found out that that was the quickest way to squelch Lalonde. From then on he never bothered me. His boss, George Kennedy, the owner of the Canadiens, wasn't impressed. He called Newsy over to ask why he didn't argue with me and Lalonde answered, "George, you pay the fines and *then* I'll argue."

That incident marked a turning point in my career because if I had given in to Newsy I'd have been through as an official. The players would have spread the word around and I wouldn't have been worth much anywhere.

But from that game on Frank Calder began giving me lots of work. In fact, I liked officiating so much I began using my holidays to referee hockey, which kept me away from home quite a bit. Don't forget, I had a full-time job while all this was going on, so if I had a game in Ottawa one night I'd have to catch the 4 p.m. train out of Montreal, eat on the train, referee the game, go to a hotel, catch the 5:50 a.m. train, and be back in my Montreal office at 9 a.m. Then, I'd do the Boston games on weekends.

Of course, seasons were a lot shorter at the time and the rinks were completely different. In Montreal, teams played at the old Westmount Arena, one block west of where the present Forum is today. Westmount had a good rink, but its ice was natural; everything depended on the weather, so the season didn't actually start until December, and only ran through March. Even so, the weather got warm once and they had to move the Stanley Cup series to Toronto where they had artificial ice.

Refereeing was a lot different, too. When you handled games in Ontario you had to use a bell instead of a whistle and that was awkward. Imagine racing from one end of the rink to the other, lugging a big bell along with you. The trick was to carry the tongue of the bell between your fingers, but it was still a clumsy procedure.

Unlike today's referees, we didn't have contracts; we got paid by the game. My position was a little different, however, because of my full-time job. The other fellows refereed because they needed the money. But I used to tell them, "If you don't like the way I'm working, well, get somebody else."

Nobody ever gave me any advice on officiating, so I had to pick up tips along the way, and one of the hardest was learning to take abuse from the fans. My wife had her lessons in that, too. For her it was no fun sitting in the stands watching me referee because lots of fans knew who she was and they'd give her as hard a time as they'd give me.

I once bought her a new squirrel coat which she wore to a game. The fans didn't like my work that night so they pelted *her* with missiles. When we got home we had to cut the gum out of the fur with a pair of scissors.

We also had to put a "stopper" on our telephone. Anybody who called our house after midnight couldn't get a connection unless they asked for Mrs. Smeaton. The operator would then call her and tell her who the caller was. Sometimes I think my refereeing made it tougher on my wife than anybody. Whenever we'd go out to eat somebody would inevitably recognize me, come over to the table, and start an argument.

Fans were worse then than they are today. In the Forum there'd be one side completely filled with the French-speaking spectators and the other side with the English. It was brutal on nights when the Canadiens and the Maroons played because the Canadiens were supported by the French and the Maroons were clearly the team of the English. I'm English myself, but I took more abuse as a referee from that group than I ever did from the French. Of course, there were those who said I bent over backwards to show I wasn't favoring the Maroons. Others claimed that because I was English I was crucifying the French.

One night my wife just barely escaped injury thanks to Hap Day, the former Toronto defenseman who wasn't playing that night and was sitting beside her. I had made a few calls on the ice that angered the fans and one guy approached my wife with his fist cocked. Luckily Day had a set of crutches next to him, because he'd just come out of the hospital, and threatened to whack the fellow with one if he came any closer.

This is not to suggest that I was having an easy time of it myself on the ice. Besides Newsy Lalonde there were others who could be difficult. The Cleghorn boys — the two I grew up with and played with in New York — gave me the most trouble. They figured that because they knew me so well they could get away with more. But I knew their tricks; they couldn't fool me.

After you officiate for a while you get to know how players will react. I recall a fight between Battleship Leduc of the Canadiens and Hooley Smith of the Maroons. Just as it began, the players automatically formed a ring around the pair. The two sparred a little at first, and then they both started to laugh. That's what happened in many fights!

I'm sure I saved myself a lot of trouble by making it a practice to talk to the players before every game. I also convinced Calder to let me visit training camps at the start of each season to go over the rules. It's amazing the amount of ignorance among players when it comes to simple rules. That's why referees had so much trouble; the players would get mad at you for calling something they didn't know was in the rule book.

One night I gave Aurel Joliat of the Canadiens a penalty of an automatic goal against his team for throwing his stick in his defensive zone. The next game I saw him he skated over to me and said, "Cooper, you were wrong the other night." I immediately pulled out the rule book, opened it to the right page, and pointed it out to him. "Can you read?" I asked. He read it, handed the book back and just buzzed off. He didn't even know the rule was there.

I didn't spare anybody, not even the big shots like Conn Smythe of Toronto. Once I was in the Toronto Maple Leafs' dressing room, trying to explain the rules to them and Smythe was sitting in the corner, ignoring me, just reading the paper. "Connie," I said, "this is just as good for you as it is for these others. So, please put down your paper." And he put it down. He learned something and, as a result, we didn't have any arguments.

By the mid-'20s I had a considerable reputation throughout the league. I'd be sent to referee in Boston and Pittsburgh and I even refereed the first game at the old Madison Square Garden. It opened in 1925 with a match between the New York Americans and the Canadiens, and it was a spectacle of pomp and circumstance, black tie and tails. Quite a show. It was so hot that night everybody nearly passed out. Howie Morenz of the Canadiens was so warm he'd lie on the wet cement between shifts just to keep cool.

While all this was going on my wife kept trying to persuade me to quit hockey, but she didn't make much headway. My company was also giving me signals. They said I'd never get a big promotion until I devoted full time to my job. But hockey in the '20s and '30s was great, and I enjoyed the trips and the players . . . well, most of them. There were a few I could have done without, like Eddie Shore.

Shore was nasty and, as far as I was concerned, a threat to the life of other players, a real danger. He was a madman when he got out on the ice and almost killed Ace Bailey of the Maple Leafs. I know Shore would have liked to have hit me; once, during a game in Chicago, when he shoved me around I threw him out of the game.

Art Ross, the Bruins manager, protested my decision. The league upheld Ross because Shore was a drawing card and I wasn't. When I heard their verdict I resigned, but the league governors asked me to come back, and I did.

Another guy who gave me a bit of trouble was Frank Nighbor when he was playing for Ottawa. I remember one game when every time a pass was made by the other team he'd yell, "Offside, offside!" That irked me and I skated over to the Ottawa bench and told him, "Nighbor, if you yell 'offside' once more, I'm going to let it go."

Sure enough, on the next rush Nighbor yelled "offside" and, even though it was offside — by about 10 feet — I ignored the whistle and the other team nearly scored. After that Nighbor stopped screaming.

It was tougher being an official in those days because the referee also had to break up the fights, unlike now where the two linesmen come in. One night I stepped between two guys in Boston and had three ribs broken.

Another time I fell on a stick early in a game and broke my ankle. Instead of going to the hospital I hung on. Literally. I'd face off by leaning on a player and then skate on one leg to the boards and hold on there until there was a stoppage of play. That night the players were wonderful; they didn't try to take advantage of me at all.

Those were the golden days of hockey when you had fellows like Howie Morenz, Nels Stewart and Georges Vezina. Howie was sensational then and he'd be sensational now. They talk about Bobby Hull's speed, but Morenz would whip around his net like a flash and be up the ice before you could blink your eyes.

Take a goal-scorer like Stewart. In today's game he'd score 100 goals. He was terrific in front of the net, a big strong fellow who had moves like a cat. Stewart never seemed to be paying any attention to where the puck was and, if you were checking him, he'd even hold little conversations with you. But the minute he'd see the puck coming his way he'd bump you, take the puck, and go off and score. For great lines I'd say the Cook brothers and Frank Boucher were right up there. They made a science out of the game; today that science is gone. In the old days if a team was a man short it would stickhandle the puck until time expired. Now they just heave it down the ice. You don't have to pay a guy $400,000 to do that.

For years I argued that the club a man short should have to carry the puck out at least into the center zone before icing it, but nobody listened.

We had a more appealing game with lots of stickhandling and nice passing. Now it's all speed. If you ever put the seven-man game on display today, the crowd would boo because it's too slow; they wouldn't go for the old-fashioned style.

Everything is different. The referees today get paid over $100,000 a season ($50,000 for younger referees in 1993). The most I ever got was $7,500 and you were lucky if you got $100 for a playoff game. One thing remains the same though — the referees never seem to please the coaches or managers or owners. To this day, nobody is perfect.

I remember blowing a call one night at Madison Square Garden. The Rangers were playing the Bruins and I was too fast whistling dead a play that really hurt Boston. After the game Art Ross came into my dressing room and began complaining, "Smeaton, you made a fine blooper out there." I looked at him and said, "Yes, I did." With that, Ross turned right around and walked out. He had no further argument.

Another time I made a few calls that annoyed Jim Norris, owner of the Detroit Red Wings and a powerful man in the league. He stormed into my room complaining about what a bum job I had done until I'd had it up to here.

"Norris," I said, "if you think you can do any better, here's the whistle, go out there and do it yourself!" And he turned around and walked out.

By 1937 Sun Life was pressuring me to pay more attention to them and less to hockey. They wanted to make me an assistant branch manager and, as hockey was changing, I began to think more and more about getting out. It wasn't an easy decision, because the league had made me referee-in-chief during the early '30s and, except for one time when a railway locomotive broke down in a snowstorm, I never missed getting back to work on time.

Attitudes were changing in the mid-'30s, however. They put in a rule that referees couldn't mingle with the players, which I didn't like. After all, I'd known some of these fellows for more than 20 years. True, we would argue on the ice, but after the games were over we were friends again and spent time off-ice together. When they put in that non-fraternization rule, I finally decided to get out.

One thing about leaving, however. I had a farewell lunch with some of the other referees and they brought along a new fellow who was going to take my place. That fellow was none other than Clarence Campbell.

So, as soon as I left the NHL I got my promotion and became an assistant branch manager. I never had any second thoughts about returning to hockey, never even got the urge.

Of course, I still kept going to games and, in 1946, when Clarence Campbell became president of the NHL, I was named the senior trustee of the Stanley Cup.

And so it goes. Every once in a while I wonder what it would be like to referee today. My conclusion is that I couldn't last two games because it's too strict. Nowadays when a referee makes a decision, he's got to skate halfway around the rink to get away from some goof who wants to argue about it.

I used to tell them, "You open your mouth and out you go!"

Chapter 5

BOBBY HEWITSON

To many who grew up listening to the "Hockey Night in Canada" radio broadcasts during the 1940s, the name Bobby Hewitson was as familiar to listeners as the legendary play-by-play master Foster Hewitt.

Hewitson, then sports editor of the Toronto Telegram, appeared between periods of Toronto Maple Leaf home games on the popular segment, "The Hot Stove League."

But Hewitson's hockey significance transcended the airwaves. Born January 23, 1892 in Toronto, Hewitson was among the first outstanding NHL referees while also officiating in football and lacrosse. Hewitson spent a decade in the NHL officiating corps while also developing into one of Canada's foremost journalists.

It was not unusual for Hewitson to spend part of a day behind a typewriter, another part at the editor's desk, a couple of hours in the press room and the rest of the night on the ice. His later years were spent as a sports archivist — the first curator of both the Hockey Hall of Fame and Canada's Sports Hall of Fame. Stan Fischler, who spent many a night listening to Hewitson dissect hockey games on CBL-Radio, Toronto, interviewed Hewitson at his Toronto home. He regaled his visitor with stories of his journalistic and sporting career with gusto. The following is the result of their discussions.

Hewitson died in 1969.

In a sense I was more fortunate than a lot of other youngsters who grew up and learned hockey in Toronto; my friends at public school were the Conacher brothers — Lionel and Charlie — two of the finest athletes in Canada.

Lionel was the better football player and Charlie, the younger one, was best at hockey. When we were five years old, we started playing hockey together on an outdoor rink. There weren't many rinks in those days with artificial ice, so when it got mild we couldn't play at all. Generally, we'd start our season in the beginning of January

Bobby Hewitson   **(Hockey Hall of Fame)**

and end about the middle of February. We had only a month and a half of really hard ice.

I was something of a curio among the neighborhood skaters because I didn't really play hockey that much. In fact, my road to refereeing in the NHL began in a newspaper office. From there I went to hockey. I had to earn a living, so I went to work for the *Telegram* in Toronto and eventually became sports editor. When I had some extra time I skated and then one day it happened — a whole change in my life.

I was at a neighborhood rink, watching a game, when one of the Conacher boys came over and suggested "Bobby, why don't you referee a few games in your spare time?" Well, I decided to think it over and a couple of days later I began in earnest my long refereeing career.

At first I handled a lot of collegiate [high school] games and then moved to junior hockey. For one thing, I didn't have a whistle; when I wanted to call a penalty I would ring a small bell and then send the player off the ice. I found that some players didn't fancy my calls and began to threaten me. My solution was to get a bigger bell, which I used for protection. If anyone — fan or player — got tough with me, I'd just wave the big bell at his head and that calmed him down. It was much more effective than a little whistle.

Of course, the big bell also had its drawbacks. It was heavy and when I wanted to call a penalty I'd have a devil of a time shaking it. Occasionally I'd drop the thing and crack the ice — or a toe.

I refereed mostly for the Ontario Hockey Association, an amateur league, but with some very fast teams. They had a junior division, with kids up to 20 years old, plus a senior league for those from 20 on. I wasn't keen about refereeing in the senior league because I weighed only 120 pounds and was 5-foot-7. But I took the gamble and did well enough to finally make it to the NHL in 1925, the same year Madison Square Garden opened.

There were only about four or five referees in the entire NHL in 1925. Lou Marsh was a hot-tempered fellow. Mickey Ion, by contrast, was quite cool. The tougher the game, the tougher Mickey became. He once advised a young linesman handling a game with him: "There are 14,000 people in the building but only two sane men — you and me!"

When I broke into the NHL they used a two-referee system. Each referee would take half of the rink and be responsible for all infractions in his area — penalties and offsides. That could be difficult if one fellow was strict and the other lenient. As a result there might be lots of dirty play in one half and nothing but clean action at the other end. Occasionally, the two referees would try to work things out beforehand. Lou Marsh might approach me before a game and say, "Lemme know in advance. Are you goin' to be tough tonight, or lenient?" And I'd tell him how I felt and he'd work out his style to match mine. After a while the league tried to assign referees who worked best together, and the two-referee system improved a bit.

Refereeing was a lot simpler then. There were fewer rules — now the NHL rule book has 10 times the number of pages it used to — and fewer arguments. Mind you, we had a lot of tough players like Eddie Shore, Red Horner and Red Dutton, but they didn't fuss so much over calls as players do now.

My problems took on other forms: travel and bad ice. Even though I moved up to the NHL I didn't leave my job at the newspaper. This meant I had to arrange my refereeing schedule around my free time at the *Telegram*. I could only get away when the paper said it was okay to do so.

At one point Frank Calder, president of the NHL, liked my work so much he offered me a pretty good contract to work exclusively with the league, which meant I'd have to give up newspapering. "No thanks," I said. "The paper is my first love. Hockey comes after."

To keep my sanity while doing both jobs. I tried to work out a schedule. I'd be home on weekends if I could and at the paper on Monday, usually a busy day. If I was refereeing out-of-town on a Saturday night I'd make a point to be home on Sunday. I always worked out the schedule two or three weeks in advance, but managed to complicate matters by also refereeing some amateur games. So it wasn't unusual for me to referee a Tuesday night NHL game in Montreal, then show up in Galt, Ontario on Wednesday night to handle an amateur game. I'd be going all the time.

It was tough, but fortunately my publisher was a big hockey fan so nobody at the paper ever criticized my refereeing. The staff was a small friendly one; not like today when you don't know who's writing the stories from week to week. And we had good times together.

Apart from travel, the other difficulty during the '20s and early '30s was the ice in the various arenas. It was artificial ice, but it wasn't shaved and cleaned after each period the way it is now. As a result we'd get a lot of snow and, although the maintenance men would clean it with a shovel, that wasn't enough to eliminate the ruts.

On cold nights the ice would crack, and on mild ones it would get soft and mushy, giving everybody a lot of trouble. Skating became a hazard and puck control almost impossible.

That's why I believe the policy of resurfacing the ice after each period was the biggest achievement in hockey history. Now you get even conditions throughout the game, instead of starting off with good ice and ending up with stuff that isn't worth skating on.

One other problem in refereeing in those days was money; I didn't always agree with President Calder about the salary I was getting.

Since I also had the job at the *Telegram*, I worked on a per game basis. The Stanley Cup playoffs were a high point because I got paid a hundred dollars clear as well as traveling expenses.

But I enjoyed the work, so the money didn't matter all that much. You had to enjoy refereeing to do it because it certainly wasn't easy. One night I was handling a game at the Forum in Montreal when Dit Clapper, the big Bruins defenseman, accidentally rammed into me along the boards. Clapper must have been about 6 feet and weighed 200 pounds and I was just a little guy — and they didn't have the plexiglass along the side the way they do now. Instead, there was this rough chickenwire with lots of points sticking out.

Well, when Clapper put me into the boards my face rubbed right against the wire and was cut up like a railroad map. I was bleeding all over the place and had to visit the Forum hospital for repairs. Another time I got hit in the head with the puck while looking the other way. I was out for a half hour and thought I was a goner that night, but I recovered and kept on refereeing.

Other than that I didn't have much trouble. When fights broke out I never did anything about breaking them up because I was too small. The bigger referee always stepped in and I would just stand to the side and try to figure out who deserved the penalties. If I went into it, I'd have gotten killed.

I don't know whether the players respected my size or not, but nobody really tried to push me around. The league used to ask me to referee a lot in Montreal when there were two teams in that city, the Canadiens and the Maroons. The Canadiens represented the French-speaking people and the Maroons were the English-speaking team. They always were rough games and many referees tried to avoid them. The league leaned toward officials from Toronto on the theory that we'd be neutral.

I suppose I was neutral because I never had any trouble at the Forum and in one season refereed nine out of 10 games between the Canadiens and Maroons. The big kick in handling a Canadiens game in those days was to watch the great Howie Morenz in action.

My recollection of Howie goes back a long way because I actually saw him play as a kid with the Stratford, Ontario juniors. Even then Morenz was a whiz, but he got better as he went along. When he played for the Canadiens, speed was his game. He moved down center ice giving a little hop every once in a while as he would literally skip over the opposing players' sticks.

Morenz was hot-tempered, though, and the other team would try its best to rile him. They often succeeded. Howie would retaliate and wind up getting penalized simply because he couldn't control himself.

Most people say that Morenz was the greatest, but the best player I ever saw was a fellow named Berger who came from Howie's home town, New Hamburg, Ontario, near Stratford. One day I said to Morenz: "Howie, do you know there once was a better hockey player than you?" To my surprise he answered, "I know who you're talking about — Berger." And he was, too, but Berger died when he was 21 and we never got to see him in the NHL.

Morenz was tops, but there were lots of good ones. I always had trouble with Eddie Shore of the Bruins but I have to admit he was an excellent player. Then there was Bill Cook, the marvelous right wing on the Rangers. He was a real tough man who could play the game any way you wanted — rough or clean. He was a good skater, very fast on his feet, always shifting from one foot to the other.

My favorite goaltender was Charlie Gardiner who played for the Chicago Blackhawks when they had a very weak team. He wasn't a big guy but he sure could stop those pucks. I think his biggest asset was his disposition. He was a breezy sort of chap who took everything as a big joke. One night during a game in Toronto, some fan threw a big bowler out on the ice. Charlie skated over, picked up the hat and wore it for the rest of the game. Can you imagine that happening today?

Others, however, weren't quite as pleasant. Jack Adams, who coached and managed the Red Wings, was a tough man. He gave the refs a hard time although he didn't bother me all that much. Once again, I think my size saved me, but I did have a pretty good refereeing style. My philosophy was to be as consistent as possible. I always tried to crack down at the start of the game to show the players I wouldn't take any nonsense from them.

Once I knew I had them under control I'd ease up a bit. Some guys would try to call everything one night and then let up the next, which really confused the players. To my mind that isn't the way to referee a hockey game.

Of course, this didn't mean every game was a breeze for me. One night I had an International League game in Detroit and disallowed a goal for the home team. Detroit lost, and when I started out of the referee's room a policeman grabbed me. "I wouldn't go outside if I were you," he said. "There's a crowd out there waiting for you who want your hide."

I told him, "I don't care," held one skate in each hand and declared, "I'll look out for myself." When I walked through the door a bunch of people started yelling at me. I took the rubber scabbards off the skates, just in case, and then positioned myself between two policemen. Lots of yelling and screaming took place but nobody threw a punch at me.

In between the times I was refereeing I'd do quite a bit of hockey writing and sit in the press box. That gave me a different perspective. And the style of hockey writing has changed a lot since then, too.

In the old days you'd describe exactly how a goal went in — off someone's body, if somebody flipped the puck in with his stick or if it bounced off some guy's shoulder. Nowadays when a goal goes in it's almost impossible to tell how it happened because the play is so fast and there are so many skaters scrambling around. It's just too quick. So the hockey writers don't know what's happening on the ice much of the time and it's reflected in their stories. It's not their fault; it's that scrambly hockey that is played today.

I don't say the players aren't as good nowadays as they were in my time. There were only six or seven outstanding ones when I was refereeing and there are about the same number today. You had a few good players, a lot of ordinary ones, and a few hangers-on. There were some who had exaggerated reputations. Take Nels Stewart of the Maroons. He held the career goal-scoring record [324] before Rocket Richard broke it, but I never thought he was such a great player. Nels was big and tall but awfully lazy. He wouldn't back-check and he'd just stand around the net waiting for the centering pass, then flip the puck in. That much he could do. We used to say that Nels stood in one spot all the time.

King Clancy of the Maple Leafs was a favorite of mine. When he quit playing he became a referee and a good one at that. He had a pleasant Irish way about him and, even though he made mistakes, he got by because players liked him.

As for myself, I could have continued refereeing though the '30s but my job at the paper was getting tougher each year. In 1931 I refereed the entire Chicago-Canadiens Stanley Cup series. Every game. The players had requested me before the series started and didn't seem to care who the second fellow was. You know, in the playoffs you don't often get that.

So I felt on top of the world as far as my officiating was concerned and, when the series was over, I decided to quit. I was still able to hop around pretty well and could do everything any other referee could, but I said to myself, "Bobby, there's got to be a quitting time sometime, so you might as well quit while you're on top."

I never regretted it. I had more time to devote to the paper and I became a member of "The Hot Stove League," the group of newspapermen who discussed the Leaf games on radio between periods. I enjoyed big league hockey until expansion came along. Then suddenly we were watching teams from bad hockey towns and things started to go sour.

It's getting ridiculous nowadays. The seasons are so long they overlap. A man can go to the beach during the day and to a Stanley Cup game that night. Then, before you know it, training camp has started — and it's still summer!

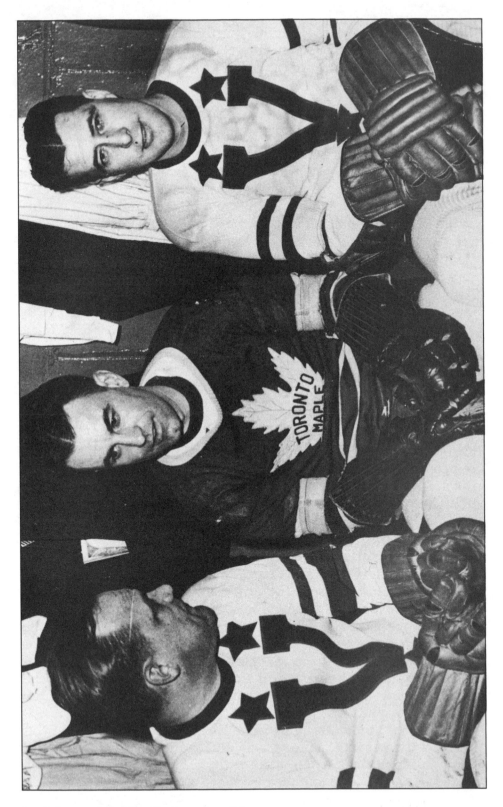

**Joe Primean (c.), Charlie Conacher (l.)
Busher Jackson (r.).**   **(Hockey Hall of Fame)**

Chapter 6

JOE PRIMEAU

He wasn't called "Gentleman Joe" for nothing. Joe Primeau, who starred for the Toronto Maple Leafs from 1928 through 1936, was one of the cleanest and most efficient players to step on NHL ice.

A deft playmaker, Primeau was a virtual clone of Frank Boucher, the Rangers center who had a lock on the Lady Byng Trophy. Like Boucher, Primeau centered a classic threesome — in this case The Kid Line of Primeau, right wing Charlie Conacher and left wing Harvey "Busher" Jackson. The trio paced the Maple Leafs to their first Stanley Cup in 1932 and dazzled viewers with their extraordinarily fluid play.

Following his playing career, Primeau became a businessman, but eventually returned to hockey as a coach. His accomplishments in that realm were as extraordinary as his playing feats. No other coach ever matched the Primeau hat trick; he became the only coach ever to lead a team to the Memorial Cup, emblematic of junior hockey supremacy; the Allan Cup, senior hockey's major trophy; and the Stanley Cup. His most notable triumph took place in 1951 when he directed the Maple Leafs to the Stanley Cup in a five-game final series against the Canadiens, of which all five games went into sudden-death overtime.

Stan Fischler interviewed Primeau late in the summer of 1969 at Joe's ranch-style house in a residential Toronto neighborhood. It was a warm afternoon when Joe hosted his guest on a veranda where the interview was conducted. Joe and Mrs. Primeau later invited the visitor into their living room for tea. Primeau spoke enthusiastically about his NHL career and only occasionally asked to go off the record when dealing with negative subjects.

True to his nickname, he was ever the gentleman.
Primeau died in 1989.

My development as a hockey player differed somewhat from that of the average Canadian because I was raised in Victoria, British Columbia, where the winters are relatively mild. Most Canadian youngsters are on skates when they're five or six; when I first got on ice I was about 13.

My parents moved to Toronto and we lived directly across from a city park. At the time, 1917, an uncle of mine went to war, leaving a pair of his skates at home. They were big for me, but by putting a pair of woollen bedroom slippers inside I managed to keep them nice and snug on my feet. Each winter day after school I'd put the blades on and skate in the park until called in for supper. I'd come in through the back door and have dinner — still with my skates on — and then go back out and skate until I had to return home to do my homework. Usually, I was able to skate another three-quarters of an hour after I had eaten.

The name Primeau does have a French-Canadian background but we never spoke anything but English in our house. My grandfather was a Frenchman from Valleyfield, Quebec, who married an Irish girl from Cork. My mother's people came from Galway, Ireland. So, actually, three of my grandparents were Irish.

As long as I can remember there was hockey talk at our dinner table. My dad used to manage the hockey team in Lindsay, Ontario, but I didn't really get interested in the sport until we moved to Toronto. In those days you needed a permit to play hockey in the park; this would allow you to have the ice for an hour. At first, I wasn't good enough to make any team in the park which was a big disappointment since I wanted to play hockey very badly. One day, though, I got an idea and went downtown to the permit office and told the man I represented the Grenadier A.C. I think he must have known I made it up, but he had a kind heart and gave me a handful of permits allowing me to have the rink for an hour seven or eight Wednesday evenings. Then I got a group of boys together who were just about as bad as I was to form a team, and we began challenging other teams.

None of the fellows I started out with in those days went on to the pros; maybe they didn't have the will to go on or maybe they just had to stop playing hockey and start earning money. I was lucky; my parents didn't interfere with my playing. My mother believed I should have a go at anything that interested me. Once she complained about my having a black ear, thinking I hadn't washed myself properly, but actually the ear was black and blue because I had gotten hit with a hockey stick.

I made my high school hockey team and, even though we only played about eight games all winter, we practiced quite a lot. There were only eight or nine boys on the team so we got a good deal of ice time.

I was playing right wing then, and was one of the last ones to make the team. But as the season went on I improved and ended up playing center. Eventually, I finished school and tried out for the Marlboros, a Junior A team run by Frank Selke who eventually became manager of the Montreal Canadiens. I played two years for the Marlboros, then one year of senior hockey.

While all this was happening I was perfecting my stickhandling. This was something I first learned in the city parks, not so much in the game themselves as in the practices and just fooling around. For instance, there were often 15 guys on the ice in the park and 14 would be against the one who had the puck with the idea that the guy with the puck had to keep it as long as possible. This meant he had to be able to stickhandle especially well or else he'd lose possession.

My inspiration was an NHL star by the name of Frank Nighbor. When we'd get on the ice somebody would pretend to be Frank Boucher, or somebody else would be Howie Morenz, but I used to say "I'm going to be Frank Nighbor." He played for Ottawa and I never dreamed that someday he'd actually be a teammate of mine, but that's what happened.

In my junior days with the Marlboros I began to think I'd be a better-than-average hockey player and that I had a chance to break into the NHL, but found out this wasn't as easy as it looked. So before going to the NHL, I played minor league hockey with a club called the Toronto Ravinas.

At that time it was considered a great honor to be playing in the NHL, and I can remember my mother's reaction when I came home one day and told her I had signed up with the New York Rangers. Conn Smythe, who wound up running the Maple Leafs, had been asked by the people running Madison Square Garden to organize the Rangers, and I was one of the first players he signed. He gave me $500 in ten $50 bills as a bonus, and it was the first time I had seen that much money. Since I distrusted banks as a matter of personal policy, I pinned the cash in my inside pocket, went home, and gave the money to my mother.

She said, "Joe Primeau, you take that right back. You have no right to take that money." I knew she thought I should be paying *them* for the privilege of playing. Eventually, Smythe had a dispute with the Garden management and returned to Toronto to organize the Maple Leafs. So as it turned out, I started with the Leafs and played with them until about Christmas time when I was sent down to London, Ontario to finish the year. I was discouraged, but finished the season at London and went to the Maple Leafs' training camp the following year. One night we were playing an exhibition game against Buffalo when some people from the Pittsburgh franchise came over to watch us. At that time Pittsburgh was in the NHL and needed players pretty badly.

Before the game, one of the Pittsburgh bosses came into the dressing room and said to Smythe, "How much do you want for Primeau?" Smythe replied, "Well, you can have him for $3,500." Benny Leonard, the great boxer, was the owner of the team and one of the Pittsburgh fellows said they had to phone him first to see if he would okay the deal.

In the meantime, we went out on the ice and I scored several quick goals. At the end of the period the man from Pittsburgh came bouncing into the dressing room to say, "Okay, it's a deal!"

"Sorry," answered Smythe, "the price is now $5,000."

So I wound up staying with the Leafs and, sometime late in 1929, I really began to feel I belonged in the NHL.

Early that season I was playing on a line with Charlie Conacher, then in his first year of NHL hockey, and Harold Cotton, whom the Leafs had obtained from Pittsburgh the year before. Then, as 1929 came to an end, Harvey Jackson was signed, but he reported with a charley horse and wasn't able to play until the end of December. That was the beginning of our "Kid Line" of Conacher, Jackson and Primeau, although at the time we had no idea how well we were going to go.

We didn't jell right off, but I knew before too many games that this was a pretty fair line. Harvey was a natural; he did things with the puck without having to think about them. As for Charlie, he was aware of every move he made and could tell you about each one. The pair of them had lots of fire and confidence which I think helped me quite a bit since I needed both at the time.

Charlie was what we called "The Big Boomer." He was to hockey what Babe Ruth was to baseball; just as the Babe could knock the ball out of the park, Charlie could win a hockey game by making the big play. Sometimes he'd cruise in on a goalie who, expecting his tremendous shot, would stiffen up; then, Charlie would cross him up and just shoot that thing along the ice and it would be in — so simple. Sure, it looked easy, yet it was a play well-formulated on Charlie's part. He'd never do the same thing twice; he'd mix his plays beautifully, and with great timing.

To me, timing is the essence of everything in hockey and it was something Charlie and I worked on for a long time. The plays themselves were not complicated; they were basic but depended on timing. For example, he'd get the puck in our end and pass it up to me just inside our blue line. He was such a scoring threat he knew the opposition would put a man out just to check him.

Naturally, that man would glue himself to Charlie. Meanwhile, I'd be moving the puck out from our end, trying to shift my way around the opponent checking me. If I was successful in shaking him, Charlie would give his own shadow the big elbow — Charlie was a huge, powerful man — and all he needed was one stride to be free.

The man would be knocked off-balance and Charlie would be moving full speed ahead on their defense.

If the defense was playing well out, a nice early pass would beat them, because as Charlie would pick up that puck on the fly, he'd be around the defense; then he could make several plays on the goalkeeper, either by shooting or stickhandling.

If the defense backed in, we would use such other plays as the dump-pass behind the defensemen or shooting to Harvey on the left wing. Both Charlie and Harvey were keen and anxious and both would be hollering for the puck at the same time, so it was a job for me to keep them both happy by setting them up for plays.

We weren't named the "Kid Line" immediately. In fact, when I think back I can't remember who gave us the nickname; it just seemed to come up one day in the local papers and it stuck.

Of course, in my early years of hockey I wasn't sure we'd be a big success so I made a point of getting into another business in case hockey didn't work out. Concrete blocks. When I did make it to the NHL the pay wasn't bad for those times; I believe it was something in the neighborhood of $3,000 a year, not exactly peanuts in 1928 or 1929.

Things got better financially as our club improved. We had a terrific Stanley Cup series in the spring of 1932 against the Rangers. Those were tough times for the New York hockey teams, the Rangers and Americans, because if they made the playoffs they were only able to play one game in New York — after that the Garden was booked for the circus. So for their second home game, the Rangers booked Boston Garden.

As I recall, in the first game in New York we were out to a comfortable lead, something like 5-2, when suddenly the Rangers came back and scored two goals making it 5-4. The game got terribly exciting, ending up at a furious clip. Naturally, the Rangers were trying for the equalizer and, in so doing, they left plenty of openings. We got the sixth goal and won 6-4.

Then we went to Boston and the Rangers surprised us by getting a 2-0 lead. It really looked as if we were going to be in for a licking. Suddenly, however, we started to roll and scored six straight goals, winning the game 6-2. And then we came back to Toronto to finish up the series. In those days, we played a best three-out-of-five series, not the modern four-out-of-seven. We won the final game 6-4 and Smythe, who loved horse racing, named one of his two-year-olds "Six-to-Four," another "Three Straight," and a third one "Stanley Cup" — all because of that series.

We always had a keen rivalry with the Rangers and also with the Boston Bruins. Once, in a game against Boston, Ace Bailey almost died as a result of an incident on the ice at Boston Garden. It involved Ace and the Bruins' great defenseman, Eddie Shore.

We were playing two men short at the time and Ace was on the ice killing off the penalties with Red Horner and King Clancy. I was on the bench along with Harold Cotton; in fact, we had actually clambered on top of the boards ready to go on the ice to relieve Ace because Ace had just done a tremendous job of checking. He was tired and we were trying to get him off, but with two men short it was difficult to leave the play to make the change.

I believe the play leading to the accident happened as Shore started a rush toward our zone. When he reached the defense, Horner stopped him with what seemed to be a trip and Shore slid into the end boards. Horner recovered the puck and moved up ice with it; meanwhile, Ace took up Horner's position. Since Ace was tired, he leaned over to catch his breath. To this day I'll never know whether Shore mistook Ace for Horner, but in any event Shore came up and ran into Ace from the back, and Ace fell forward, hitting his head on the ice. Shore had given him a good shot from behind with his body.

I dashed out on the ice immediately after Ace was hurt and I knew he was badly injured — he was having convulsions. Right after that Horner turned around and belted Shore. Bailey, who was a complete player, one who could work nearly every position, was lucky to recover. But he never played hockey again. It was a terrific blow to the club since he was a no-nonsense player, a great competitor who hated to lose.

But the team recovered because we had a lot of great guys and there was plenty of horseplay. One memorable incident was the time Conacher hung Cotton out of a hotel window in New York. They were roommates at the time and also were related through marriage. The whole thing started on a Saturday night in Toronto during a game against St. Louis. Cotton had been in position to score several goals — at least that's what he claimed — but no one would pass him the puck. After the game we showered and I heard Harold barking something about "I'm not going to pass the puck to anybody on this club!"

Nobody paid much attention to him because it was Saturday night and we all looked forward to going home since there was no game for us Sunday night on the road. But we had a practice Monday morning and Cotton still was harping on the same thing — he wasn't going to pass the puck to anyone. That evening we left for New York to play the Rangers on Tuesday night, and by then it was sort of a joke.

After we got on the train the players started going around saying to Cotton, "Harold, you're going to pass the puck to me, aren't you?"

And Harold would reply, "No, I'm not going to pass the puck to anybody." This went on all evening. Well, we arrived in New York at about eight in the morning, then took a cab to the hotel and were assigned to our rooms.

Harvey Jackson and I were on the 20th floor and when we got to our room we opened the window to let some air in. We then put our stuff away and were getting ready to go down to breakfast when, suddenly, I heard this terrible screaming from outside.

I looked out the window and couldn't believe my eyes. Cotton was hanging there from Conacher's hands. What made the whole scene so implausible was that I knew Harold had a great fear of heights, so much so that when he normally looked out a window it was usually from about two or three feet back.

Anyway, there's Conacher, holding Cotton by the waist, head down, 21 stories above the street, saying, "Are you going to pass the puck to me, Harold?" And Harold is gasping, "I'll pass the puck to anybody; just take me in out of here. I'll pass to anybody."

Charlie wasn't the only practical joker on the team. He had plenty of help from Hap Day, King Clancy, and a few others. Needless to say, I didn't always escape being a victim. Once I stupidly listened to Conacher after a game in Montreal. Right after the games there we'd normally go onto our train where most of the guys would congregate in the smoker. Charlie and I were the only ones in the body of the car.

So he says, "Okay. Okay, Joe, come on and help me. Get all the grips out. All the grips out." I helped him and we had all the valises out of the berths, all along the floor. As I'd take one out, he'd open it and start mixing up all the clothing. He'd take a handful out of one bag and put it into another until he had everything mixed up real good; all the toothbrushes, clothes, shaving equipment completely switched about. "Now," he said, "we'll put them all in different berths." And I helped him.

I put the grips in whatever berths I was near. Charlie then said, "Okay, now I'm going to take the fuses out." If you removed the fuses all the lights would go out and it was just about this time that I suddenly came to my senses and said, "No, there's going to be a lot of trouble." So I quickly went to my berth because I had my pajamas on, pulled my clothes over my pajamas, and put on everything I had — overcoat, hat, shoes — took my grip and started heading out of the car, which was a good thing because just about this time the lights came on. As I reached the end of the car the fellows were all watching what was going on, and by this time a few of them had discovered that the bags were mixed up and they started hollering.

Meanwhile, I was up at the vestibule of the car and could hear them screaming, "Who's done this? Who mixed these things up?" Then they realized their clothes were all different. And Conacher was right in the middle of them asking, "What's wrong fellows?" All they could say was, "Look at the mess we're in. Who did this?"

The next thing I heard was Conacher commenting, "Well, I haven't seen that Primeau around for quite a while." That's when I took off. I went to the very far end of the train and stayed there; I don't even remember how long. Finally we passed a station called Smiths Falls, which is a long way from Montreal, so I figured they all were asleep at that point and I crept into the car. By then I had realized it wasn't very smart of me to "help" Conacher.

Meanwhile, I'd been building up my business in Toronto and after we were eliminated by Detroit in the Stanley Cup finals of 1937, I decided to quit hockey. Smythe talked to me about staying, but my mind was made up. I felt I had given my best to hockey and gotten the same in return, and thought that if I continued playing I wouldn't be giving as much.

I also had my eye on coaching in those last years as a player; in fact, I started to coach two or three years before I decided to stop playing. In 1935 I coached a club called the Toronto Dukes and we won the Ontario Hockey Association's senior championship, but lost to the Quebec champions.

Then, in 1937, 1938 and 1939 I had a team called the Toronto Goodyears that won the championship two years in a row. In 1942, I coached a Canadian Air Force team with a lot of ex-big leaguers such as Neil and Mac Colville, Alex Shibicky, Kenny Reardon and Joe Cooper. We called ourselves the Ottawa Commandos, and we won the national championship. From there I went to coach the St. Michael's College junior team and we reached the Memorial Cup finals three years in a row, winning it twice and losing out in the last three minutes of the seventh game in the other series. The first Memorial Cup win was in 1945, the second in 1947.

I had some great players in junior hockey. Tod Sloan, who went on to play for the Maple Leafs and then the Blackhawks, was outstanding. Eddie Sandford, Ed Harrison, Les Costello, Johnny McLellan and Rudy Migay were also up front. On defense I had Jimmy Thomson, Gus Mortson and Red Kelly. Actually, Kelly started out as a forward, but we were hard up for a defenseman once and I asked him to drop back, which he did.

In 1947, Conn Smythe asked me if in addition to coaching for St. Mike's I'd coach the Toronto Marlboros senior team. I said "Yes," and in 1947 we played off for the OHA championship and lost to Hamilton. A year later we beat the Northern Ontario representative and played off with Ottawa but lost to them. Then, the next year we went right through to play Calgary in the West for the Allan Cup. That was a really memorable series.

I flew out West on Friday and we practiced Saturday with the series scheduled to open Monday night. On Monday at noon, I got a call from my brother that my father had been hit by a car and killed. So I flew home right after the game for the funeral, and missed the game that was played on Wednesday night. But I did get back for the Friday game.

We had a marvelous team that year with players like George Armstrong, who went on to become captain of the Maple Leafs, Danny Lewicki, Bobby Hassard, Hughie Bolton, Frank Sullivan and old Flash Hollett. We got great goaltending from a boy named Pat Boehmer who had previously played for that St. Michael's team. Johnny McLellan also played for me. It was quite an outfit, and we went on to win the Allan Cup. Then I became coach of the Maple Leafs in the fall of 1950.

That was about the time that Turk Broda, the great Leafs goalie, was approaching the twilight of his career. But Toronto also had a young goalkeeper named Al Rollins, and I alternated them about evenly over the year. On defense I had Jim Thomson and Gus Mortson, who had played so well together on the Toronto Cup winners in 1947, 1948 and 1949. The other defensemen were tough Bill Barilko, Bill Juzda, a veteran who had been with the Rangers, and Fernie Flaman, another rough boy.

Up front we had three good centers with Ted Kennedy, the captain, leading the way; he was a tremendous competitor and a marvelous man on face-offs. Cal Gardner and Max Bentley were the other centers and, of course, Max was one of the most exciting centers who ever played hockey.

Then there were such solid forwards as Tod Sloan, Sid Smith, Joe Klukay and Danny Lewicki. They were an interesting bunch of characters. Bentley was a worrier, thinking there was something wrong with him all the time, and Broda had a weight problem. I had orders from Smythe to weigh Broda the first and 15th of every month, the days on which paychecks were handed out. Turk had to be under 190 pounds or else he was fined. Actually, I think they were doing him a favor because this discipline kept him playing and he was the type of individual inclined to put weight on. But, as a goalkeeper, he was simply great. He had the knack of coming back after a bad loss with a terrific game; his mental outlook was excellent in that respect.

My boss was Smythe, regarded as a hard man in some quarters of the NHL. Personally, I liked working for him, even though it wasn't any bed of roses. If Smythe had anything to say, he said it; there was no holding grudges or anything like that. You knew exactly where you stood at all times and I liked such treatment — it's always good to know where you're at with someone. But he made it clear he expected a lot of you; he made it tough.

During a game he'd send messages down to the bench from his private box at Maple Leaf Gardens. Once I told him, "Connie, you're my boss and I'm willing and anxious to listen to anything you have to say between periods and after the game. But when the game is on *I* have to run the team."

We finished in second place that year, right behind Detroit, then went up against Boston in the first round of the playoffs. I had Rollins in the net, but he didn't last too long. A chap named Pete Horeck who played forward for the Bruins came sailing in on Rollins when he'd come quite a ways out of the net to clear the puck. Horeck hit him dead on and put Rollins out of commission, so I had to put Turk back in goal. He played well and we beat Boston to advance to the Stanley Cup finals against the Canadiens.

They say that series was one of the best of all time because every single game went into sudden-death overtime. But the last game and winning goal were certainly among the most memorable in hockey history.

The Leafs had won the first game in Toronto, then Rocket Richard scored a breakaway goal to win the second game for Montreal. We then switched to the Forum for the third and fourth games. Ted Kennedy broke up the third game in overtime and Harry Watson won the fourth again in sudden death, bringing us back to Toronto for the fifth.

One of my defensemen was Bill Barilko, a big, rough chap who had come up to the Leafs around 1947 from the Hollywood Wolves of the Pacific Coach League. At first he was a very crude player, but he worked hard and by the time I became coach he was just about ready to become a real star, although he still needed a few refinements here and there.

While we were in Montreal for the third and fourth games, I had been after Barilko for what we call "getting caught up in the slot." This meant he'd skate up when our forwards pressed the puck up into the Canadiens' end of the rink and stay there too long and consequently get caught up-ice when Montreal captured the puck. This was poison against skaters like Rocket Richard and a few others. They'd break out, feed that long forward pass up, and — poof! — they were gone.

I said, "Bill, if you get caught up there once more I'm going to fine you $100, and $100 for every time after that — and I mean it."

So Barilko started playing it pretty cautious and then, of course, our fifth game went into sudden-death overtime and who was on the ice but Bill. Up front I had Howie Meeker on right wing, Cal Gardner at center and big Harry Watson on the left side. They forced the puck into the Canadiens' end, then lost it to the Montreal defense. But they kept checking and Barilko, remembering what I had warned him about, was still hanging back, outside our blue line.

Watson, Meeker and Gardner were really deep in against the boards fighting for the puck and sort of maneuvering around, when suddenly the puck came out, skimming toward the blue line. Barilko saw it and made this tremendous dive because he had to get the puck before a Canadien did or else there'd be a clear shot down the ice for Montreal. Somehow, he threw himself at the puck and swung his stick, all in the same motion. After firing the puck he seemed to hang in the air, parallel to the ice, with his eyes fixed on the net.

Gerry McNeil was the Montreal goaltender and, for some reason, he fell to the ice trying to stop the shot. The puck flew right over his shoulder and into the net. We had won the Cup.

I was so exuberant that I jumped the boards and ran onto the ice. Barilko was just getting up off the ice when I reached him. He looked up at me and remembered that I had been harping at him about playing back. "Well," he said, "you didn't want the hook on me that time, did you?"

The tragedy was that poor Bill, who was then reaching the peak of his career, was killed in a plane crash that summer in the North woods. It was a great loss to hockey. He was a tremendous competitor who was held in great respect by opponents, because if Bill nailed them, he nailed them hard. He liked to call himself "The Tough Kid," and that's just what he was.

That year was a tremendous one for me because I had won the Stanley Cup and previously the Memorial and Allan Cups which gave me a "hat trick" among the major hockey trophies. But all the while I was thinking about giving up coaching because my business had grown and I was considering building a new plant, which would be quite an undertaking. I didn't feel I could spare the time away from it that hockey would demand, and so I told Mr. Smythe about my plans. He gave me every chance to stay and as a matter of fact, when I told him I had decided to spend all my time with my concrete business, he held a press conference, made a little talk, and said, "I'm going to leave it up to Joe. He can either continue to coach the Leafs or retire. But it's up to him."

I decided to go with the business although I loved hockey. To my way of thinking, the game involves a real, honest endeavor and a hockey player is as honest as any person you can find because what he does out there on the ice is it. There's no covering up anything; his performance tells the tale.

If I had to do it all over again, I wouldn't change a thing.

Johnny Gagnon   **(Hockey Hall of Fame)**

Chapter 7

JOHNNY GAGNON

No player ever was better nicknamed than Johnny Gagnon. His swarthy looks, slicked-down black hair and piercing eyes gave him a feline look. Hence, "Black Cat" Gagnon.

A native of Chicoutimi, Quebec — also home of the legendary Montreal Canadiens goaltender Georges Vezina — Gagnon was one of the most colorful players in a colorful era.

He became a Montreal Canadien in 1930 at a time when the Habs were painting some of the prettiest hockey pictures on the NHL palette. Gagnon was teamed with center Howie Morenz, already a superstar, and left wing Aurel Joliat, who also had earned a niche in the NHL years earlier.

The trio clicked almost immediately with the result that the Canadiens battled their way to the Stanley Cup with successive three-games-to-two series victories over the Bruins and Blackhawks, respectively.

The "Black Cat" was ubiquitous throughout the playoffs. He scored six goals, tying Cooney Weiland of the Bruins for the goal-scoring lead, and his eight points was second best.

Gagnon remained a Montreal fixture until 1934 when he had a brief stint with the Bruins before returning to the Habs. He finished his NHL career in 1939-40 with the New York Americans.

Gagnon remained in hockey as a Providence-based scout of the New York Rangers.

He frequently visited Madison Square Garden where he regaled sports writers with tales of yesteryear. The Gagnon stories were well-coated with his French-Canadian accent. "I don't think," chortled Gagnon, "dat I'll ever be a professor of English."

Stan Fischler often interviewed Gagnon about his NHL exploits, and Johnny's narrative follows.

Johnny Gagnon died in 1984.

There were 11 kids in our French-Canadian family — five boys and six girls — and we grew up in a Quebec town called Chicoutimi. Naturally, the language in our house was French. Life was tough in those days, the early '20s, and my father kept wishing that somebody would leave home and go to work.

I was the first one to say "I'm going," but I didn't know where. All I knew was that I was a good hockey player, so I figured I could get myself a job doing that. I had heard there was good hockey in Trois Rivières, so I went down to the railroad station and bought myself a ticket.

When I got there I headed for the arena and asked the boss for a job playing hockey. "We don't know you," he said. That didn't bother me. "Listen," I told him, "you may not know me now, but you'll know me later." He liked that and said he'd give me a chance to make the big team in town. I was very small and, when they saw me, they said I wasn't good enough for the big team. "How about putting me on another club?" I asked. So they put me in what was called the Bank League, because each bank in town had a team. The competition was good and I didn't mind that at all.

The big Trois Rivières team kept an eye on the Bank League to see if there were any good prospects and, in the middle of the season, they asked me to come along to Quebec for an exhibition game against the Montreal Victorias. That's where I got my big break.

I was only brought along as a spare, so I wasn't going to play unless one of the regulars had to come out. In the middle of the game one of our players broke his skate. The coach turned to me and said, "Johnny, you'd better go on the ice and take his place."

At the time the score was 1-1, and I went out and got the winning goal. The coach came over to me after the game and said, "Johnny, I think you're going to make the club next year." That was in 1923-24.

By that time I was a very good skater. I had lots of practice from skating in an outdoor rink near our school. It was a very crude kind of hockey then because nobody had much money. I couldn't afford to buy sticks so I would walk around town picking up all the broken hockey sticks and nail them together to make some good ones. Nor could I afford pads to protect my legs. Instead, I'd stuff old magazines into my stockings. Some kids could talk their fathers into getting them equipment, but I couldn't. My father didn't like me to play hockey because I was breaking too many windows in the neighborhood, always practicing my shot. Whenever he'd see me with the hockey equipment he'd chase after me and, if he caught me, he'd break my stick. Naturally, I couldn't let him see any hockey equipment around the house, so I'd have to sneak it in and hide it somewhere.

All this did was strengthen my desire to become a pro hockey player. I'll never forget one day I told my mother, "Ma, someday I'll be playing for the Montreal Canadiens."

She wasn't very impressed. "Leave me alone," she'd say. "You've been telling me that too many times."

Nobody was really that interested when I got back from Trois Rivières. My father was still putting the wood into the burner at the local paper mill and I knew I didn't want to stay in Chicoutimi to do that kind of work. I wanted to play hockey and couldn't wait for the next year. My big obstacle was a player from Montreal that the Trois Rivières club was after, but it turned out that he wanted too much money. So they told him to forget it and gave me the job. "Johnny," the coach said, "you're going to play right wing on the first line."

For me that was terrific. This was called Senior A hockey; it was something like first-class minor league baseball. If you were good in Senior A you knew that, sooner or later, you'd make it to the NHL. Then I suddenly heard that Trois Rivières was making another try to get that Montreal player to sign with them just as the season started. Before he answered them, we opened against a Montreal team. I scored two goals and we won 4-2. Right after the game our coach called the guy in Montreal and told him to stay home; Gagnon had taken his place.

You didn't get big money playing senior hockey. The club was giving me $10 a week, but $8 of that went for room rent and that left me with only $2 a week to spend on myself. That was tough so I had to make sacrifices. It was worth it, though, because sooner or later I expected somebody from the Montreal Canadiens to hear about me.

I got lucky again when Georges Vezina, the great Canadiens goaltender, died. He came from Chicoutimi, so the funeral was near my home and all the big-shots from the Canadiens came.

One of them was Leo Dandurand, the president of the Canadiens. After the funeral, Dandurand noticed me and started talking hockey with me. "Johnny," he said, "I hear you're a pretty good hockey player — but you're too small for the National League."

That made me mad, but I was thinking and I said, "Mr. Dandurand, why don't you see for yourself how heavy I am. Before you leave for Montreal come to my house and I'll get on a scale and you can judge for yourself." Later that day he came around and I suppose he expected me to be about 135 or 140 pounds. Well, I got on the scale and weighed 150 pounds. "Jesus," said Dandurand, "that's not bad at all. You come to training camp next fall."

After Leo said good-bye and left I took the five pounds of rocks out of my pocket and threw them away.

In the fall, when training camp was about to begin, I made it my business to get there a week earlier; that way I'd be in shape ahead of everybody else. The camp was in Montreal and when the veterans started to arrive, they ignored me. They never gave a kid much chance of making the NHL club. The first two days were really tough; I didn't know anybody there and felt like a real outsider, but I knew that making the team was entirely up to me and after about five days the veterans started coming up to me saying, "Johnny, you're doing all right. Don't worry about a thing."

Competition was very stiff and there were guys who wanted the same job I did. One of them was a really big fellow, and really mean, but some of the other guys took care of him for me and then I knew I had some friends on the club. Still, I wasn't good enough to make the Canadiens on the first try and they sent me to play in Quebec City. I was a little disappointed, but I played hard and wound up leading the league in scoring with 27 goals and six assists.

Our Quebec club made the playoffs, but we were beaten in the finals by Springfield because a strange thing happened. Originally, the final game was scheduled for our home ice in Quebec City. But the rink there used only natural ice and it had gotten very warm in Quebec and the ice had melted. So the game was moved to Springfield where they had artificial ice. We lost by one goal.

Right after the game I got a call from the manager of the Providence team. He said he wanted to talk to me about playing an exhibition game there. "How much do you pay?" I asked. "Johnny," he said, "I'll give you $100."

I couldn't believe it — I was only getting $75 for playing two games in Quebec — but said, "I'll take it right away." Then, I began thinking: Why was he willing to pay me so much just for playing an exhibition game? Finally, I asked him.

"Well, Johnny," he said, "next year we want you to play hockey for Providence. I don't care how much the other teams are willing to pay you, we want you here."

"Look," I told him, "you're going to have to talk to the boss of the Montreal Canadiens." He didn't seem worried about that. Later he talked to Leo Dandurand and it was agreed that I would play for Providence in 1927, but I was on loan to them from the Canadiens.

At first it seemed okay with me. I had a pretty good year — scoring 20 goals — but after a while I began getting a little mad because nobody in the NHL wanted me and the Canadiens never gave me a chance to play. Then I hurt my knee and the Canadiens traded me to Providence. So, in 1928, I belonged to Providence.

I was very disappointed at the way my career was going, but my coach in Providence kept reassuring me. "Johnny," he'd say, "I know you're feeling bad, but if you play very good hockey with me, I promise you that you'll be in the big league next year."

"Coach," I replied, "I've heard that before. But don't worry; I'll play for you the same as anybody else and maybe even a little harder because you're the first one who really got behind me this way."

Well, it turned out he was right. Four NHL clubs were after me: Boston, Detroit, the New York Rangers and the New York Americans. Even better, the Canadiens knew about it all, because news travels fast along the hockey grapevine. The next thing I knew, Montreal had offered Providence $10,000 for me. I was the first hockey player they ever bought for that sum of money. In fact, the Canadiens said they wanted me right away, to finish the 1929-30 season.

But Providence wasn't going to let me go so fast. They wanted me to finish the season with them because they had a shot at the championship and they finally convinced the Canadiens to wait until the following season. That was good, because we won the championship.

I showed up at the Canadiens' camp in the fall and before I knew it they had me playing on a line with Aurel Joliat, who was a great hockey player. At first I was a little nervous, but I settled down and had a good year, scoring 18 goals and nine assists, and was named "Rookie of the Year." Then, as the Stanley Cup playoffs were about to start, my mother phoned me with the news that my father was very, very sick.

"Your father's dying," she said. "I don't think you'll have to come and see him, but at least talk to him on the phone." I'll never forget that conversation. My father said, "Johnny, never mind coming back here to see me. Keep going in the playoffs because you won't be helping me at all by coming home now."

He was dying of cancer at the time, but I didn't know it. He wanted me to keep playing because he felt I was more useful to the Montreal Canadiens than to him. "Go to Chicago" were the last words he said to me.

The team went on to Chicago and in the first minute of the opening playoff game I was about to jump on the ice when somebody called me back to the bench. I didn't know what was going on and said, "What's the matter with you guys? What's the matter with the coach? Why doesn't he play me now?"

I was on the bench for the rest of the game and I got madder and madder. We lost 2-1 in overtime and I walked into the dressing room and threw my stick and my gloves on the floor in disgust. All of a sudden one of the guys called me into another room and told me my father had died and that was the reason they didn't put me into the game. "Look," I told them, "my father was the one who told me to come here and play."

"Oh," he said, "we didn't know that."

I'll never forget that. Then, I had to take the train to Montreal, call my wife, get some clothes ready, and go to Chicoutimi. Then, after the funeral, I went back to Montreal.

By the time I arrived I was very tired. Chicago scored two quick goals in that fourth game and we were in trouble. The series was only a best-of-five playoff, so if we lost, we would be eliminated from the Stanley Cup round. Then, I got hot and scored twice to tie the game. Next, I gave Pit Lepine a perfect pass and he scored to put us ahead, and we wound up beating Chicago 4-2 to tie the series, and forcing a fifth game.

I guess the most disappointed man in the rink was Major Frederick McLaughlin, president of the Blackhawks. He thought he had the series won and he was pretty upset when that game was over. He should have been, because we won the next game and the Stanley Cup. Aurel Joliat fed me a perfect pass to put me in the clear; I took my time and put it in the net, giving us a 1-0 lead. With two minutes left in the third period I scored again and we won the game and the championship. To think, my father never wanted me to be a hockey player and my mother always thought I was foolish when I'd tell her I was going to make the Canadiens!

Sticking with the club was no problem. I had Joliat as one linemate and Howie Morenz as the other. Morenz was a very fast hockey player, extremely fast. He'd skate so fast sometimes that you'd think he was going through the endboards. As far as I'm concerned Morenz was the Babe Ruth of hockey. Joliat, on the other hand, was more of a stickhandler; he always made beautiful passes. He wasn't as fast as Morenz, but he could move when he wanted to.

My style was speed, stickhandling and shooting; and I had to have a little guts to go with all that, too. Someone as little as I was had to have guts, otherwise you'd get run out of the league. It's the same in hockey today.

At first I had a little trouble playing with Howie. He wasn't too good as a playmaker, so I'd play more with Aurel. He always used to get the puck and pass it to me, and then I'd pass it to him. We had pretty much the same stickhandling style and I always knew what kind of moves he'd make. For instance, as soon as he'd hit the blue line he'd throw me a pass behind his back.

We had a good line, but there were a lot of other good ones. Toronto had Joe Primeau, Busher Jackson and Charlie Conacher — "The Kid Line." On the Rangers there was Frank Boucher and the Cook brothers, Bill and Bun. The Montreal Maroons also had a good one with Babe Siebert, Hooley Smith and Nels Stewart, "The Big S Line." Hockey was a lot better in those days; every club had four or five big stars at least.

The best player? It wasn't Morenz. I would say Boucher, the Cooks, Charles Conacher and Aurel. Howie wasn't the best, but he was the fastest and the biggest star. I wasn't in that class.

In my first season with the big club my salary was $35 a week and I really had to pinch pennies. When I got to Montreal I needed a coat very badly since the one I had wasn't heavy and I was cold all the time. So I went to a pawn shop and got a nice one for $5 — that was my start in Montreal.

A player in the National Hockey League didn't have the kind of security a player has today. There was no union, it was Depression time, and there were no jobs anywhere, so hockey was a good thing. If you weren't good enough, however, they'd get rid of you right away because there were so many good amateur players. Still, I was hard to handle; I had a bad temper and I fought with my coach, Newsy Lalonde.

Newsy was a great hockey player, but as a coach he was something else. He never patted me on the back, and in my case that was bad, because I was the kind of guy who would stop playing if you didn't encourage me or if you hollered at me. But I got along pretty well with the other players.

The coach didn't want us to drink if we were on the train. Once, we were heading for New York and he caught us with a bottle and gave us hell; he took the bottle away and hid it in his compartment. But I watched where he put it and got it back without his knowing it and we all had our drinks. Next morning he saw us at breakfast and said, "Who stole the bottle?" Nobody talked and he never found out.

Those train trips were a lot of fun. We'd play cards and kid around with the newspapermen. There was one guy from the *New York World-Telegram* named Jim Burchard who was friendly with the boys on our team. He was a great storyteller and he'd spend a lot of time with us. You don't see that too much today. The old newspapermen didn't care about the story; they'd just go out and have a good time with us. Today, those guys aren't so friendly; they're just interested in doing their job.

Still, we gave them plenty to write about. In my case it was partly because I was such a little guy playing with the big ones and consequently I got hit a lot. Lots of times I'd come to the bench with my mouth bleeding and my teeth loose because somebody put an elbow in my face. There was nothing I could do about it, though, because if I wanted to stay in the National Hockey League I had to forget the pain.

One guy who really gave me trouble was Busher Jackson of the Toronto Maple Leafs. We were playing in Toronto one Saturday night and Conn Smythe, who ran the Leafs, figured he could beat us by having the big guys on Toronto continually hit the little guys on our line. Before the game Smythe told his players, "I don't care about the puck; just hit Morenz, Joliat and Gagnon. You, Jackson, you get Gagnon." Well, the game started and those guys from Toronto didn't touch the puck at all. The second we went after the puck, we got hit.

After a period and a half Jackson had knocked me down 15 times. Finally, I said, "What's the matter with you guys tonight?" He looked at me and replied, "Sorry, Johnny, that's orders from Connie Smythe."

I answered, "Busher, how long are these orders gonna last? I'm getting tired." He started to laugh; he enjoyed that.

Eddie Shore of the Bruins was worse; he was sneaky. In those days there used to be only one official and naturally he couldn't see everything. So when he wasn't looking Shore would give it to me. I'll never forget the first time I played against him; he knocked me cold. When I got up he said, "Kid, next time you keep your head up!" That turned out to be good advice and I kept my head up after that.

In my first year I scored 18 goals and seven assists and got paid $3,000. A year later, after we won the Stanley Cup, I asked for $5,000 but Leo Dandurand couldn't believe it. He kept saying, "Five thousand dollars!" as if I had asked for the world.

"Look, Leo," I said, "I had a good year."

"You know, Johnny," he observed, "if I gave you all that money you'd be making more than a judge."

"Don't tell me a judge makes only $5,000," I replied. "You gotta be kidding."

Actually, I didn't know how much judges were making but figured if Leo told me I was going to make more than that I'd be all right. We finally settled for $5,000. That was the most money I ever made in one season of hockey. After that I started to go down. I had a few bad years and Newsy Lalonde was tough and kept picking on me. He finally sold me to Boston and Morenz to Chicago, but he was wrong in the way he handled me. Just like my father, he was too strict and was after me all the time. I didn't listen to my father and I couldn't listen to him, so I wound up losing a few good years in the NHL.

The Canadiens finally fired Newsy and they called Morenz and me back to the big club in 1937. It was just like old times; the three of us were together again and I scored 20 goals. We finished on top of the league and everything was going great until Howie got badly hurt and eventually died.

The accident happened in a game against Chicago when Howie skated down my side of the rink on the right. When I saw him there

I decided to cut left to center. Then Earl Siebert of Chicago tripped him and at the time we were only five minutes into the first period at the Forum and the ice was still very smooth. Once Howie hit the ice he started sliding directly into the sideboards; the point of his skate hit the boards and went through the wood.

Siebert was right behind Morenz and fell over him onto Howie's legs. Earl was a big man and when he fell he broke Howie's leg; after the game we heard from the doctor that it was a bad break.

Howie was taken to the hospital and the word got around that Morenz was through as a hockey player. It soon became official and his son brought him the news. Howie took that hard and a lot of people think it broke his heart. Then, one night, I got a call from our manager, Cecil Hart, telling me that Howie had just passed away.

I couldn't sleep all night; it was as if I'd lost a brother. Many other people felt the same way; in fact, when they had his coffin at the Forum there were 5,000 people waiting outside just to get in and pay their last respects. I knew why — he was the best guy in the world. I always said he was the Babe Ruth of hockey, but you wouldn't think it, because he never acted like a big shot. Losing Morenz was a terrible tragedy for hockey.

There were laughs, too. For a while we had a very funny Frenchman on the team, Jean Baptiste Pusie. Once he got in a mood and just sat himself in the middle of the ice and wouldn't move. My favorite story about him occurred when we were playing in New York and the guys were taking a walk down Fifth Avenue on the afternoon of a game. Suddenly we looked across the street to see Jean holding a monkey on a string.

"I bought it for five bucks," he said. "I'm going to bring it to the dressing room."

That night we all got to the dressing room before Jean so we could see what would happen when Cecil Hart spotted the thing. When Pusie showed up Hart shouted, "Take that monkey outta here!" So Jean threw it outside and somebody must have picked it up because it wasn't there when we went out on the ice. Jean got even with us later, however.

We were on the train sleeping when I felt something in my bed. I soon realized what it was and yelled out to one of the guys, "Look, I got a white rat here!" He hollered back, "I got one, too." Soon, all up and down the train guys were yelling, "There's a rat in my bed." Jean had somehow gotten hold of seven rats and put them in the sleepers before anyone arrived and we wound up chasing white rats all over the place.

After Howie died my career really went downhill. In fact, the whole team fell apart, and they had nobody to replace us except for Toe Blake who took Joliat's place. Toe was a hard worker and a good left wing. I played with him for a few years and then Montreal sold me to the New York Americans in 1940. By then I was only making about $4,000.

Those Americans were an interesting team; they had a bunch of old superstars like Eddie Shore, Charlie Conacher, Harvey Jackson, Hooley Smith and Nels Stewart. Ten years earlier you couldn't have bought that club for a million dollars and, let me tell you, a million dollars then was what $20 million is today.

Since I didn't play the whole season with the Americans it looked like I wasn't going to get a full playoff share. I mentioned this to Red Dutton, the owner. "The players voted you a half-share," he told me. I answered, "Red, if I only get a half share I'll be losing money. I'm gonna quit."

Dutton said he'd suspend me if I quit. He then told me that the club was flying to Detroit for the opening playoff game. I had never been in a plane in my life and I thought to myself that that alone was worth the trip.

"Look," I told Dutton, "I'll stay, but if we get beat in Detroit I'm going home."

"You do that," he replied, "and I'll suspend you just the same."

Well, we went to Detroit and we scored a goal but they got two, so we lost 2-1. After the game I came back to New York, packed my bag, and went home to Montreal. I never played in the NHL again. I figured that when a man starts losing money he's better off quitting — and that's just what I did.

When I look back I can remember a lot of good hockey players. To me, the best goaltender I ever saw was Charlie Gardiner of the Chicago Blackhawks. He was a stand-up goalie with a good pair of hands; many thought he was the game's greatest. Somehow, though, I had his number. I'd score on him a lot but he'd still laugh; he was that kind of guy.

One time I said to him, "You shouldn't be smiling at me; you should be mad."

He shrugged. "What are ya goin' to do? You fool me a lot and that's all there is to it."

Another guy who laughed a lot was Ching Johnson, a Ranger defenseman. He was big and almost completely bald. He'd check you to the ice with a huge grin on his face, smiling all the time.

I thought I was through with hockey when I walked out on the Americans. I had gone back to Montreal and gotten myself a job, but the war came and it was hard to get hockey players then because most of the younger guys went into the army. Meanwhile, my wife took a trip to Providence to see some friends and while there she met Lou Pieri, the owner of the Providence Reds.

Pieri asked about me, and my wife mentioned that I was working in Montreal. "I'd like Johnny to play hockey for me," Pieri said. At that time the American League was one step below the NHL.

My wife told Pieri that I had quit hockey, but he insisted. "I don't care; I need some hockey players. You call Johnny and tell him to come and see me."

I guess I couldn't resist the temptation because I got on a train for Providence and, when I met Pieri, I told him I didn't think I could play good hockey anymore. He said, "I don't care" and signed me.

I played eight games and I could tell it was too much. "That's enough," I told Pieri. He agreed and said he'd give me a job as a scout. One of my first assignments was to go watch an Eastern League game in Boston. That was lower than the American League but it was still good hockey since the kids were just out of junior hockey in Canada and hadn't yet gone into the service. The team was the Olympics and its coach was Hago Harrington, one of my former teammates. As soon as I saw him he claimed he had a player for me.

"His name is Allan Stanley," said Harrington. "He's a defenseman. Look at him for a period. Then come and see me."

Right after the period was over I saw Hago and told him that Stanley was so good he should play for the Boston Bruins. Hago said that Art Ross, the Bruins manager, didn't like him and felt that I might be able to get Stanley for Providence on loan from the Bruins. So I went home and related the incident to Pieri and he said, "Johnny, you're kidding. But if you think you can get him, go ahead!"

Sure enough, Art Ross let us have Stanley on loan, but he was still interested in him. He came to watch Stanley play one night that season and if Stanley played well Ross would bring him back to Boston. Luckily for us, Stanley had a bad cold that night and played a terrible game. Pieri asked Ross what he thought of Stanley and Ross said, "Eh!" and left it at that.

"Okay," Pieri said, "I'll give you $2,500 for him."

"It's a deal," agreed Ross.

So we got Stanley who played great hockey for us and in 1948 we sold him to the Rangers for about $80,000. After that I found lots of good hockey players for Providence. One was Jack Stoddard, a fellow who wore a number 13 jersey — that's one thing you didn't see many of — and who the Rangers also bought for a good price later on. I scouted 13 years for Pieri and then the Rangers hired me, and I scouted with them for over 14 years.

I'll tell you this: the game has certainly changed since I broke in with the Canadiens. When I played we didn't have a center red line, just two blue ones, and we couldn't shoot the puck into the other guy's zone until we skated over the blue line. Now, all you have to do is skate over the center red line and dump it in. The game has opened up a lot and they don't worry as much about defense; today the big thing is the slapshot. Slap, slap, slap — and if the puck goes wide of the net they go in the corner to get it. In my day timing was more important; today there's none at all. But the public likes it and there aren't many people around who remember what it was like in the old days.

They think that this is better hockey but, to me, it seems that the kids don't have the desire we did. When we came up the ladder we had nothing — now they have everything. Everybody owns a car and has places to go. We didn't have cars and we didn't have money.

When I started playing they gave me two dollars as expense money and I was glad to get it. If you gave a kid anything like that today, he'd laugh at you. No, they're just not hungry anymore.

Chapter 8

EBBIE GOODFELLOW

Young historians of the Detroit Red Wings tend to think that the first great Motor City hockey player was the incomparable Gordie Howe. This is understandable in view of the fact that Mister Hockey spanned four decades of NHL action.

Actually, there were a number of earlier Detroit heroes, including members of the first top Red Wing line of the mid-'30s: Larry Aurie, Herbie Lewis and Marty Barry. But nobody stood the test of time better than Ebenezer Goodfellow, a towering center who came to Detroit in 1929 when the club was called the Cougars and left in 1943 as a Red Wing.

What Goodfellow may have lacked in glitz, he more than compensated for with remarkably sturdy play and an adept scoring touch. During the 1930-31 season, he finished with 25 goals and 23 assists. His 48 points were only three behind league-leading Howie Morenz. Goodfellow was a member of the Red Wings' two Stanley Cup-winning teams and found himself in an unusual position in 1942 when Detroit and Toronto met in the finals.

Red Wings coach Jack Adams was suspended by NHL president Frank Calder after the Detroit leader attacked referee Mel Harwood at the conclusion of an already tumultuous Game Four. Goodfellow went behind the bench, after which the Red Wings lost all of the remaining games in the best-of-seven series.

Goodfellow turned to full-time NHL coaching for the 1950-51 season, directing an abysmal Chicago Blackhawk team. Ebbie handled the club for two seasons (1950-51, 1951-52). Chicago finished last both times with appalling records (13-47-10, 17-44-9). Following the second stint, he was relieved of his duties and never returned to the coaching ranks.

Ebbie Goodfellow   **(Hockey Hall of Fame)**

Goodfellow was named to the Hockey Hall of Fame in 1963. Shortly before that, Stan Fischler interviewed him on tape. He was exceptionally cooperative and well prepared. Ebbie had armed himself with notes and occasionally referred to them to refresh his memory. It was evident to the interviewer that his happiest years were spent in Detroit as a player and his unhappiest nights were those spent behind the bench with the pitiful Blackhawks.

Ebbie Goodfellow died in 1985.

I can thank my father for getting me interested in hockey. He was a farmer in a small hamlet and before I grew up he took a job on an experimental farm run by the government in Ottawa, and we moved there. He was the biggest hockey fan in the world, with my mother right behind. Consequently, there was no problem in my finding ice time, and in those days Ottawa was famous for its hockey players. Frank Boucher, King Clancy and many other stars came from the area.

Around 1919 a big, new indoor arena was built called the Auditorium. Before that we had only one hockey building — Dey's Arena — but it had natural ice; the Auditorium was the first to have the artificial stuff. Still, I didn't really care because I played on the outdoor rinks where we had ice from November to March. And even if the park rinks were crowded we could always go out on the Rideau Canal and skate in the shadows of the Parliament buildings. Now the winters are a lot milder and all the kids play on artificial ice.

I started playing organized hockey when I was a teenager in school leagues and, finally, with a senior league team called the Montagnards. I must have been pretty good because the Detroit Red Wings scouted me and I wound up playing for their farm team, the Olympics, in the old International League.

Getting there wasn't easy, however. For one thing, I came from a poor family and hockey equipment cost money, and to us money was scarce. My first pair of skates cost 25 cents. They were called spring skates, the kind you put on right over your shoes, and they had heel clamps on the back and two clips on the side that you tightened with a key, something like roller skates.

When the snow fell it would get packed down hard on the sidewalks because nobody bothered to shovel them and we could skate on them and play hockey after school. Those spring skates weren't very steady, but they were good enough to learn on and better than nothing. After that I graduated to tube skates and made my pucks out of hardwood.

I played whenever I could, sometimes three games in one day: morning, afternoon and evening. When I was 17 I played intermediate hockey and can remember a game at an outdoor rink in −30 degree weather and riding home afterwards 15 miles in a hay sleigh, pulled by a team of horses.

A year later we travelled to a neighboring town for a game in a blizzard. Drifts were 20 feet high in places, but this time we had cars. Unfortunately, we had to push them practically the whole distance and didn't arrive until midnight. We started the game at 1 a.m. and finished about 3 a.m. or so. But we won.

Then I played two years in the Ottawa senior league before I got my big break and signed with the Detroit Olympics.

Jack Adams, an old Ottawa boy himself who was coaching the Red Wings at the time, scouted me with the Olympics and decided to sign me for the big team. Before he did, though, I looked up my friend Pat Kilroy, who was playing for the Ottawa Senators and got his advice on what to ask for. Adams came up with an offer of $6,800 for two years which was a pretty good contract. In fact, it was a hell of a lot of money then.

That really set me up for the NHL because word gets around to the old pros about how much the rookies are getting. They all knew I was an All-Star center in the IHL and had won the rookie award and stuff like that. Everybody expected me to be a hotshot. The write-ups all said I was a great prospect and claimed that Boston offered $50,000 for me, an unheard-of sum in 1929.

Naturally I arrived with a big chip on my shoulder. I remember my first night in the NHL; we were playing in Boston against a strong Bruin team that included such big fellows as Eddie Shore, Lionel Hitchman and Dit Clapper. Right in succession Shore hit me, then Hitchman, then Clapper. I came off the ice after the game a very cooled-off rookie. "Ebbie," I said to myself, "you'd better start picking your spots if you want to stay alive up here."

That made sense and I wound up with 17 goals in 44 games; not bad at all considering I played with a lot of different wingers. Jack Adams' theory was to balance the team, have equal strength. So I never played with the best wingmen for long.

Some fellows objected to Adams' style; they figured he was too tough a guy. He was a hard competitor — all he thought about was winning and I can't blame him for that. We'd say about Jack, "All he can ever do is win."

I don't mean we won big right off the bat. It wasn't easy at the start because our team was not that good, but each year Adams made it stronger, and in 1932-33 Jim Norris bought the team and Adams was able to bring in good players like Syd Howe, a forward, and Wilf Cude, a good goaltender. We made the playoffs that year and knocked Toronto, the favorites, out in the first round. Then, when we went up against Chicago, it was touch and go until I lost the whole thing for us. The score was tied 1-1 in sudden-death overtime and I was back on defense.

Clint Smith of the Blackhawks came skating down at me and I jabbed my stick, and he more or less fell down while I came up with the puck. Anybody would say in fairness that I didn't deliberately trip him, but I was still given a two-minute penalty.

There I was, anxiously sitting in the penalty box, watching the clock tick away, hoping we could kill the penalty until I got out. But then just as I was about to leave the box one of the Chicago players got off a long shot from the blue line that our goaltender should have handled. He didn't, though, and there went the game and the playoff for us — all because of my penalty.

Still, that wasn't as memorable as another game I was involved in, the longest one in NHL history. It was on March 24, 1936, at the Forum in Montreal. We were up against the Montreal Maroons, a pretty good club with scorers like Hooley Smith and Jimmy Ward, and we had a big line then of Larry Aurie, Herbie Lewis and Marty Barry. Neither team scored in regulation time, so it went to sudden death.

I know that game is considered a classic because of its length, but as for quality, it wasn't much after the first three periods. Both teams were very cautious and in those days they didn't resurface the ice, just swept it with brooms after each period. By the time we got to sudden death the ice was full of cracks and sticky as hell; there just wasn't any possibility of spectacular play.

Nobody scored in the fourth and fifth periods, but we nearly broke the tie in the sixth when Herbie Lewis worked his way through for a shot at Lorne Chabot, the Maroons goalie. Herbie beat him and it looked like we had the game, but the shot bounced off the goalpost — no goal!

It went on and on into the evening, past midnight with still no goal. Montreal had a few chances, too, but Normie Smith, our goalie, played well and stopped them all. Meanwhile, it was past 2 a.m. and the guys were so tired they were just walking around out there; a lot of fans had left, too.

Finally, we got a break. Mud Bruneteau, our youngest player, got hold of the puck in our zone and passed it up to Hec Kilrea who moved past center and in on the Maroons. Hec carried the puck around their defense, but was checked by one of the Montreal players as he circled in the corner. Yet he managed to get the puck out in front of the net — and that's just where Bruneteau was standing. He put it in past Chabot at about 2:30 a.m., after more than nine periods of hockey.

Afterwards we all got cleaned up and, instead of going to sleep, went to a night club to have a few beers. It wasn't unusual for us to go out drinking after a game because times were different then. We didn't play nearly as many games as they do now, and there was a lot more camaraderie. When we were home in Detroit, for instance, it was quite common to go across the border as a group to Windsor to some place where we weren't known and just have a lot of fun. We might not have a game for three or four days, so we could let off a little steam this way. Today it seems that everything's out-of-bounds for the players.

The whole atmosphere was more conducive to laughs. Like when Harry Jacobson used to hang around our dressing room. He was a coal dealer and he'd come in before every game and say, "Well, you guys, I'm going to pay you 10 dollars for every goal, and 10 dollars for every assist and 25 dollars for a shutout."

Once, he came in on a night we were playing the Montreal Canadiens. That was when Montreal had its terrific line of Howie Morenz, Aurel Joliat and Johnny "Black Cat" Gagnon. At the time Gagnon was really hot and he happened to be wearing number 14 on his jersey, so Jacobson announced: "Fourteen dollars for every time Gagnon is knocked down." Of course, everybody on the team liked that, especially our big defenseman Bucko McDonald who really knew how to bodycheck.

Well, Bucko really did a job on the Black Cat that night, and when the game was over he came tromping into the dressing room over to Jacobson who said, "Bucko, I think you got him four times!"

Bucko roared so loud he nearly blew Harry out the door. "Hell," he said, "I got him five times if I got him once!" So Jacobson coughed over 70 bucks together with about 300 dollars more for goals, assists and knockdowns.

Naturally, this got around to newspapermen as well as some others and Harry started to worry because he was planning to go with us to Montreal and was afraid the French-Canadian fans would try to get him. He was known as a health addict; he never wore a coat or hat in winter and everybody in Olympia Stadium would recognize him. But he wanted very much to go with us to Montreal so he put on a coat and a hat, bought a false moustache, and got away unnoticed.

If Bucko was our hardest hitter, I must have fit in somewhere right behind him, although my style of roughness was a bit different. Ching Johnson, the great old Ranger defenseman, once said I was the dirtiest player in hockey. He must have decided that because of the way I'd developed the knack of cutting him when I played center. I'd skate down the ice, see Ching coming at me with his two arms spread out, and knew I had to protect myself.

At the last split-second I'd bring my stick up and down he'd go. Luckily for me, Ching was a lot like our Bucko McDonald; he was a nice guy, too nice to really give me the business. True, he hit hard, but he wasn't ever mean and wouldn't hurt a fly if he could help it.

A bit later we had a real tough cookie in Jimmy Orlando, a defenseman who came from Montreal. He was a lovable guy off-ice, but in a fight on skates he was the best puncher I've ever seen. Before him there was Lionel Conacher who was amateur champion of Canada. Lionel once fought an exhibition with Jack Dempsey; it was just a few rounds, but Lionel took a crack at Dempsey which almost floored him. Dempsey stared a good hard look at Conacher and said, "One more like that, kid, and you're gone!"

Remember, though, fighting wasn't everything. The name of the game is scoring goals and winning, and I think I did my share. I don't believe a really mean guy lasted in the league very long because his reputation would get around and somebody would say, "That dirty sonofabitch gave me the stick," and the other guys would then lay for him and straighten him out.

Playing forward and defense, I saw both sides of the action. Forward seemed a better position because a man can make more mistakes there and not be criticized as much for it. When you're back on defense and somebody skates by you, then you're the goat. That happened to me one night in Madison Square Garden and some guy yelled down from the balcony, "Goodfellow, you look like one of Jake Ruppert's brewery horses!"

Another time in Detroit, Charlie Conacher of the Maple Leafs, who weighed about 210 pounds and came down on you like a freight train, shifted around me and scored. "Hey, Adams," some guy shouts at our coach, "why don't you try Ebbie as a referee?"

You hear a lot about how much tougher the game was in the '30s — and it was — but there were also some funny things happening on the ice that you don't read about. There was a game one night with Toronto and it was brutal. At one point both benches emptied into a terrific brawl. We had a player, Connie Brown, who stood only about 5-foot-5, and the Leafs had a fellow named Pat Kelly; they were good friends and didn't want to fight, but when they saw everybody else paired off and battling, Connie said, "Pat, you tackle me." Kelly obliged and they went down and started throwing fake punches at each other, rolling all over the place until Connie wound up on top, looked around, and saw that all the action was at the other end of the ice. "I'll get up," Connie suggested, "and you chase me and tackle me down there where the action is." And that's what they did.

Off-ice we always had to be careful of Jack Adams. Once, we had some trouble with him on a trip to Montreal after we'd had a bad game at the Forum. He was good and mad and told us to be back at our hotel no later than 12:30. About six of us, including Eddie

Wiseman, a rookie who was making his first trip to Montreal, went to a tavern where we got something to eat, then headed back to the hotel. In those days we stayed at the old Windsor Hotel which had two entrances: one for the main lobby and the other for the back. It was about a half hour after our deadline and we figured Adams would be waiting for us in the lobby.

At the last minute the other guys decided to duck around to the rear but I was brave — I was a veteran — so I went in through the front door and saw Jack. "Where is everybody?" he asked. I told him, as innocently as I could, that I didn't know. All of a sudden he let out a howl. He had noticed some of the guys scooting in from the back entrance.

Jack jumped out of his chair and raced upstairs with me right behind. When he got to our floor he arrived just in time to hear one of the doors slam shut. He figured it must have been one of his players so he dashed to the door and barged in. Eddie Wiseman was there lying peacefully in bed, snoring to beat the band with his blanket pulled up to his neck. Adams didn't care. He walked right up to him, pulled the blanket off, and there was Wiseman with all his clothes on, even an overcoat. Before Adams could say anything, Eddie looked up, rubbed his eyes, and said, "Geez coach, it's awfully cold in here!"

Adams and I usually got along, but there was one night when he took a dim view of me. It occurred in the mid-'30s — I can't remember the exact time, just that we all were wearing helmets — and I got in a mix-up in front of our bench. All of a sudden my helmet slipped over my eyes and I couldn't see a thing. I was afraid of getting belted so I yanked it off and, in the same motion, heaved it over the boards in the direction of our bench. Naturally, it hit Adams right on the head, knocking his glasses off. Everyone on the bench thought it was a riot and they sat there laughing their fool heads off, but Jack was furious.

Like everybody, Jack was at his best when he was winning and he hit his peak in 1936 when Detroit won its first Stanley Cup. That was the first year I switched to defense and it was a memorable team with Aurie and Lewis and Barry, the Kilrea Brothers, Syd Howe, Johnny Sorrell and Normie Smith. Beautiful. We beat the Maroons in three straight games — including the longest one on record — in the first round, then went up against Toronto in the finals. We took them easily in the first two games at the Olympia, but they beat us at Maple Leaf Gardens in the third one. At that time it was only a best-of-five series, so we still needed only one more win.

The final game was on April 11, 1936, at the Gardens, and we won it 3-2. Toronto had a marvelous team that season but I remember Adams' explanation of how we took them: "We played aces against aces," he said, "and our aces topped theirs. It was decided when the Lewis-Aurie-Barry Line held their Kid Line of Joe Primeau, Busher Jackson and Charlie Conacher to one shot in two games."

When we got back to Detroit after the game the town had gone wild. There seemed to be thousands of people at the railway station and we were driven in a procession to Olympia where another celebration took place. It was thrilling, but we had just as good a time the following year when we beat the Canadiens in the first round three games to two — the final game went into sudden death — and then faced the Rangers in a best-of-five final.

They called that "The Broken Leg Series" because our captain, Doug Young, and Aurie had broken legs. I had a bad knee, and our goalie, Norm Smith, had an arm injury. The opening game was at Madison Square Garden and the Rangers beat us 5-1, but then we got a break. The Ringling Brothers Barnum and Bailey Circus came into the Garden so New York had to play the rest of their games with us at Olympia. We split the next two, but Normie Smith wasn't available for the fourth so we went with sub-goalie Earl Robertson. He shut out the Rangers 1-0 in the fourth game and we won the Cup when we shut them out again, this time 3-0.

Age didn't seem to bother me; in fact, when I was 35 — in 1941 — I won the Hart Trophy, probably because I led all defensemen in scoring. I don't know how much longer I could have played if I hadn't been hit with a knee injury then. It required an operation and afterward I played only 12 or 13 games. Adams got some mileage out of me, using me as his assistant coach when we were losing; when we were winning, however, he was the coach.

One time, though, Adams had no choice. It was during the 1942 Cup finals with the Maple Leafs — that notorious series where the Red Wings won the first three games and Toronto took the next four. Never before had a team made such a comeback.

If I'm not mistaken, we got beat in the fifth game and Jack thought we took a lot of lousy penalties from referee Mel Harwood. At the end of the game he charged across the ice and took a swing at the ref. There was quite a scene, and when the dust cleared NHL president Frank Calder suspended Adams for the rest of the playoffs. That's when I was made coach.

But Jack even got around that by managing to seat himself right behind the bench where he could call all the plays. I was on the bench itself, more or less in charge of changing the lines. We should have taken the series with the lead we had, but Toronto was really up once they'd won the fourth game and their coach, Hap Day, did some interesting things. For instance, Bucko McDonald was playing for the Leafs then and since we knew his style, and that he'd gotten slow, we took advantage of him in the first three wins. Then Day benched Bucko and stuck a rookie named Ernie Dickens in the lineup; he also benched his leading scorer, Gordie Drillon, which really was a surprise, and put in another unknown named Don Metz.

Well, those two Toronto kids just went like hell. In the end, though, the difference was that the Leafs had more depth than we did, because when they benched four veterans and came back with the kind of hockey they did, that's remarkable.

I tried one more season after the series with Toronto, played 12 games, and decided I'd had it. Management had something to say about it, too, I'll admit. They wanted me to go down to the minors and be a playing coach for Indianapolis in the American League — except by then Adams and I weren't getting along too well and I think he had something to do with the suggestion.

One of Jack's failings was that if you started slipping over the hill, you immediately fell out of favor. And I wasn't the only one who suffered. Of course, my knee had been giving me trouble and I couldn't play a game without having it swell up for three or four days. So playing in the minors was out.

At that point I could have done a lot of things. A friend of mine was in the tool and die business, and I tried that for a few years but somehow I had hockey on my mind. Coaching still looked glamorous to me and when Jim Norris, who owned the St. Louis Arena, asked me to try it with his team in the American League, I said I would.

I spent three years learning the trade in St. Louis, and then Norris asked me to coach the Chicago Blackhawks in 1950-51. That sure was a dismal period for them. Jack Stewart, who had been my teammate in Detroit, was at the tail end of his career, and there was a guy named Ralph Nattrass on defense who was one of the worst hockey players I ever had.

It was a tough hockey team to coach because the players weren't good and, on top of that, they liked to "go." I remember one time when we checked into Montreal for a game the next night and I gave them orders not to stay out late.

"Have a beer or a sandwich or something," I told them, "and be back at the hotel by midnight."

Bill Tobin was the club's manager then, and the next day I got a call from him telling me that a lot of our guys had spent the night at Jimmy Orlando's club. I told him I didn't know a thing about it.

"Well," he said, "Clarence Campbell [the NHL president] just called me and said somebody had reported it to him."

All I could do was tell Tobin that we had checked the players into the hotel, but they must have sneaked out afterwards. That kind of stuff just tore my heart out. However, there were a couple of guys I liked on the club. One was Bill Mosienko, a real pro and a terrific little hockey player; he gave me a great thrill before I finally quit.

It was the last night of the 1951-52 season — March 23, 1952 — and we were playing the Rangers at Madison Square Garden. I'll admit our opposition was no bargain. New York had finished just ahead of us in fifth place, and they had a kid named Lorne Anderson in goal that night who was up from their farm team in the Eastern League.

It was in the third period when the Rangers were leading 6-2 that "Mosie" got going. He was playing on a line with Gus Bodnar and George Gee, two pretty good hockey players, and there was about six minutes gone in the period when he got his first goal. Then they came back to center ice for the face-off. Bodnar won the draw and sent it to Mosie. You have to go pretty straight to score that fast and he did. He scored his second goal only 11 seconds after his first.

It's funny, I was thinking of pulling Mosie off the ice but decided to let him stay on for another minute. This time Bodnar took the face-off and gave the puck to Gee. He relayed to Mosie who got around Hy Buller, the Rangers defenseman, and beat Anderson for the third time in 21 seconds. It's a record that's never going to be broken as I see it.

I left him out there and Mosie damned near scored a fourth goal, but he shot wide and finally came back to the bench. "Get off the ice," I shouted at him, "you're in a slump!"

That was the last game for me. I just couldn't take that Chicago club anymore and I prefer to win, so I quit and felt really good about it. I came back to Detroit, lived a normal life, and began to watch hockey simply as a spectator and to look at it a little differently.

I still like seeing a good hockey game but, given a choice, I'd much rather watch one the way we played it in the '30s or early '40s. They have too much scrambling now; we had set plays. In our day the defense would more or less stand back at their blue line while we'd get organized and our three forwards would go down and pass the puck back and forth much more than they do now. Fellows like Bill Cook and Charlie Conacher could stickhandle through a whole team, throw fancy shifts, and score a beautiful goal. You seldom see that type of play now. We had a hell of a lot more beautiful goals, nice passing and good stickhandling.

I've got to admit that the players today are bigger and stronger, and skate and shoot faster; I also think they're in better condition. Personally, I wouldn't want to play today because hockey is all big business, whereas we seemed to have more fun.

This doesn't mean I don't enjoy watching some of today's players. Bobby Orr is the best I've ever seen on defense. My all-time favorite is Gordie Howe — I thought he was the greatest! It's just amazing what he could do and the stamina he had. He could shoot, he was tough, he could skate, stickhandle and pass. I don't think he had a failing.

Times change, though, and so does the game. If I had to do it all over again I wouldn't have gone to St. Louis or coached Chicago; I would have stayed where I was. Chicago was a bad set-up. We had no players and, since Jim Norris owned the Red Wings and the Blackhawks, we only got the castoffs.

Otherwise, I enjoyed every minute of it.

Chapter 9

BABE PRATT

Rare is the National Hockey League player, past or present, who combined such a high level of total skill with rich humor as Walter "Babe" Pratt.

A native of Stony Mountain, Manitoba, Pratt was the natural successor to an earlier funny man All-Star, Ivan "Ching" Johnson. It is noteworthy that both broke in on the New York Ranger blue line. Ironically, it was Pratt who replaced Johnson in the Ranger lineup during the 1937 playoffs against Toronto and made headlines by scoring the winning goal in the deciding game. Pratt was a stalwart on the Rangers' last Stanley Cup-winning club in 1940. Babe went on to an illustrious big-league career, first with the Broadway Blueshirts, then the Toronto Maple Leafs and finally the Boston Bruins, with whom he concluded his career in 1947.

After many private battles with Rangers manager Lester Patrick, he was dealt to the Maple Leafs and helped them win the Stanley Cup in 1945. Pratt scored the Cup-winning goal on a power play in the third period of the seventh game against the Red Wings.

He remained a Maple Leaf until 1946, whereupon he was traded to Boston. Following his stint with the Bruins, he played minor-league hockey and eventually settled in British Columbia, where he worked for a lumber company.

When the Vancouver Canucks were granted an expansion franchise, Pratt joined the new club as a goodwill ambassador and was a frequent laugh-getter at sports dinners. Pratt once asked for questions from the audience after addressing a banquet.

"How many goals a season would Cyclone Taylor score in today's watered-down NHL?" somebody asked.

"Seven or eight," Pratt replied.

"How can you say that?" the man cried. "Taylor was one of the greatest players who ever lived."

Babe Pratt (l.) with Frank McCool and happy fans
(Imperial Oil-Turofsky/Hockey Hall of Fame)

*"Certainly," Pratt said, "but you must remember the
man is 90 years old."*
*Stan Fischler interviewed Pratt in 1968 in his office at
a lumber company in New Westminster, B.C. He regaled
the listener with stories for hours and displayed all of the
rich humor for which he was beloved. Pratt died in 1988.*

Winnipeg, which is where I grew up, was a terrific hockey town;
they had great teams there going back to the 19th century and always
seemed to be winning the Allan Cup for supremacy in senior
amateur hockey. There were also several Winnipeg teams who
received the Memorial Cup for the Canadian junior championship.

In those early days of pro hockey, I think Winnipeg Amphitheatre
had the only artificial ice plant outside of Toronto. In fact, the city
was such a hotbed of hockey that when I was a kid they had a saying:
"No matter where you were in the world, you could find a Swedish
match, an English sailor, a German beer and a hockey player from
Winnipeg."

I wasn't the first hockey player in my family; my older brother
was pretty good, but he was even better as a soccer player. In those
days a fellow could make more money in soccer than hockey, so he
went to England and played there. But then he found out he could
get paid even more money in Scotland for playing hockey so he
wound up in that country. He might even have made it as an NHL
player, but he never cared about hockey as much as I did.

Naturally, we had a lot of hockey heroes in Winnipeg; mine was
Frank Frederickson, who had come from Iceland and lived near us.
I watched Frank play and felt I wanted to be just like him. Luckily,
it was easy to practice in Winnipeg since we had something like 64
rinks for kids 12 years old and under.

We always played outdoors on natural ice and there was no
problem in getting the ice because it would get as cold as 30 or 40
degrees below zero. Our games were held every Saturday morning
and I can remember some of them vividly. In fact, I recall how we
once won the local championship even though we got beaten 8-0 in
the final game. We had found out that there were six guys on the
other team who were over-age, so they forfeited to us. The following
year we played in the playground league and got beaten legitimately.

When I reached the age of 15, I began to play for real winners. I
was one of the junior champions of Manitoba and, even though I
played defense, I led the league in scoring. As a puck-carrier I was
pretty good; any time I had the puck I'd go down the ice with it,
something like Bobby Orr did many years later.

There wasn't enough hockey around for me to play — that's how
much I loved it. Once I played four games in one day. Between noon
and 1 p.m. I played for the high school; then at 4:30 p.m. I had a

game at another high school; at 7 that night I played in the church league and there was a taxi waiting to take me to an 8:30 game, played in 30-degree-below-zero weather. I think I won every game that day.

On nights when there weren't regular league games, we'd have to wait until the public skating sessions were over in the local rinks. Usually it would be about 10 at night before we were able to get on the ice. My father often came down to watch me; he loved hockey. Lester Patrick always said that an athlete's greatest asset is healthy parents; I was lucky enough to have them.

I eventually went to Kenora, a town in Western Ontario not that far from Winnipeg, and played junior hockey there. There are lots of Indians in that area and my coach was a full-blooded one named Sandy Sanderson. He was a fine coach with great compassion for youngsters, something that's missing today. All we seem to have in junior hockey coaches nowadays is a bunch of fellows who want to do nothing but win and send players to the big leagues, completely ignoring character-building in the boys. They're so interested in pushing into the majors that they haven't got the understanding to work with the player who isn't that good.

When I played in Kenora I was scouted by Al Ritchie who worked for the New York Rangers. Lester Patrick was then the Rangers' boss and he was to hockey what John McGraw was to baseball. Lester had friends everywhere in Western Canada. When any of his buddies saw a hockey player he thought might make a good pro, he'd get in touch with Lester who would send his head scout, who happened to be Al, out to investigate. Well, Al told many people I was the greatest prospect he'd ever scouted and invited me to the New York Rangers' training camp in 1934.

Lester had asked 23 amateurs to that camp and, as things turned out, 16 of them made it to the big leagues. Neil and Mac Colville, Alex Shibicky, Bert Gardiner, Joe Cooper, Lynn and Muzz Patrick, Don Metz, Phil Watson and Mel Hill were there, among others. At the time Lester wanted me to turn pro, but I still had two years of junior hockey left. Then he got stuck because two of his regulars, Ching Johnson and Earl Seibert, were holding out for more dough and he needed an extra defenseman to work out with the team. He asked me to stay with the club and I worked out with the Rangers for 10 days.

After practicing with Bill and Bun Cook, and Frank Boucher, I really felt I belonged with the big club. However, I decided to go back and play junior hockey for another year — and it was a fabulous one. Our team finished first and I led the league in scoring with 20 points.

The next fall I went back to the New York training camp and turned pro with the Rangers, although Lester farmed me out to

Philadelphia for two months along with the Colvilles, Shibicky and Phil Watson. That was the first year the Rangers didn't make the playoffs, but the following year Lester got together a sprinkling of oldtimers — Boucher, Johnson, Murray Murdoch and Butch Keeling — and a bunch of youngsters, and we easily made the playoffs. We reached the Stanley Cup finals only to get beaten in the fifth game of a three-out-of-five series.

From that point on Lester went with youth. He brought up Bryan Hextall, Art Coulter, Clint Smith and, in the following year, Muzz Patrick. When I started playing with the Rangers, Lester alternately teamed me with Ching Johnson, Art Coulter and Ott Heller.

By the end of the '30s Patrick had really developed a powerful hockey club; we could play terrifically, offensively as well as defensively. Conn Smythe, who was then running the Toronto Maple Leafs, said that the 1940 Rangers were the greatest hockey club he'd ever seen. In those days, whenever we came to Toronto, Smythe would advertise us as "The Broadway Blues, Hockey's Classiest Team."

Our club was so well-balanced that our first line scored 38 goals, the second, 37, and the third line, 36, over the season.

On that Ranger team we had three great centermen — Clint Smith, Phil Watson and Neil Colville — plus so many good wingmen that we were able to put the pressure on the other team when we were a man short. Our power play was so strong that once the Toronto Maple Leafs took a penalty we kept the puck in their end of the rink the entire two minutes — and scored two goals.

It was a different kind of game, then. Today they stress board-checking and checking from behind, both unheard of when we played. We'd hit a man standing right up, and now the players don't seem to want to take that kind of check. The only check they want is on the first and 15th of the month.

Sure, we played a tough game, but we also had a million laughs. There was a newspaperman from the *New York World-Telegram* named Jim Burchard who liked to drink, tell stories, and do wild things, like swim across the Hudson River. Once, we had Ukelele Ike travelling with us and, naturally, Burchard had his own ukelele which he played every night we were in a Stanley Cup round. We also had quite a few jokers on the team. Ching Johnson was one; he was also one of the finest players when it came to working with rookies. Ching was from Winnipeg too, and he sort of took me under his wing.

That was quite unusual when you consider Ching was getting old and was on his way out of the NHL and I would be the one to take his place. Of course, you can never take the place of a great athlete who retires; you can simply do the job in your own way. Ching was not what you'd call a "picture player" — he wasn't a beautiful passer or stickhandler — but he was one of the hardest hitters in the history of the game, a great leader, and an absolute bulwark on defense.

He'd hit a man and grin from ear to ear, and he'd be that way in the dressing room, too. There was never a time when Ching didn't have itching powder in his pocket, ready for a practical joke. One time he gave Lester Patrick a hotfoot and Lester's shoe caught on fire; Lester was half asleep at the time and after they put out the fire he couldn't walk for a week. It took a lot of nerve to do that to Lester Patrick.

Of all the players on the Rangers, Muzz Patrick became my closest friend; he was the flamboyant type and I was no Little Lord Fauntleroy, either. In fact, Lester classified me as "Peck's Bad Boy" from the time I joined the team. I remember when Lester came to Winnipeg and a little redcap said to him: "God, you keep Pratt in terrific shape; he ain't had a drink all summer." Lester answered, "I think that's great for a 17-year-old boy!"

Lester reacted to Muzz the way he did to me. Once Muzz's name appeared in Walter Winchell's column; it was about his being in the company of a beautiful showgirl. Shortly thereafter we had a meeting and Lester throws the paper over asking Muzz if he'd seen the item.

Muzz looked at it a few seconds, then replied: "Isn't that marvelous, Lester? And very well-written." Knowing his father, Muzz anticipated that Lester would harangue him about the article so he said, "Lester, I just want to ask you something — how many hockey players have ever made Winchell's column?"

"None," Lester answered. Muzz smiled and said, "Well, I'm getting you the greatest publicity you've ever had." At that point, Lester thought about it for a moment, then admitted, "You got me pal, you got me."

Both of Lester's sons, Muzz and Lynn, were with the Rangers at the same time and in one way it was quite a handicap to them. People would keep mentioning Lester and Frank Patrick to the young guys and reminisce about how great they were.

On the other hand, Lynn and Muzz got a lot of help from their father. I always look at it this way: If your father isn't going to help you, who is? It's the same in almost any business controlled by a family — it's handed down to the sons. You don't see a Rockefeller digging ditches.

Even though he called me "Peck's Bad Boy," Lester liked me and I loved playing in New York. It was a great hockey town then and still is. Lester made sure that the new Rangers appreciated the place. He'd tell them, "Where's Helen Hayes? Where's John Barrymore? Where are all the great stage actors? The great singers and the Metropolitan Opera? Where does anybody go who's good? What do they do — they go to New York."

But you can't sell a kid a bill of goods like that anymore. He'll just turn around and say, "I'll go where the dollars are." If they're in Manitoba, that's where he'll play.

After a while, though, I think Lester got a bit disturbed at some of my extracurricular activities. I was having fun but I got hurt; that was during World War II when talent was scarce and he had an opportunity to make a deal with Toronto whereby he'd get two players for me. Since the team wasn't winning, I was expendable. That's how I wound up with the Leafs.

As it turned out I went from one great character to another — Conn Smythe, the Leaf manager. I guess Conn was the greatest exhorter hockey has ever known, and he had the greatest coach in Hap Day. What made things really unusual was that I was the only player in hockey to room with his coach.

Lots of people think that happened because then I'd be under the coach's thumb, but I didn't feel that way. I always thought Hap was a lonely man who needed my company. In any event, I had some great times with the Leafs. I won the Hart Trophy as the NHL's most valuable player and got 57 points in 50 games as a defenseman; it was 20 years before that record was broken by Pierre Pilote of the Chicago Blackhawks. He scored 59 points in 70 games.

But my greatest thrill was beating Detroit for the Stanley Cup in 1945. In 1942 Toronto had lost three straight games in the Cup finals to Detroit, then bounced back to take the next four — the only time that ever happened in Cup play. In 1945 the Leafs won the first three and lost the next three to Detroit. I'll always remember the seventh, deciding game.

It was in Detroit and whenever we played there we usually left for the rink at about 7:30. I was rooming with Hap Day as usual and was snoring away when Hap came in and kicked me right out of bed. I woke up on the floor, looked up, and said, "What the hell's with you, Hap?"

"How can you sleep when the final Cup game is going to start in less than an hour," he demanded. "How do you do it?"

"Well, Hap," I said, "it's simple because the game doesn't start until 8:30. That's when I'll go to work."

He wasn't upset anymore. "Well, Babe," he replied, "I'll tell you one thing, you were never short on building yourself up, so I'll look forward to a good game from you."

The score was tied in the third period when Detroit had a man off with a penalty. I started toward the Red Wing net and took a pass from Nick Metz, a great but underrated player. Harry Lumley was the goalie for Detroit and Earl Siebert and "Flash" Hollett were on defense. When I got the puck I skated in from the point, made a double-pass with Metz, and received it back on my stick. I slid a long one into the corner of the net — it turned out to be the winning goal.

I always felt that if any one person could have been given the Stanley Cup to keep for himself that year, Hap Day should have gotten it for the way he handled our club. We had great goaltending from Frank McCool plus some good players like Wally Stanowski, Elwin Morris, Gus Bodnar, Teeder Kennedy and Mel Hill. But, to me, Hap Day was the man who made it all work.

During the 1946-47 season, the Leafs traded me to the Boston Bruins, a move I considered very fortunate. Winding up with a club like Boston was discouraging; still, I had a chance to play with the Kraut Line of Milt Schmidt, Woody Dumart and Bobby Bauer, and with guys like Bill Cowley, Dit Clapper and Johnny Crawford. The Bruins' problem was that they never practiced. With a team like Toronto I could keep my weight down because we worked out every day for two hours; in Boston, I had no control over my weight and was never in the condition I used to be. This hurt me and I became susceptible to injuries. I always feel that when a player gets hurt, it's usually because he's not in shape.

In my case, Art Ross, the Boston manager, sent me down to the minors for a couple of weeks, thinking I'd come right back. But I arrived in Hershey and got injured again, and when it came time to return to the Bruins I was in the hospital, so they took somebody else instead.

On the other hand, it was somewhat fortunate that I stayed there because the Bears won the American League championship and we got $1,800 apiece as a playoff check while Boston got beaten in the first round of the playoffs, and I think their players received only $600.

I never did play in the NHL again. In 1947-48 I spent part of the season in Cleveland, then in 1948-49 I went west to play three seasons for New Westminster in the Pacific Coast Hockey League. My last year was with Tacoma in 1951-52.

Over the years I saw a lot of hockey and many good hockey players. Looking back, I'd say that Milt Schmidt of the Boston Bruins had the most drive. Schmidt, Syl Apps of the Maple Leafs, and Neil Colville of the Rangers were the three greatest puck-carriers I've ever seen. Of course, the greatest goal-scorer was Rocket Richard, but he wasn't the greatest player; to me that was Jean Beliveau. He was a polished performer who did everything — stickhandle, shoot, the works! As for the smaller men, Stan Mikita of the Blackhawks was a little guy who could shoot the way Doug Bentley used to and make plays like Bill Cowley did for Boston.

Looking back at the defensemen, Doug Harvey ranks as the greatest along with "Black Jack" Stewart who played for the Red Wings and Blackhawks. Stewart never was the puck-carrier that Harvey was; just a real, fine, sound defenseman.

Then you get to Bobby Orr. His roaming up the ice at will hurt him and it got him hurt, too. If a defenseman doesn't start picking his spots to rush instead of randomly attacking, he'll get hurt a lot more. Defensemen should never rush against five men; they should rush when they get a break.

If you ask me, today's game could be improved with a rule change here and there. I'd love to see them do away with the blue line. I really think this would open up the game.

I'd also like to see the nets put right in the backboard. That would eliminate the habit modern defensemen have of going behind the net and standing there. With everything in front of them they'd have to go up the ice with the puck and this would also stop a lot of that body checking behind the nets. The puck would be alive and there'd be more sustained action.

Let's face it, the game is different today and so are the players. In my day you had to be able to stickhandle; some of these fellows I see now couldn't stickhandle past their mothers without losing the puck — and some couldn't pass it to their mother if she were starving to death and it was a piece of bread they were handing her.

But they do a heck of a job on defense by slamming into guys, going down, and stopping pucks. They earn their money there; but for real hockey — the way the fundamentals were originally taught by people like Lester Patrick and Art Ross — these fellows playing today can't do the job.

When I played we were taught not to shoot the puck until we saw the whites of the goaltender's eyes. Now they blast from anywhere, hoping the puck will hit somebody's skates or ankles and bounce into the net. And when they go to sign next year's contract, the manager never asks whether the player stickhandled through the whole team, faked the goaltender, and tucked the puck in the net; all he says is, "How many did you get?"

Another difference is that the modern players don't have the laughs we used to — and that includes the hockey writers, too. Believe it or not, I once wrote a story for Burchard in the *World-Telegram*. We'd been playing the Maple Leafs in the playoffs and Toronto had just brought up a rookie named Hank Goldup. After one of the games, Burchard came over to me and said, "Babe, make me my story; c'mon, write it for me."

I said, "I was on the ice the same time as Goldup and it was the first time I played against him. I wanted to see if he could shoot. He did, and he scored the winning goal." The next night I picked up the paper and there was the headline: PRATT FINDS OUT ROOKIE CAN SHOOT, POPS IN WINNER. I was only kidding around and Burchard made me the goof on the play.

One year — I think 1936 — the writers were the ones who gave out assists on goals, something like official scorers in baseball today. They were so funny — they once gave *three* assists on one goal.

It happened when we were playing the New York Americans and little Roy Worters was their goalie. Sweeney Schriner put the puck in for the Americans and the scorer gave the assists to Art Chapman and Lorne Carr. Carr went over to the scorer and said, "Hey, why don't you give an assist to Worters; he's a nice fellow." So he did. Three assists on that one goal.

As I said, things were different then; even the arenas have changed. They used to be noisy and the fans were closer to the ice; now they're big and new, but they're not the same. I went to the opening of the new Madison Square Garden, and when I got inside I looked around and thought, "Jesus, this is a cold-looking joint."

The crowds have changed, too. You don't get the same funny cracks we used to, especially from the gallery gods. I remember once at the Garden there was a game with the Red Wings who we were beating 6-1. Jack Adams, Detroit's manager, had just gotten his citizenship papers and suddenly a fan yelled out, "Hey, Adams, it's a good thing you got citizenship; now you can get home relief!"

Another time we were leading the Americans by about six goals. A voice from the stands yelled down to me, "Hey, Walter, why don't you turn the net around; nobody's looking!"

The attitudes have changed; everything is all business. When a hockey player gets on a plane he's as apt to pick up *The Wall Street Journal* as anything else. And when business gets more important than the sport itself, that's not right.

Chapter 10

FRANK FREDERICKSON

*It was a late summer day in 1968 when Stan and
I interviewed Frank Frederickson at his home in
Vancouver. Tall and slender, the silver-haired Icelander
looked and spoke more like a retired university professor
than a retired hockey player.*

*When he and his wife — also of Icelandic extraction —
discovered that my paternal grandmother had been born
and raised in the Icelandic enclave of Gimlee, Manitoba,
not far from Winnipeg, they took great pleasure in
showing us how to make the Icelandic cheese they served
us that day. We stood for some time in their homey
kitchen, Frank reminiscing about his life while his wife
hung a huge cheesecloth-wrapped ball of forming cheese
to drain liquid into a large bowl.*

*Like others Stan and I spoke to that summer so long
ago, Frank Frederickson had not played professional
hockey for many years. Still, the memories — of games,
triumphs and defeats — appeared at moments to be as
fresh and vibrant as though they had occurred a mere
month before.*

Frank Frederickson died in 1979.

Learning hockey was easier for me than learning English. Although
I was born in Winnipeg, Manitoba, my parents came from Iceland
and only spoke Icelandic in our house. As a result I couldn't speak
a word of English until I was six years old and started school.

Being of Icelandic descent was also difficult because of the attitude some of our neighbors had. They looked down on our family
as "those white-haired Icelanders" and would make fun of us in
various ways. Coming home from school frequently turned into a
battle as the kids would gang up on us and start fights just because
we were Icelandic.

My best outlet was hockey. I got my first pair of skates when I was
five and had a great time learning to play. My dad, who probably
didn't weigh more than 140 pounds soaking wet, used to come home

Frank Frederickson   **(Hockey Hall of Fame)**

and pump water into the backyard and flood the place. After a while it froze and we would have a little rink, about 15 by 20 feet. Dad didn't reserve it just for me; there was also my sister, my younger brother, and a lot of other kids from the neighborhood. My father was vitally interested in giving all the youngsters an opportunity, and eventually he and some friends built a community rink with shacks, pot-bellied stoves and everything else we might need to be comfortable.

I didn't get away with playing hockey all the time. Those Icelanders were very insistent that their children have the opportunity for the best education possible, and apart from school this included violin lessons. On my way to instruction I'd always walk along the back lanes to keep away from the rest of the kids; I was so afraid they'd see me with the violin case and call me a sissy.

School came easy for me. I especially remember my eighth grade teacher, Miss McLeod, who was one of the most marvelous persons I ever met; she actually used to come out on Saturday mornings and play hockey with us. I wasn't such a good hockey player at the time, but my break came not too much later when I quit school.

After finishing grade eight I decided I ought to earn a living and got a job as an office boy in a law firm. This turned out to be an excellent move. All the firms sponsored hockey teams then, so naturally we had one, too. It was a seven-man team because in those days a rover was the seventh player in addition to three forwards, two defensemen and a goalkeeper.

I didn't get to play right away, but one day our club was a man short and they asked the senior office boy to play. He couldn't, though, because he had a game leg. Then they tried another boy who had a different excuse; that brought them finally to me.

As things turned out I played well and captured the attention of two of our attorneys. They took a great deal of personal interest in me, not just as a hockey player, and urged me to go back to school. So in 1914 I enrolled at the University of Manitoba, took a liberal arts course, and a year later was named captain of the hockey team. Everything was moving along well in school and I would have graduated in 1918 except that World War I had broken out and a lot of my chums were joining the 196th University Battalion.

I felt a duty to go along so I joined up, but before they sent me overseas I switched to the 223rd Scandinavian Battalion. When I got to the other side I joined the air force, which was really a laugh. In those days the planes were more like box kites. I'd climb in the front, peer around and see a rudder that looked like two organ pedals. The joystick was like the top of a pair of scissors. My plane was a Maurice-Farman that had pusher-type engines and a top speed of about 75 miles per hour. We did our training in Egypt of all places, and if we were good enough we graduated to Bristol Scouts and

Avros, which I did. Then they transferred me to Italy. I was enjoying the trip across the Mediterranean when my hockey career — and all my other careers — nearly ended.

I had been in a depressed mood before we left the port of Alexandria because I had just heard of my sister's death, but once on the ship I felt a little better. It was a beautiful moonlit night and the sea seemed so peaceful. Then there was a terrific explosion and the captain announced we had been hit on the starboard side by a torpedo and were sinking. The cry went out: "Everybody to the lifeboats!"

I looked around and discovered there was no lifeboat left for me to go to. So I began thinking about what was important to me and went back to my bunk to get my violin. I gave it to one of the captains of another lifeboat and told him to take care of it. Just when I thought all was lost, I found one of those canvas-sided boats and along with some other fellows scrambled in.

At first we couldn't get it to move straight; the thing kept going around in circles and it looked like we might be caught in the swell of the sinking ship. We straightened out just in time, but then looked up to see a Japanese destroyer coming right at us. I said to myself, "Oh, God, that's everything!"

The destroyer swerved in the nick of time and came right alongside us. Japanese sailors dropped a few ladders and we climbed aboard. Were we ever happy to see them! They gave us saki and pajama tops to bandage some of the fellows who were hurt.

Eventually we made our way to Italy and from there were told to report to England, then on to Scotland. What I wanted to do was get on a plane called the SC-5 because I had heard they were doing a marvelous job; however, orders were for me to instruct. So, from that time on I was an instructor and never a hero.

It took a year from the time the war ended before I could get back to Winnipeg. When I returned in 1919, a bunch of us led by Mike Goodman, the speed-skating champion of North America, and Slim Halter, a great big, gangling six-footer who was a beautiful stickhandler, organized the Falcon hockey team and applied for admission to the senior league.

The leaders of that league wouldn't let us in because they claimed we weren't good enough to compete with teams like the Monarchs and Winnipegs. So we did the next best thing and organized our own league composed of such teams as Selkirk that had "Bullet" Joe Simpson as captain. We later found out the reason we couldn't get in the senior league was because the players there were from well-to-do families and wanted no part of us. But they couldn't quite get away from us that easily. We finished in first place, then played the winners of the big league in a two-game series. In a terrific upset we beat them in two games straight, 14 goals to two. We then defeated

Lake-of-the-Woods, Head-of-the-Lakes, and Fort William, and went on to Toronto where we won the Allen Cup for the senior championship of Canada, beating the famed University of Toronto!

That was quite a triumph because it qualified us to represent Canada in the 1920 Winter Olympics at Antwerp, Belgium — the first time ice hockey was ever included on the Olympics program. That trip was certainly memorable.

We played indoors at the Palais de Glâce, a rink that wasn't full-size by our standards, but was big enough. Unfortunately, the boards weren't really boards, but rather wood paneling of a delicate nature, and sometimes when we'd bounce a hard carom off them we'd smash them to smithereens.

Some of the teams were relatively new to hockey and showed it, even in their gear. The Swedes wore ordinary leg pads and their goalkeeper had on his cricket pads. We loaned him our goalie's extra set of pads and he was very grateful.

The Americans had a pretty good team, mostly of Americanized Canadians, but we beat them 8-1 even though we were trying very hard to keep the score down and played only two 20-minute periods. It was a highly gratifying win because the Americans were a very disliked team. They were running up scores like 21-0 and 25-0 against the weaker countries since there were some pretty poor players in those days. Some were so bad they didn't even know how to stop — they just skated headlong into the boards!

Winning the Olympic championship was quite a feather in our cap and gave us all a lot of publicity. I had the world at my feet, but instead of returning immediately to Canada I was asked by the Icelandic government to go there to do some experimental flying. As it turned out, I became the first pilot of Icelandic extraction to fly in Iceland.

I flew from May to September and had to give it up at that time because they couldn't get petrol supplies. Then I went to England to try and get some of the English concerns interested in flying to Iceland, but I failed in that and returned to Canada, making a stop in Toronto.

When I got there, Mayor Church entertained me and asked, "Now that you're back, Frank, what do you want to do?" I told him I wanted to join the Canadian air force, but didn't think I could get in because there were many senior officers ahead of me. Church was a wonderful guy and a very influential man; when I got home to Winnipeg there was a telegram advising me to report to camp for duty. So, in 1920 I joined the Canadian air force.

For all intents and purposes it appeared that my career was set for years to come. Life is funny, though, and out of the blue I received a letter from Lester Patrick, the old Silver Fox of hockey, who was in Victoria, British Columbia, where he had a team in the old Pacific

Coast League. It was top-notch hockey and Lester offered me what was a substantial contract in those days — $2,500 for 24 games. I call it substantial because the rest of the boys were playing for $800 and $900. I couldn't resist the offer and so found myself right back in the middle of hockey again.

It was quite a selling job on Lester's part. After all, he was just taking a gamble on my reputation and the fact that I had played on the Olympic teams. But he believed in me and gave me a big ballyhoo, telling people I was the highest-paid player in the Pacific Coast League.

My first game with Victoria was quite something. There I was, a young center-ice man just fresh from the Olympic win, teamed with Cyclone Taylor, who was 10 years older and widely known as a great player. Lester himself still played — he was a rover — and that made things a lot easier for me. We won the game and I went on to have a terrific season, finishing in a tie for the goal-scoring championship.

Playing in Victoria was very worthwhile and kept getting better until 1925 when we won the Stanley Cup. Our opponents were the Montreal Canadiens who had players like Georges Vezina in goal and the Cleghorn brothers, and there was terrific interest in those playoffs. We played some of the games in Victoria and others in Vancouver because our home rink could hold only 4,500 people while the Vancouver rink held about 11,500, and it was absolutely packed. At the time it had the largest seating capacity in the world. Excitement was so intense that people would come there the night before a game and build fires to keep warm until the ticket wickets opened.

All the sportswriters, both Eastern and Western, had conceded the series to Montreal because they thought the Canadiens had the superior team and deserved to win. But we up and beat them and the city was ours; the people simply gave us everything we wanted.

We nearly did it again the following year, but this time we faced the Montreal Maroons who had the big "S" line of Siebert, Stewart and Smith, and lost by a small margin.

I remember that series for its freak goals. In the first game Nels Stewart, who had been moved back to the Maroon defense, started a rush up the ice but, in heading for the Victoria goal, he slipped and fell flat on his face. Instead of staying alert, our goalie relaxed and Stewart, while still flat on the ice, swung his stick at the rolling puck and bounced it into the net, and Montreal went on to beat us.

Then again, in the one game we did win in that series, I took a high shot that went over the cage and smacked against the wire mesh netting above the backboards, about 10 feet over goalie Clint Benedict's head. Somehow the puck rebounded off the wire, hit Benedict on the back of the neck, and rolled into the goal. It wasn't enough, though, and the Maroons outscored us the rest of the way to win the Cup.

But we had played well and, of course, we had Lester behind us with that analytical mind of his. He had quite a way with players; he'd never come into the dressing room and bawl the hell out of you or anything like that. He would just sit down and chat with the fellows and then he might turn to me and say, "Frederickson, why don't you come down to the office tomorrow?"

The next day I'd see him and he'd go over my mistakes in a very fair and understanding manner. He liked to win, there's no question about that, but he wasn't unjust in his criticism. However, the next year Lester decided to sell all his players to the NHL, which was in the process of expanding throughout the United States. Patrick had made arrangements for his players to go to Detroit, and the Detroit club signed up everyone but me. Meanwhile, Boston's Art Ross, who was a great friend of Patrick's, arranged to have me play with the Bruins along with Eddie Shore and Harry Oliver. But I wouldn't sign up with Boston and Ross sent me a wire threatening me with expulsion for the rest of my life. So I signed with Detroit and got $6,000, which was a lot of money then.

When I got off the train from the West and picked up a paper in Detroit, I saw a lead story entitled, "Frederickson Gets $10,000." You can imagine how my teammates must have felt — they were getting only $2,000 and $2,500. But that newspaper story was just the same old bunk; they always have to add a little.

As things turned out I didn't do well in Detroit. Previously, I had been first, second or third in scoring, but now was 24th and getting nowhere at all. The problem was dissension on the team, but I didn't last too long and was traded to Boston for two good hockey players.

As soon as I arrived with my new team, Art Ross scheduled a meeting with me. At first I thought he'd give me the business but instead he said, "I'm taking Dick Ferguson off the first line and I want you to take it with Harry Oliver and Perk Galbraith and work with them." At that time Boston was the second tail-end team in the American Division, but after I got there we took the lead.

Now, I don't say that this good fortune was due to their acquiring Frank Frederickson; it resulted from fellows working together in a collective effort. I learned one thing: by cooperation and joint effort you can do an awful lot more than when you're just by yourself.

My first game as a Bruin was against the New York Rangers who were now managed by my old boss, Lester Patrick. We beat New York 3-2 and I got three goals. Those days with Boston were outstanding from the viewpoint of competition because there were great players all over the place. New York had Frank Boucher and the Cook brothers, Bill and Bun. Frank was as sweet a hockey player as you could find, and that line, well, there was nothing like it. But on our club we had Eddie Shore and he was really something.

Shore was a very colorful hockey player who put everything he had into the game, but also used every subterfuge he could to win the sympathy of the crowd. He'd fake getting hurt and would lay down and roll around in agony. Then he'd get up and be twice as good as ever. To me, Shore was a country boy who had made good; he was a good skater and puck-carrier, but wasn't an exceptional defenseman like his teammate Lionel Hitchman. Hitch was better because he could get them coming and going. But there wasn't another character like Shore. I remember once when he decided to take saxophone lessons. Art Ross, Harry Oliver, Sprague Cleghorn and myself were playing bridge and there was Shore alone in the hotel drawing room, playing his saxophone with the damnedest noise in the world coming out.

Finally, Ross said to Harry Oliver: "Jesus Christ, Harry, go and tell that silly bastard to *blow* on the goddamned thing and not suck on it."

One night we had a game and Shore came skating out on the ice — wearing a bathrobe. It was crazy and I think Art Ross encouraged him. Of course, Art himself was quite a character. Once we were playing a Stanley Cup game in Ottawa and Ross objected to some bad calls the referee had made. We lost the game — and the Cup — but after it was over Ross got us together in the dressing room and said, "Okay, the first man who gets that referee gets a $500 bonus." Well, we had a big French boy on our team named Billy Coutu who was straight out of the woods; the minute he saw the referee he let him have it unmercifully and absolutely knocked him out. Sure enough, Ross gave him a $500 bonus.

But in the final analysis it was a tragic episode. The matter was brought up before the NHL board of directors and Coutu was suspended for life; yet it was Ross who was responsible. I've never forgiven Ross for that, and it was the beginning of the end for us. Not long after that incident a story appeared in the *Boston Herald* saying that Frank Frederickson would be handling the Boston club. It was ridiculous and I had no idea why it was written. Naturally, Ross didn't like it and when we got to New York he didn't put me on my regular line.

With each game he would use me less and less and finally relegated me to killing penalties. Then he went to Charles Adams, owner of the Bruins, and suggested I be traded to Pittsburgh.

The deal was for me to go to the Pittsburgh club in exchange for Mickey McKay and $10,000. When the trade was approved I was heartbroken, not only for myself but also for McKay because his pride was very much hurt when he heard about the terms. Besides, I loved Boston and my family was very much settled there.

I sent the family home and then Adams called me into his office to say, "Frank, I'm awfully sorry, but I more or less have to take the advice of my manager and that's that." He then handed me a check for $1,000, which was wonderful. I still have letters from fans and teammates saying how badly they felt that I had left Boston, but I had to make do and so moved on to Pittsburgh.

I went directly to my new team, run by Odie Cleghorn. He was a colorful chap, always dressed with top hat, spats, cane and gloves — the works, like a Beau Brummel. But I wound up getting double-crossed in Pittsburgh. I had a three-year contract with them at $8,000 a year, but my first season was a poor one and I ended up tearing the cartilage in my knee. By hockey standards I was old — 37 years — and they decided to cut my contract. They gave the club to Cooper Smeaton and moved to Philadelphia in 1930.

If they had dropped me like that today I'd have sued. I even met with Lester Patrick, told him what happened, and said I wanted to sue. He replied, "It would cost you more to sue in the courts than to get your contract."

And that was it for the NHL and me.

Frank Boucher   **(Hockey Hall of Fame)**

Chapter 11

FRANK BOUCHER

Frank Boucher was a hockey player right out of a Boy Scout manual. There has never been — and likely never will be — a player who epitomizes all that is lyrical, artistic and thoroughly magnificent about the game of hockey. Boucher not only was an extraordinarily skillful player, but he was also one of the most cerebral and likeable.

His claims to fame are innumerable. He helped the New York Rangers to their first Stanley Cup in 1928; centered a remarkable line that included Bill Cook on the right and brother Fred "Bun" Cook on the left; coached the Rangers to their last Stanley Cup in 1940; helped rewrite the NHL rule book; introduced the center red line to the game in 1943; and won so many Lady Byng trophies for good conduct — seven times in an eight-year stretch — that Lady Byng gave Boucher the trophy to keep and then bought another one for other players.

Although he weighed only 134 pounds, Boucher was a fearless competitor, perhaps because he previously served as a member of the Royal Canadian Mounted Police.

Born in Ottawa, Boucher followed in a long line of stars who learned their hockey in Canada's capital city. Boucher's idol during his youth was Hall-of-Famer Frank Nighbor, who made a name for himself with the Ottawa Senators. "Nighbor," said Boucher, "was every young lad's hero in Ottawa in those days. He was a magnificent center who rarely lost his temper, who could hookcheck and pokecheck like nobody else."

Boucher starred for the Rangers from 1926 until 1938 when he moved into the coaching realm. When a large number of Rangers left the team for the Canadian armed forces during World War II, Boucher put on the Ranger livery again and at the age of 42 played 15 games for his Blueshirts. Incredibly, Frank outscored 19 other players the Rangers had tried that season. In time, Boucher gave

*up coaching to manage the Rangers. In September 1954,
a 22-year-old just out of Brooklyn College was hired
by Boucher to be the Rangers' assistant publicist. Stan
Fischler worked under Boucher's regime during the
1954-55 season, during which time he obtained much of
the narrative below. Additional stories were gathered on
Boucher's return to New York after his retirement.
Frank Boucher died in 1977.*

Are you kidding? Get a bonus for signing my NHL contract? Not on your life.

Back in 1921, that's the way it was — attitudes were different then. We didn't have the agents, attorneys and what-have-you that the Bobby Orrs and Bobby Hulls of today have. When the Ottawa Senators asked me to play for them in 1921, I signed a one-year contract for $1,200 and considered myself very lucky and happy to be playing hockey. Nobody cared about images and stuff like that. It's not that way anymore, though; today, hockey players are all business. Why I've even heard that Phil Esposito gets paid for a one-hour speaking engagement what I got paid for a whole season! Imagine that. And here I won the Lady Byng Trophy seven times and never made more than $8,500 in one season.

Of course, we didn't have a players' association in our day and weren't wrapped up in all those other trappings. Frankly, I don't know whether it was dedication to the sport or if we were just damn fools. But there's one thing I'm sure of — I know we had a heck of a lot more fun than they do today. That's where we had it over them, in the laughs.

I'll never forget that first Rangers training camp. It was the fall of 1926 and Conn Smythe, our manager, had booked us into the Peacock Hotel which was right on the outskirts of Toronto. Smythe was later replaced by Lester Patrick, but at that time he was organizing the club and he was a real stickler for discipline. One of the first things he did was to set an early curfew. That was fine except that I had been out having a good time with Ching Johnson, and by the time we got back to the hotel that night the place was completely locked.

No matter how hard we tried we couldn't get into the place, so we decided to do the next best thing and head for a hotel downtown. Since there were no cabs around, we walked a few blocks to an intersection and discovered a trolley car about to start on its first run of the morning. It was about 6 a.m. when we got on the trolley, and the motorman was an awfully friendly chap. We offered him a bit of the applejack we had been drinking and he proved to be a very congenial host.

After about 10 minutes he had to start the trolley on its run and asked, "Where are you gentleman going?" I told him we'd like to head for the King Edward Hotel, but at the time I didn't realize it wasn't exactly on the same route as the trolley normally would go. The motorman said he'd oblige, and before you could say "Jack Robinson" he turned off all the lights except those up front and started downtown.

We had gone about three blocks when we came to the first trolley station where a half-dozen or so people were waiting to get on, but our man didn't slow down one bit; he just plowed straight ahead as if the only thing that mattered was getting us to the King Edward Hotel.

We passed enough passengers in a mile or so that somebody surely must have phoned the Toronto Transit Commission to complain but, as I said, our motorman didn't seem to care — at least not until we reached a corner where there was a switch. At that point he must've realized the tracks weren't going to take us to the King Edward even though his route was supposed to go directly ahead.

Suddenly he gets one of those big steel rods, runs out onto the tracks, and pulls the switch and off we go toward the hotel. By this time the three of us made quite a barbershop trio and were singing every good song in the book until we looked up and saw the King Edward ahead. Our friend stopped the trolley directly in front of the hotel, shook our hands, and then took off into the early morning!

I was associated with the Rangers for 28 years as a player, coach and manager, and I can say without hesitation that the 1927-28 New York team and the 1939-40 team were the best Ranger clubs of all time and among the finest ever seen in the NHL. Naturally, I'm a little partial to the 1927-28 team because I played on it and was in my prime then. What made it so great was its two very strong lines — in those days we didn't have a three- or four-line system as they do today — plus a defense that no club could equal and good goalkeeping. You knew we were good because we won the Cup in strange circumstances.

We couldn't play any of the final Cup games in New York then because Madison Square Garden had other commitments, so all our "home" games had to be played on the road, making it tremendously difficult. We eliminated Pittsburgh and Boston in the opening rounds, then went up against the Montreal Maroons and had to play all the games at the Montreal Forum.

That was the series where our regular goalie, Lorne Chabot, got hurt and old Lester Patrick went into the nets. From my own standpoint that was unforgettable because I scored the winning goal at 7:05 of sudden death in Game Two of the series and scored the only goal of Game Four.

After Lester went in as goalie and won, we got Joe Miller to
goaltend for us. He'd been nicknamed "Red Light" Miller because
he'd played for the Americans and they were losers at that time. I
personally never thought he was that bad and, as things turned out,
he was pretty terrific in that last game. Right off the bat we were
behind the eight ball. We got a penalty and I was sent out to try to
kill the clock until our man returned. For quite a few seconds we
did pretty well and then somebody got the puck to me and I found
myself at center ice, skating in on Red Dutton, a Maroon defenseman. I knew Red's weakness — if you pushed the puck through his
legs he'd give his attention to it instead of watching you. I tried the
trick and, sure enough, he looked down. By the time he looked up,
I was around him and had picked up the puck, skated in on their
goalie, Clint Benedict, and flipped it into the right-hand corner.

Not very long after that we got hit with another penalty and Lester
sent me out again. My only concern was to stickhandle the puck as
much as possible at center ice; however, I suddenly found myself
in a position where my only play was to shoot the puck off the
boards, and hope to pick up the rebound and keep possession. I
miscalculated and shot the puck too far ahead — so far that Dunc
Munro, the Maroons defenseman, thought he could intercept it.

The puck was now about midway between Munro and me, and as
I watched him I realized he was going to try to beat me to it. He came
on for quite a run and I could almost hear him thinking, "By God, I
can't get there in time." He seemed to stop in one motion, then
change his mind and go for the puck again. All the while, I was
skating madly toward it and, by this time, had reached it. I just
swooped over to one side and let Munro go by; I had the whole ice
to myself, straight to the goaltender.

I moved directly in on Benedict and landed the goal in almost the
exact place as I did earlier. We won the game 2-1 and the Cup. It
certainly was a tribute to Lester — if he hadn't gone into the nets
when Chabot was hurt, I don't know what we would have done. But
that was Lester: a very, very interesting man and a tough taskmaster
as well.

One memory of him really stands out in this regard. We had
played in Ottawa one night and won the game with some fantastic
score like 10-1 and went to a party afterward in Hull, Quebec, the
town across the river. I guess we stayed long past our curfew, but
finally decided it was time to get back to our Pullman sitting in the
Ottawa station. We all knew that Lester must have been asleep so
we tiptoed onto the train and kept passing the word along in
whispers, "Don't wake Lester!"

It seemed to us that we managed to sneak in without disturbing
him — or so I thought until the next morning when I walked into
the diner for breakfast. Lester, who was sitting there alone, looked

up and said, "Good morning, Mr. Boucher." As soon as he called me by my last name I knew something was wrong. I sat down next to him and nothing was said for about a minute until Lester off-handedly mentioned to me, "Did you know that Butch Keeling walks in his sleep?"

I said, "No, Lester, I didn't." To which Lester replied, "Y'know, Frank, that's very interesting because at about four in the morning Butch walked into my compartment, peed on the floor, and whispered something about 'Don't wake Lester!'"

There wasn't much I could say after that, but if you think I was tongue-tied then let me tell you about another situation that really put me on the hot seat for quite some time. That occurred in the 1930-31 season that Cecil Dillon joined the Rangers as a rookie. It didn't take long for me to discover I was his idol, but not just as a hockey player.

Cecil had been crazy about the Royal Canadian Mounted Police ever since he was a kid, and when he found out that I had once been a Mountie there was nothing I could do to discourage him. It became embarrassing because I was only a Mountie for a short time, as all the other Rangers knew, and had never served in any of the wild, Northwest outposts. Dillon nevertheless began to press me to tell about my experiences. At first I thought I'd just let him know that nothing much really had happened to me, but I could tell that he was really keen to hear something so I began with a few honest-to-goodness yarns of incidents that actually did occur. They were my true stories and I hoped they'd be sufficient.

I didn't know whether to be happy or sad about it, but Dillon thought my stories were just the greatest things in the world and began begging me to tell some more. Unfortunately, I ran out of true stories and had to make a decision: either let on to Dillon that absolutely nothing else happened that was interesting, or start to fabricate stories. My mistake was in deciding to do everything possible to make the rookie happy. The next time we sat down I told him a whole pile of fictitious tales.

You name it, I did it. Boucher battled the Indians; Boucher commanded a dog team in the Arctic; Boucher was all over the Northwest. When my imagination ran dry I went to the nearest newsstand to pick up a few Western magazines to restore my supply. After a while I even began to hope that Lester might trade Cecil, just to get him off my back. That didn't happen, though; Dillon was an awfully good hockey player and just a nice a guy to boot. His problem was that he kept wanting more Mountie stories and I had to keep telling them.

Once and only once I was nearly exposed. The Rangers were in Atlantic City for some reason and several of us took a stroll on the Boardwalk. When we passed a shooting gallery Dillon asked me to join him in a few rounds, figuring that as a former Mountie my shooting would be super. Actually, I couldn't shoot the side of a barn.

Cecil started shooting first and he was deadly accurate. He had done quite a bit of hunting back home in Ontario, so this was second nature to him. When he got through he handed me the gun and I couldn't touch a thing — not one bloody target! It reached such a point that I could tell Cecil was wearing a long face because he was horrified at my performance.

I was about to let on to him that I had been telling a pack of fibs when I suddenly thought of something. I took Cecil aside and mentioned that while he was firing at the targets I had spoken to the fellow running the gallery and had told him to put blanks in my rifle. Cecil fell for it, and as long as he played for the Rangers he remained convinced that all those Mountie tales were true.

Maybe that helped me later when I became the Rangers manager, because we needed all the imagination we could get during those bad years. But they didn't come till later; we had some marvelous teams in the '30s. After I retired and was made coach, we had a wonderful bunch of boys in the 1939-40 season. Yes, that was one of the greatest teams in history.

Tops in every position, it started with Davey Kerr in goal, Art Coulter and Murray Patrick as one defense team, and Babe Pratt and Ott Heller on the other. The three forward lines were just fantastic: Phil Watson-Bryan Hextall-Lynn Patrick; Neil and Mac Colville-Alex Shibicky; and Clint Smith-Kilby MacDonald-Alf Pike, with Dutch Hiller as the spare. They were perfect players for a coach because you could encourage suggestions and they'd always come up with something good that we'd practice and eventually use in a game. One result was the "box defense," where the four players killing a penalty arrange themselves in a box formation in front of the goalkeeper. We had another strategy called offensive penalty-killing which turned out to be the beginning of modern forechecking. In this one, we tried for goals when we were a man short instead of going into a defensive shell. We'd send out three forwards and one defenseman, and we'd forecheck in their own end. Our team was so good it scored more goals over a season than it had goals scored upon it during penalty-killing. Once, though, it backfired on us.

We had perfected this system — or so we thought — and went into Chicago with a 19-game unbeaten streak. In that 20th game we played rings around the Blackhawks and should have won by a big margin, but for some strange reason we couldn't score a goal. We were down 1-0 going into the third period.

During intermission we were batting around ideas in the dressing room when the guys came up with another new one. It was decided that if we were still down by a goal in the final minute of play, we'd pull the goalkeeper and send out an extra skater. Up until that point, the way the system worked you never put the extra man on the ice until there was a whistle for a face-off. But we thought it'd be better not to make it obvious that we were pulling the goalie; in other words, do it on the fly while the play was still going on. That was the plan.

I made one big mistake; I forgot to tell Lester our plan and on this particular night he was sitting on our bench, which he very rarely did in those days. Toward the end of the game, though, he walked over to the Chicago Stadium timekeeper because he didn't trust him and wanted to keep an eye on the clock.

We still were down a goal and had the puck in the opposition's end of the rink. This was the time to try the new plan and the signal was given for Davey Kerr to come off the ice and for the extra forward to go on. That's exactly what happened and nobody in the rink knew what was going on except my players — and then Lester. *But he didn't realize that Kerr was removed from the goal.* So Lester thought I had made a mistake and put too many men on the ice and started screaming for me to take the "extra" man off before we got a penalty.

Paul Thompson — the Blackhawk coach — heard him, and when he saw six men in his zone he started screaming too. Meanwhile, we had moved the puck into scoring position and the plan was working perfectly. We were about to put it in the net when the referee blew his whistle to give us a penalty. Then, he turned around, saw that Kerr was out, and realized there shouldn't be a penalty at all. But it was too late. The attack was stopped and we lost the game 1-0.

As things turned out we won the next five games in a row for an over-all record of 24 wins or ties in 25 games and went on to win the Stanley Cup. Then the war came and we lost most of our really good players. When it was over a lot of them came back, but they had lost a step or two and weren't really the same. That's when we had to start rebuilding, which took quite some time. Naturally, when times were bad we used to resort to all kinds of tricks to get people into the Garden.

There was one period during the war years when things hit an all-time low. We had lost such fellows as Jim Henry, Murray Patrick, Art Coulter and Alex Shibicky to the armed forces and, by the time October 1942 came around, more than half of our roster that had finished first the previous spring was gone. It was time for training camp to start and, believe it or not, we didn't have a goalkeeper on hand — not one! Lester was just as worried as I was and I told him the only thing we could do was to check out every town in Canada to see if we could find one. We sent telegrams to all our scouts telling them to wire us if they came across a goalie and, three days later, we got word from our man in Saskatchewan, Al Ritchie. He said he had a chap named Steve Buzinski who'd play goal for us, so I told Ritchie to get him to our camp immediately.

Camp was in Winnipeg, as it had been for years, and when we got there and started workouts I discovered that nobody named Buzinski had arrived. Well, there was nothing much we could do but sit around and hope that he'd show up; meanwhile, we sent the boys through the practice skates and light workouts. After a day or so I really began to get worried, but on this particular afternoon we were on the ice when I looked over towards the sideboards and got the surprise of my life.

In the Winnipeg Amphitheater the sideboards were quite a bit higher than in other rinks, and as I looked at them I saw this tiny fellow walking along, wearing a black helmet — but all I could see was the helmet over the sideboards. At first I thought it was a "rink rat," one of those lads who hang around the rink and clean the ice between workouts. But soon I saw one goalie pad, then another, climb over the boards and, sure enough, this little chap skated directly to the net. I remember saying to myself when I looked at him, "Oh my gosh, it can't be him!"

This was Steve Buzinski; he was not only small, but he was bowlegged too! And when he stood in front of the net, you saw nothing but holes. We didn't have much choice since there were no other goalkeepers around, so Steve was our man when the 1942-43 season started. I can't say he was the greatest, but he did try and he had a strange sense of humor. One night we were playing in Detroit and the Red Wings were scoring on him left and right. Sometime late in the game one of the Detroit players took a long shot and Buzinski nabbed it in his glove and casually tossed it aside, as though he were a Vezina Trophy-winner. Just as he did, one of our boys skated by and heard Steve say: "Y'know, this is as easy as picking cherries off a tree!"

I can't honestly say our losing was entirely Steve's fault, but when we found out there was another goalie available with more experience — Jimmy Franks — we got him. But we kept Buzinski on the payroll because he was good for his humor and in those days we needed all the humor we could get. Lester finally got rid of him after he refused to attend a practice with our farm team, the Rovers. I believe he told Lester he had some letters to write home and that's all Lester needed. Buzinski was on the next train to Saskatchewan.

The fun didn't end with Steve. We had some lulus after the war, too. Remember Dr. Tracy, the hypnotist we brought in to help the team win? That was when we were running into tough luck again, in the early '50s. Tracy was a big bloke who thought he could give the Rangers a winning complex. The night of a Bruins game he talked to Buddy O'Connor and a few of the other players, and then they went out and lost the game in the final minute; we didn't see much of Dr. Tracy after that, but it wasn't the end of the gimmicks. Gene Leone, the owner of Mama Leone's Restaurant, tried to help us once with what he called "a magic elixir." He concocted some combination of clam juice — or broth — and a few other items, put it into a big black bottle, and offered it to the boys in the hopes it would get us going.

It worked a lot better than Dr. Tracy had, and we actually started winning after Gene created it. Pretty soon the black bottle became a big thing around town and Jim Burchard, who was covering hockey for *The World-Telegram*, decided we should also take it on our road trips. We had a Saturday night game in Toronto and Jim took a plane there, bottle in hand.

Damned if we didn't beat the Maple Leafs 4-2. Now, everybody's talking about Leone's black bottle and wondering what's in it. I don't think Gene expected it to become so popular and, since he was a busy man, he wasn't able to brew it every time. Once we didn't have the magic elixir and lost to the Red Wings. Burchard claimed that without the bottle we were at a psychological disadvantage.

After a while, bottle or not, we got into the old rut and eventually finished in fifth place, out of the playoffs. That was the end of the era of the magic elixir. Of course, my hope was to fill the Garden because we had a good hockey team, not a gimmick. At the same time, I was always trying to think of ways to improve the game. One of my ideas was the use of two goaltenders on a team instead of one. I was a good 20 years before my time since it's standard practice today, but in the late 1940s it was somewhat revolutionary.

At that time I had two good goalkeepers: "Sugar" Jim Henry and Charlie Rayner. Not only were they teammates, but they were also good friends off-ice and it was always a tough decision whenever I'd have to consider which one to play. I decided to alternate them during the game, so I started to change goaltenders every five minutes and it worked. Except I ran into an odd thing once against Toronto when there was only one pair of gloves for them both to use, and every time they passed each other during a change they'd transfer gloves — which looked kind of funny at the time.

They both lasted with us for a while until we got rid of Henry while keeping Rayner. Charlie was a good goaltender who helped take us to the Stanley Cup finals in 1950. But then things got rough again.

By 1953-54 we had a horrible hockey team and I had to figure out how to keep the fans from dropping off; that's when I signed Max Bentley and later talked his older brother, Doug, into coming to New York, even though both were past their prime.

I got Max at the start of the season and he still was good, but a funny sort of character. He was a hypochondriac, always carrying boxes of pills around for all his imaginary illnesses. I had a hell of a time just keeping him playing because of some trivial thing that happened to be bothering him at the time. I felt if I could get Doug to play for us as well, he'd get Max to do things he wouldn't ordinarily do.

Without Doug, I had to pamper Max. We even brought his cousin in to New York as our spare goalkeeper, just to try to keep Max happy. The Bentleys believed in traveling together, like a tribe. If you invited them over it was nothing for 12 to 14 Bentleys — the whole shebang — to come along. So I kept after Doug, trying to get him away from Saskatoon where he was player-coach. Phone calls didn't work, so I finally decided to fly up to Canada and talk directly to him. It took a while — and a lot of money — but I managed to persuade him to take a fling at it with the Rangers.

It was worth every penny of it just to see Doug and Max back together again after all those years, with Edgar Laprade on the line with them. I remember Coley Hall of the Vancouver team coming all the way from British Columbia just to see the Bentleys together once more. They scored a whole bunch of goals between them and we beat the Bruins; after it was over Hall said, "That was the greatest thing I ever saw."

Personally, I didn't think they'd be sensations right off the bat. But they were fantastic, passing and shooting and skating just like in the old days. Doug was the one who put the desire in Max when Max would lose confidence in himself.

After they teamed up together we gave the Bruins a good run for fourth place, but Lynn Patrick was coaching Boston at the time and knew what to do to stop them. Realizing that he couldn't make Doug back down, he had his players lay for Max. "As soon as Max goes for the puck," he told them, "you go get him!" They managed to slow Max down, but Doug still played beautifully right down to the end. I wish I could say we made the playoffs but it didn't happen that way; we finished fifth.

Just watching those Bentleys convinced me of one thing — the biggest mistake ever made in hockey was breaking up that team, Max and Doug, when they played for Chicago. They were a funny pair of brothers.

While all this was going on I was trying to build up the farm system, especially the juniors in Guelph, Ontario. A year after the Bentleys we began to show real progress. Andy Bathgate, Dean Prentice, Harry Howell and Lou Fontinato all came out of the Guelph Juniors, but were still a little green. We missed the playoffs again in 1954-55, my last season as manager of the Rangers. After that the Guelph kids really developed and the Rangers had a good run of playoff teams. It did my heart good to see how they turned out.

PART II

THEY CAN STILL LACE 'EM UP

Ed Sandford (c.), Zellio Toppazzini (l.), Dave Creighton (r.).
(Imperial Oil-Turofsky/Hockey Hall of Fame)

Chapter 12

ED SANDFORD

In the immediate aftermath of World War II, all six National Hockey League teams re-grouped as former stars who had served in the Canadian and American armed forces returned from active duty.

Once they had determined who could successfully make the varsity lineup, the clubs began looking to new, young players to fill the gaps. In the case of the Boston Bruins, they were concerned about their Kraut Line (Milt Schmidt, Woody Dumart, Bobby Bauer) which had helped them to pre-war Stanley Cups but appeared somewhat jaded upon return to the NHL.

With that in mind, Bruins general manager Arthur Ross began scouring the Canadian junior leagues for talent. One of his most promising finds was Edward Michael (Ed) Sandford who hailed from New Toronto, Ontario and had been a successful junior star in Ontario.

At 6-foot-1, 190 pounds, Sandford was unusually tall for hockey at the time. At the age of 19 he was promoted to the Bruins and remained in the NHL for his entire career. He played for the Bruins until he was traded to Detroit in a huge deal involving nine players on June 3, 1955. After playing only four games with the Red Wings, Sandford was dealt to the Blackhawks.

Sandford's NHL career ended in Chicago with the 1955-56 season.

Over a period of nine seasons, Sandford epitomized the honest, tenacious big-leaguer. While never a superstar, he performed nobly for the Bruins and in the spring of 1953 Ed helped Boston to one of the NHL's most astonishing upsets.

That spring the defending Stanley Cup champion Red Wings iced one of the best teams in hockey history, finishing high atop the standings in the regular season. But the Bruins upset them four games to two in the opening round before losing to the Montreal Canadiens in a five-game final.

Sandford reached his peak that spring, scoring eight goals and three assists for 11 points in 11 playoff games.

Following his retirement, Sandford remained in the Boston area and stayed close to the hockey scene. He became an NHL off-ice official and during the 1993 playoffs between the New York Islanders and Washington Capitals, Ed handled games at Nassau Coliseum. Still hale and hearty, Sandford sat down for the interview in the off-ice officials' sanctuary two hours before the playoff game began.

Where I grew up, in Toronto, everybody inherited a pair of skates and I was no different. We had an outdoor rink nearby where everybody skated — the neighbors, the kids, everyone. Of course, there was a competitive team and when I was about 11, I made the team. From that point on, I was playing plenty of hockey.

In those days all the games were played outdoors at night, against teams from neighboring towns. At the time I had no idea I was going to be a professional hockey player. Sure, I was interested in the game and we all listened to Foster Hewitt broadcast the Maple Leafs games every Saturday night.

When spring came and the ice melted, I switched to lacrosse, which was very popular where I came from. Other places had baseball as the big warm weather sport, but not us; it was lacrosse, which was a wonderful conditioner for hockey.

At that time junior hockey was extremely popular in Ontario and the Ontario Hockey Association's Junior A league was the top of the line. If you could reach that level, you knew that you had a chance to turn pro because a whole bunch of guys from the OHA had made it to the NHL over the years.

I was very fortunate. I kept improving and finally made it to Saint Michael's College, which was a Catholic boys school in Toronto. St. Mike's was renowned for its terrific hockey teams, so I considered myself in very good company. Grade nine was my first semester at St. Mike's, and I remained there right up until I joined their Junior A club.

We had a wonderful team and one year actually won the Memorial Cup. By that time I knew that pro scouts were looking at us, but I still had no thoughts of an NHL career. My first thought was about getting a good education — not that I had anything against hockey.

World War Two was at its peak then and I was getting very close to being drafted. My father worked in a munitions plant, so you can imagine that the war was uppermost in our minds. In 1944 the Allies invaded France [D-Day] and, thank goodness, the war began to swing in our favor. Meanwhile, I was still playing hockey and getting better at it all the time.

There were lots of top players in juniors then. Tod Sloan, who later became a big player with the Maple Leafs, was with us at St. Mike's and Gus Mortson, who was a very good Maple Leafs defenseman, and Jimmy Thomson as well. Red Kelly, who eventually made it to The Hockey Hall of Fame, was also a St. Mike's grad. In fact, I played defense with Red in juniors.

Then, right out of the blue, I got an offer to play for the Bruins — contract and all. At first I wasn't sure that I wanted to go to Boston. The idea of giving up school weighed on me and then there was the possibility of taking night courses. I finally decided to give the Bruins a shot, and am I ever grateful that I made that decision. It was one of the best moves of my life.

It wasn't easy to break into the big-time that year because of all the players who had come back from the armed forces. Only five or six centers broke in that whole year that I made the Bruins. It was a very competitive field and I was lucky to get a spot on the varsity.

The Bruins didn't have a championship team when I came down in 1947, but they were good. Frankie Brimsek was our goalie. His nickname was "Mister Zero" from all the shutouts he got when he came to Boston as a rookie. Frank had reached his peak when World War Two broke out and then he joined the U.S. Coast Guard. Brimmie was one of the guys who suffered from a long stint in the service, but he still had some good goaltending in him [2.80 goals against]. He was a marvelous athlete who kept himself in excellent shape. He had one concern and that was spotlights or flashing lights anywhere near him at any time of the day of a game, even hours before the game. In the dressing room he would sit with his head covered with a towel because he didn't want the lights of the room bothering his eyes. Brimsek was always concerned about not being able to see as well as he wanted. When I joined the club, he had a pretty good defense in front of him.

Our veterans were Pat Egan, whose nickname was "Boxcar," because that's what he was built like, and Johnny "Jack" Crawford. Jack was a piece of work, let me tell you. He was the only player in the league to wear a helmet at the time, but it had nothing to do with protecting his head. Jack was completely bald and he was so embarrassed by it that he decided to wear the head piece. The best young defenseman on the club was Fernie Flaman, out of Saskatchewan. Flaman had played for our minor league club in the Eastern League, the Boston Olympics, and he was a tough customer.

Up front, I had some good forwards to work with including Milt Schmidt and Woody Dumart who were two-thirds of The Kraut Line. Among the younger guys was Johnny Peirson who was from Montreal and had gone to McGill University for a year. John was the right wing on my line. He was an astute hockey player; a smart, right-hand shot and a good skater who played his position well. I'd call him a thinking man's hockey player — always watching to see what the other guy was doing and trying to offset him. I liked playing with Peirson because I knew pretty well what he was going to do when we were on the ice.

In my first full season, 1947-48, I scored 10 goals and 15 assists over 59 games. We finished third, behind Toronto and Detroit, and then played the Leafs in the opening playoff round. They had a powerful club that year with three great centers: Max Bentley, Syl Apps and Ted Kennedy. We almost beat them in the opening game at Toronto, but they won it in overtime and then took the next two. We finally beat them once in Boston before they knocked us out in five games.

A year later we finished second and I scored 16 goals and 20 assists in 56 games. As luck would have it the Leafs, who finished a poor fourth — under the .500 mark — got hot at the right time. They beat us four games to one in the first round and then swept Detroit in four straight to win the Stanley Cup for the third straight time, which was a league record.

When I think back, the real negative in my career is that I never played on a Stanley Cup-winner. The Canadiens were the power team right after the war, then the Maple Leafs won three straight Stanley Cups up to 1949, and in 1950 the Red Wings, with Ted Lindsay, Sid Abel and Gordie Howe, won the Cup.

We kept getting to the semi-finals, but not beyond. In 1951, for example, we played the Leafs and looked like we might take them. The opening game was in Toronto and we came out on top, 2-0. Our goalie was Jack Gelineau, who was rather unique in that we got him straight out of McGill University. If we had won the second game — also in Toronto — I think we could have won the series. As it happened, the second game was a real oddity. In those days the city of Toronto had what they called a Blue Law, which meant that you couldn't play a professional sport on Sundays. That was when Toronto was a very conservative town.

Well, the second game was on March 31, 1951, which was a Saturday night. That was no problem except that the score was tied 1-1 after three periods, and we went into overtime.

Into the extra session we went and still there was no score, except that now it was getting closer and closer to midnight — and Sunday, when no pro hockey could be played. Finally, the game was stopped at midnight, a 1-1 tie and a washed-out game. But the law was the law so we headed for Boston and Game Three on April Fool's Day.

Turk Broda, who was Toronto's elderly goalie — but a great one in clutch playoff games — shut us out 3-0, and then Toronto beat us again on our home rink, Boston Garden, 3-1. We lost the next two, 4-1 and 6-0 and we were out again.

We had a very competitive team, but we just couldn't get over the hump. Our coach was Lynn Patrick — father of Craig Patrick, general manager of the Penguins — and he really knew his stuff. He had coached the Rangers when they went all the way to the seventh game of the Stanley Cup finals against Detroit in 1950, and then he came over to Boston.

In 1951-52 we finished fourth and then had a terrific semi-final playoff series with Montreal, who had finished second. They took the first two games at home by big scores (5-1, 4-0) but then we bounced back and won the next three in a row. Game Six was in Boston and if we win that, we go to the finals.

This was a dandy. The game was tied 2-2 at the end of regulation. We played a whole overtime without a goal and then they beat us a little more than seven minutes into the second overtime. So, the seventh game was in Montreal and they won that, 3-1, and we were out again.

We finally made it to the finals in 1953, but only after a terrific upset over the Red Wings in the opening round. Detroit had a powerhouse in 1952-53. Gordie Howe was at the top of his career; they had a fine defense and young Terry Sawchuk was in goal.

They trounced us 7-0 in the opening game at Detroit and everyone figured that they'd run right over us. But we came right back and won 5-3 in Game Two at Detroit and, all of a sudden, a lot of things were going right for us. The line I played on — with Johnny Peirson and Fleming Mackell — got hot and we defensed very well against Howe and Lindsay.

Our old-timers — Milt Schmidt and Woody Dumart — were terrific. Lynn Patrick assigned Dumart to guard Howe and he did a terrific job shutting him down. Our reserves, particularly a fellow named Jack McIntyre, came through for us big-time. We came home to Boston Garden and beat Detroit 2-1 in overtime, and all of a sudden the hockey world was going wild, especially after we beat them again, 6-2, at home.

We returned to Detroit and they came up big, 6-4, at old Olympia Stadium, but we knocked them off 4-2 in Game Six at Boston and that was that, one of the biggest upsets in hockey history.

I got six goals in that series and my linemates got two or three, so we carried the team offensively and that put us up against the Canadiens — Montreal had beaten Chicago four games to three in the other semi-final — in the finals.

It was the closest I ever came to winning a Stanley Cup. Montreal beat us 4-2 in the opener and then we rebounded for a 4-1 win at the Forum of all places. After that it was all downhill. They took us 3-0, 7-3 and 1-0 to wrap things up. The last game was tied 0-0 after three periods, but before the overtime was two minutes old, Elmer Lach scored on a Maurice Richard pass and we were done.

That wasn't my last playoff; I had two more with the Bruins but never got to the finals again. I stayed a Bruin until June, 1955 when I was traded to Detroit. It was quite a deal; Real Chevrefils, Norm Corcoran, Gilles Boisvert and Warren Godfrey, all from the Bruins, went to the Red Wings. In return, Boston got the great Sawchuk as well as Marcel Bonin, Vic Stasiuk and Lorne Davis.

I only played four games for the Red Wings and then got dealt to Chicago for Metro Prystai in October, 1955. The 1955-56 season was my last in the NHL and I finished playing 57 games for Chicago, got a dozen goals, nine assists and 21 points.

All in all, I had a very enjoyable career and I was fortunate to remain connected to hockey and to have been able to follow the game in the 37 or so years since I played in the NHL.

Comparing today's game with that when I played is interesting. The NHL players now are bigger and stronger than we were and much faster than I ever was. The game itself has changed enormously and I doubt that our Bruins line [Mackell-Peirson-Sandford] would be able to contain any of today's big lines. They skate faster today and they shoot harder. The one thing we could do better was pass the puck. Really, we're talking about two different eras. It's like trying to compare the earlier baseball players to the current players.

It was a completely different style. We only used straight-bladed sticks — no curves or hi-tech stuff like they have now — and hardly anybody used the slapshot. We traveled from city to city by train and we had more time with each other.

Another difference was the birthplace of the players. Nearly all of us were Canadians. There was a sprinkling of Americans in the NHL, guys like Frankie Brimsek who came from Minnesota, but nearly everybody came from Canada and, of course, there were no Russians at all, although there was a Finn — fellow named Pentti Lund — who played for the Rangers and Bruins for a while.

I can remember the first time I saw the Russians playing at Boston Garden. It was about 25 years ago. They played Harvard and, to be honest, they didn't look all that good to me.

What I recall was that I wanted very much to see them practice and they were always very guarded about those things. They would never tell you when they were going to practice. They'd have a practice schedule for noon and then you'd find out that the scrimmage was another time.

I finally did get to see them practice and what I noticed is that they borrowed some of the best techniques of our pre-war teams, like the old Rangers who were so good at passing the puck and stickhandling. That was what Bill and Bun Cook and Frank Boucher had done so well when the Rangers were winning Stanley Cups in the late 1920s and early 1930s. The Russians had improved on these methods and were using them in their practices. That's how they got so good to where they could compete against the NHL All-Stars in 1972.

Getting back to my own hockey life, I retired in 1958 and got a job with an investment company in the Boston area, a small brokerage firm. In 1967-68 I became an off-ice official with the NHL, except in those days we were called "minor officials."

As a result, I've been fortunate to have seen a lot of hockey and to have witnessed the evolution of the game. When I played the shots were so much slower; now the slapshot is very, very prominent. I look back to the years when Phil Esposito led the NHL in scoring and I don't even think he ever slapped the puck. Maybe once or twice. Same with Gordie Howe.

Now the slapshot is dominating, but I don't think it should be as prominent as it is because it is so hard to be accurate with it.

When I played for the Bruins, Clarence Campbell was president of the league and remained so long after I retired. I became an off-ice official while Campbell still was president and I've worked through the John Ziegler administration and now under the new commissioner, Gary Bettman.

Big-league hockey is a whole new ball game nowadays and the accent is more on entertainment than it was when I played. In the late 1940s and early 1950s, we weren't thinking of ourselves and of marketing and things like that. We just thought that hockey was an interesting game for people to watch. Those of us who came down from Canada found that we were in competition with many other sports such as basketball, baseball and football, not to mention a whole lot of other things, but we did well. At the time we didn't think it was necessary to market our game, to encourage people to come and watch it.

Times have changed and now they look at it differently, what with television and ratings and competition. Now the NHL is doing an effective job after some troubled times.

I believe that if the NHL can educate the people in the southern States, it will become even more popular, although it is not an easy task. But I'm convinced that hockey is moving in the right direction.

Certainly, the game has done well by me and the proof that I still love it is the fact that I have remained connected with the sport for all these many years.

When I think back, I can assure you that I wouldn't have changed many things, other than the fact that I would have loved to have played for just one Stanley Cup-winner.

Otherwise, if I had to do it all over again, I would do it about the same — although I would want to be a faster skater!

Rod Gilbert   **(Hockey Hall of Fame)**

Chapter 13

ROD GILBERT

It has been said, with some justification, that Rod Gilbert is the most popular of the modern New York Rangers players.

Gifted, affable and, perhaps as important as any element, a resident of Manhattan, Gilbert has shared a love affair with The Big Apple since he played his first game at Madison Square Garden in the 1960-61 season.

Born in Montreal, the French-speaking Gilbert made his first imprint on the minds of Broadway fans in the spring of 1962 when he was promoted to the Blueshirts from their Kitchener farm club in the now-defunct Eastern Pro League.

The Rangers were down two games to none in the playoff semi-finals against the Toronto Maple Leafs when Gilbert was summoned to New York for Game Three. He was an immediate sensation, scoring two goals and three assists in his four-game stint. A year later he became a regular and remained a Ranger until the 1977-78 season when he retired following a squabble with then-Ranger general manager John Ferguson.

During his lengthy NHL career, Gilbert became one of the most productive Rangers in history. He played right wing on the GAG (Goal-A-Game) Line with his childhood pal, Jean Ratelle, and Vic Hadfield, a hulking left wing with a laser slapshot.

Although Gilbert never played on a Stanley Cup-winner, he came close in 1972 when the Rangers went all the way to the finals only to be beaten in a six-game series by the powerful Boston Bruins led by Bobby Orr. Gilbert retained his skills through the 1970s and many believed that he could have been an effective player for several more seasons had he not crossed Ferguson, forcing his premature retirement.

By that time Gilbert had become to New York hockey fans what Joe Namath had been to its football enthusiasts. He was not simply a talented athlete, but one with a joie de vivre and a genuine affection for the city in which he played.

Following his departure from the ice lanes, Gilbert became involved with a number of enterprises including a restaurant on Manhattan's East Side. He remained close to the Rangers' organization and to this day is involved with the club's alumni association.

Gilbert was interviewed by Stan Fischler, who originally met him when he came to New York in 1962, at Mickey Mantle's restaurant near Central Park. They huddled on a February night in 1993 when Rod and several other members of the Rangers' alumni had gathered for dinner.

I grew up in Montreal and began thinking about hockey at a very early age. When I was four years old, I already had a favorite player; it was Bernie "Boom Boom" Geoffrion, who was the right wing on the Canadiens. He had a terrific shot and was a very popular guy.

Boom Boom was also from Montreal and we knew him through our family. My father was a blacksmith by trade and Geoffrion's uncle used to play checkers on my dad's porch. I used to hang around them and his uncle already had been brainwashed to root for The Boomer. Naturally, he became my idol.

Hockey was a way of life for us in Montreal. My older brother, Jean-Marie, also was playing and it was logical that I follow in his footsteps, which I did.

My parents sent me to a Catholic school, Roussin Academy, where they had their own private hockey rink. One of my classmates was a tall, skinny kid by the name of Jean Ratelle. We became very good friends and by the time I was eight years old, Jean and I were playing hockey together.

Even then, Jean was something to see; the way he stickhandled and skated and managed to keep the puck. He was my favorite teammate and by the time we were 12 the two of us were doing some nice things together, hockey-wise. Our club went to the finals of the Montreal peewee championship.

It wasn't until I reached age 12 that I actually had seen an NHL game in person. The first time I walked into the building on St. Catherine Street West and Atwater Street, I was absolutely in awe. I walked inside and stared at the life-size photos of great Canadiens of other years: Hall of Famers like Howie Morenz, Georges Vezina and Aurel Joliat which were hanging from the walls in the lobby.

This was in 1954, and the Canadiens had a contending team then. Doug Harvey, one of the best defensemen of all time, was on the club along with Rocket Richard and Butch Bouchard, who was a hero to French-Canadian boys like myself. But the guy I cared most about was the one with the number 5 on his jersey, Bernie Geoffrion.

The Boomer was the first NHL player to master the slapshot and at that time was the only guy in the league to use it. The others were still taking the wrist shot or the backhander. Anyway, on that night Geoffrion scored two goals and Montreal beat Detroit, 4-2. To say the night was thrilling would be an understatement, and from that time on I set my sights on become a professional hockey player.

I soon got friendly with Boomer's uncle, Maxim Geoffrion, and chatted with him when he would visit my dad at his blacksmith shop. Once, I told Maxim that I very much wanted to meet his nephew who starred for the Canadiens, but it took two years for the meeting to happen.

One day Boom Boom came to visit his uncle. As soon as Bernie arrived, Maxim picked up the phone and told me to come over. I got there as fast as I could and could hardly get the words out of my mouth when I was introduced to the great Canadien.

The Boomer shook my hand and we chatted a bit. As I looked at him I reiterated my vow that I wanted more than anything to do what he was doing — earning a living as a big-leaguer. As I left Maxim Geoffrion's house, I wondered whether my dream ever would come true, but never would I imagine that one day I actually would be a teammate with the immortal Geoffrion on the New York Rangers!

To reach that level, I had a lot of work to do. Meanwhile, there already were some scouts keeping an eye on me. One of them was Yvon Prud'Homme, coach of a local team that included many players over the age of 20. In his spare time, Prud-Homme ("wise man" in French) scouted for the New York Rangers and he asked me if I would be interested in playing for his semi-pro team. Even though I was only 14, I agreed to sign with them and found that I could play with guys who were almost 10 years older than me. I did well enough to eventually start playing Junior B hockey. When I did well on that level, Prud'Homme recommended me for the Guelph Biltmores, which was the Rangers' farm club in the Ontario Hockey Association's Junior A Division.

This was quite a jump for me since it meant that I would leave my French-Canadian environment, in which I was very comfortable, and live in an English-speaking city [Guelph] in the province of Ontario. Even though I was a 16-year-old who couldn't speak a word of English, I decided to give it a try.

Fortunately, everything worked out well in the end. The Guelph Biltmores were coached by Eddie Bush, who had been an NHL defenseman and was a tough cookie. When I was introduced to him, one of my teammates, Al Lebrun, acted as the interpreter.

"Do you want to make this team?" snapped Bush.

I said, through my interpreter, that I did.

"In that case," Bush announced, "you'd better get a haircut or you won't get on the ice!"

I went to the barber who, under Bush's orders, cut all my long hair and left me with a brush cut. That was the beginning of basic training under Eddie Bush. He was a stickler for conditioning and insisted that we forsake cars or buses and, instead, walk the long distance from the rink to our boarding house.

Bush always insisted that we improve by making sacrifices and he also was a stickler for nattiness. "When you dress sharp," he would say, "you play sharp."

I played good hockey for Bush but he was only in Guelph for my first year. After that my coach was Emile Francis, who had been an NHL goalie with the Rangers and Blackhawks before he left playing. I kept improving under Emile — we called him "The Cat" — and it didn't hurt that I was playing on a line with my old chum, Jean Ratelle.

I had a wonderful time in Guelph — except for the near tragedy that almost cost me my hockey career. During a home game I tripped over a cardboard lid from an ice cream container and wound up breaking my back. From that point on I went through hell — trips to the Mayo Clinic, spinal fusion and doubts that I'd play again — but the Rangers stuck with me. They provided me with the best of care and, eventually, I was on the road to recovery. The Rangers, by this time, had figured that I could be an important player for them during the 1960s, and my junior record showed why they had such faith.

In my third year with Guelph, I finished second in scoring. Chico Maki, who went on to be a star with the Chicago Blackhawks was ahead of me. That was good enough for the Rangers to promote me to their pro team in Trois Rivières. It was a critical time in my athletic career because I also was being lured in another direction by my other favorite sport — baseball.

I loved baseball. Sometimes I'd pitch, other times play the infield; it really didn't matter. It was very relaxing and, besides, I was good. The reason why I knew I was good was because the Milwaukee Braves offered me a job with their farm team in Waycross, Georgia. The hangup was that they wanted me to go down south before our hockey season was over, and I told them I needed more time.

"It's now or never," the Braves' scout told me.

"In that case," I shot back, "it'll have to be never." My baseball career ended with those words.

At Trois Rivières, I played only three games but got four goals and six assists for 10 points. That told me I could play on a pro level, and the next year I was transferred to the Kitchener Rangers in the same Eastern Pro League. I averaged over a point a game with them and, as the season came to a close, I wondered how far I was from hooking on permanently with the Rangers. The answer came sooner than I had expected.

The Rangers had done well that year, 1961-62, gaining a playoff berth with some pretty good talent like Andy Bathgate, Dean Prentice, Gump Worsley, Harry Howell and Earl Ingarfield. I had no thoughts about making the big club that soon but, lo and behold, I got a call from the Rangers general manager, Muzz Patrick, who told me to come down to New York.

Patrick told me straight out that he might put me in the lineup for the playoff series against Toronto. I flew down to New York and it was like a dream coming true. At first I wondered why the Rangers wanted me since they had so many good players on their roster. Then, I found out that one of the better New York forwards, Ken Schinkel, had broken his toe in the second game of the series in Toronto and the big club needed help.

The Rangers had lost both playoff games at Maple Leaf Gardens, 4-2 and 2-1, and badly needed a win in Game Three, April 1st, 1962, at Madison Square Garden.

When I arrived in Manhattan, Doug Harvey, who now was both a defenseman and coach of the Rangers, called me into his office. "You're going to play on a line with Johnny Wilson and Dave Balon," he told me.

Balon, who was just coming into his own as a scorer, would be my center and Wilson, who was a really solid player, had been a well-respected forward for years, and once held the league's "iron man" record for consecutive games played.

That night Harvey sent us out against some of the best players Toronto ever had — Frank Mahovlich, Bob Pulford, Dave Keon, Allan Stanley — all in the Hockey Hall of Fame. What a game it was. Back and forth, thrilling playoff hockey. Our line held its own and late in the third period I skimmed a pass to Balon who beat Johnny Bower in the Toronto goal and we won the game, 5-4. I got an assist on the play and I could tell from the crowd roar that I had made an impact on the fans.

Two nights later, we beat them again. This time Harvey started our line and on my very first shift I beat Bower for my first NHL goal. It was only 41 seconds into the game and I reacted like you'd expect a rookie to react — I went wild. Later on in the same period, Wilson and Balon exchanged passes and then the puck was on my stick and, wow, in the net again. When I returned to the bench, I leaned over to Muzz Patrick who was standing behind the boys and said, "Muzz, do me a favor and give me a pinch. I think I'm dreaming!"

We beat the Leafs, 4-2, to tie the series and now we flew back to Toronto for the critical Game Five. That was a classic and it's too bad we didn't win because great things could have happened after that.

The Leafs had a 2-1 lead until late in the third period when I sent a pass to Earl Ingarfield and he beat Bower to tie the score. It sent the game into overtime and for the first 20 minutes of sudden death, nobody scored.

In the second sudden-death period it looked like we would beat Johnny Bower and take a three-to-two series lead, but "The China Wall," as they called him, was at the top of his game. So, for that matter, was our Gump Worsley.

Just after the four-minute mark of the second sudden-death period, Mahovlich took a shot at Worsley. Gump made the save but the puck slipped behind him. Not sure where it was, he fell backwards as if to smother it under his head.

Gump was waiting for the referee to blow his whistle, but there was no whistle after about three seconds, so Worsley leaned forward. Just then Red Kelly of Toronto skated by, saw the rubber and pushed it into the net. The time was 4:23 of the second sudden death and we lost 3-2 on the freak goal.

It was a terrific blow to me because I could have won the game in overtime, but I hit the post behind Bower. Then to have Toronto score on a goal when there should have been a whistle was pretty hard to take.

Normally, there should have been a sixth game played at our home rink, Madison Square Garden, but the Ringling Brothers Circus had moved in so we had to stay in Toronto for Game Six and the Leafs clobbered us, 7-1. But it was that fifth game that took the heart out of us.

Even though we lost the series, I felt good about myself. I averaged more than a point-a-game in the four games I did play and I was invited to training camp in the fall. Better still, my buddy Jean Ratelle also got a tryout with the big team but, as it worked out, he wasn't ready yet and was sent down to our farm club in Baltimore.

I played all 70 games next season, but I didn't exactly have a banner year. Part of the problem was that I still had to wear an awkward brace to protect my back. It reached from my hip to just under my armpits and had to be laced tightly against my spine. It made breathing difficult and it hurt my movement. Although I played a full 70-game schedule, I scored only 11 goals and 20 assists for 31 points; not exactly gangbusters after my hot playoff the previous spring.

A year later the doctors believed that the graft on my spine had become solid enough for me to be able to do without the back brace, so when the 1963-64 season began, I was more free, so to speak, than I had been for years. The results showed it: 24 goals and 40 assists for 64 points and another full, 70-game season.

That year I played on a line with two other French-Canadians, Phil Goyette and Camille Henry. Naturally, it was dubbed "The French Line" and we clicked very well, finishing the year as the second-highest scoring line in the league. Trouble was, we didn't make the playoffs. Doug Harvey had left the club and was replaced by Red Sullivan, and it just wasn't the same.

Actually, we went four straight seasons without getting a playoff berth and, in the interim, Cat Francis took over as general manager from Muzz Patrick. The Cat was rebuilding the organization, and by 1966-67 we were back on track.

In the meantime my back had acted up again and I needed another operation. This one was done at St. Clare's Hospital which was right around the corner from the old Madison Square Garden on 50th Street and Eighth Avenue. It was a long and agonizing affair, but I came through and was back in the lineup, full-time, for the 1966-67 season.

That was the year that, believe it or not, the Rangers signed my childhood idol, Boom Boom Geoffrion. The Boomer had left the Canadiens after the 1963-64 season and tried coaching for a while, but Cat Francis figured that Geoffrion still had some good hockey left and brought him to New York. The Boomer scored 17 goals and 25 assists for 42 points that year in 58 games, which was awfully good for a guy his age.

Needless to say, it was a joy to have Boomer as a teammate and even more surprising to wind up playing Montreal in the first playoff round. The records show that the 1967 semi-final round only lasted four games, but we stayed close in every one of them.

The last one, played at the Garden, was a classic. We had them tied 1-1 after regulation time which meant it would be settled in sudden-death. One of our top centers, Orland Kurtenbach, was out with an injury so Cat Francis used Red Berenson in his place.

The Redhead had not exactly been one of Francis' favorites that year, but this time he looked like a winner. Berenson got the puck in our end of the rink and chugged up the left wing. Just past the red line he released a hard shot that seemed to take Montreal goalie Rogie Vachon by surprise.

Berenson's shot beat Vachon cleanly but it bounced off the right goal post and stayed in play. A short time later John Ferguson came down the right side and put his own rebound past our goalie Ed Giacomin and it was all over.

The good news was that my back was holding up after the second operation, and the 1967-68 season was to prove that I was getting better all the time. Francis had put together a good group of guys and we once again were playoff contenders. My goal-scoring and point-getting had reached a career high and I felt that I had become a true New York sports hero. But never in my wildest dreams did I believe that I would accomplish what happened on the night of February 24, 1968 at my hometown rink, the Forum.

We were ahead 1-0 in the first period on a goal by Ron Stewart. Not long after, the Canadiens got a penalty and Francis sent me out with the power play. A half-a-minute later I was camped in the slot, took Jean Ratelle's pass and put us ahead, 2-0.

Next, Montreal scored but on a later shift, Jean and I managed to get a two-on-one break. Ratelle had the puck and easily could have taken the shot himself, but he shoveled the pass over to me and I slapped the puck past Vachon. Two goals at the Forum. Not bad!

That gave us a 3-1 lead which we held until late in the second period when our big Indian defenseman, Jim Neilson, skimmed a pass to me. I was about 50 feet from the net, which usually is way too far to expect to score. But I gambled and Vachon thought I was going for his right side. Instead, I fired to the left and had a hat trick. As we say in French, *"Incroyable!"* With a 4-1 lead going into the third period, we wanted more than anything to protect the margin and play smart hockey.

"Keep pressing," said Francis, and we did. In the third period, Ratelle took a pass from defenseman Arnie Brown and took a shot at Vachon. The Canadiens goalie batted it down to the ice but couldn't control it. My luck, I was right at the edge of the crease and I backhanded the loose puck behind Vachon. Four goals at the Forum. *"Double incroyable!!"*

We beat Montreal 6-1, and after I got to the dressing room, I was surrounded by reporters. Someone told me that I had a total of 16 shots on goal during the game.

"That's an NHL record," one of them said.

I told him that I had no idea. "All I can tell you," I said, "was that whenever I got the puck, I shot!"

From that point on, my career took off. In 1970-71 I hit a career-high 30 goals and in 1971-72 I almost reached a 100-point season. I finished with 43 goals and 54 assists for 97 points in 73 games. We finished second in the Eastern Division with 109 points, second-best in the league. Boston topped us, finishing first in the East with 119 points.

That was the best team I ever played for and it showed. Jean Ratelle led in scoring [109 points] even though he played in only 63 games. Vic Hadfield was second on the club [106 points] and we were strong up and down the line, from Eddie Giacomin and Gilles Villemure in goal, to Brad Park, Dale Rolfe and Rod Seiling on defense. Fellows like Walt Tkaczuk, Billy Fairbairn and Peter Stemkowski gave us tremendous balance.

In the playoffs that year, we knocked off Montreal in a six-game opening round and then took Chicago in four straight. That put us up against the hated Bruins in the finals, and what a series that was.

They went up two games to none at Boston Garden — both decided by a single goal — and then we won at home in Game Three. But they took us in Game Four and it looked like the series was over. Having returned to Boston, we came back from a 2-1 deficit in the third period to tie them and then won the game on Bobby Rousseau's goal late in the third.

So, the sixth game was back in New York and the difference was Bobby Orr. We matched up even with them from goal to defense to the forwards, but Orr just dominated the game. He put them ahead in the first period and the score stayed 1-0 until early in the third when Bobby and Phil Esposito set up Wayne Cashman to make it 2-0. They added one more near the end and that sent us to the showers.

And that said it all. We had a terrific team in the early 1970s and would have been number one for years if it wasn't for Orr. I had one more career year, in 1974-75, when I scored 36 goals and had 61 assists for 97 points again. We finished second behind the Philadelphia Flyers, but had the misfortune of meeting the New York Islanders in the opening round.

We went into that playoff as overwhelming favorites but they had an upstart team with a lot of kids and a rising young goalie named Bill Smith. They beat us 3-2 in the first game at the Garden then we clobbered them 8-3 at Nassau Coliseum in a game that was filled with fights. Everyone figured we'd come back to the Garden and finish them in the best-of-three series with ease. Instead, they jumped into a 3-0 lead.

We did fight back and managed to tie the game in the third period and almost took the lead, but Smitty was playing out of his mind so the game went into overtime tied at three.

Fans hadn't even gotten back to their seats when it was over. Right off the face-off, the puck went to them and the Islanders moved it into our right corner. We lost control of it and it went to the Islanders. There was a centering pass that got past Brad Park and onto the stick of J.P. Parise, and it was into the net at 11 seconds of the overtime. What a blow!

The club wasn't the same after that. In the following season, Cat Francis had Ron Stewart as coach and that didn't work out. Then they shook up the whole organization. John Ferguson was brought in and The Cat was gone. For me it was downhill after that. I managed 36 goals in 1975-76 and 86 points, but we didn't even make the playoffs. The following year I was down to 27 goals and in 1977-78 there was the mess with Ferguson and on Thanksgiving Day, I was told I was gone.

I would have loved to have played on a Stanley Cup-winner; that's for sure. But I had my share of thrills and, in a lot of ways, I was a very lucky guy considering my dream of making the NHL and being able to do what I did with all those back problems.

Eddie Mio   **(Hockey Hall of Fame)**

Chapter 14

EDDIE MIO

Nobody ever would suggest that Eddie Mio was one of the 10 best goaltenders of all time, but the smiling native of Windsor, Ontario would be listed among the 10 nicest netminders who ever stepped into a National Hockey League rink.

Not only was Mio affable, but he was competent, and almost a decade of goaltending at the highest level proved that.

After basic training with the Ontario Hockey League's Windsor Spitfires, Mio played four seasons at Colorado College after which he turned pro.

His start toward the top began with Indianapolis of the World Hockey Association where he teamed with a teenaged Wayne Gretzky. In November 1978, Mio was involved in a trade that would have longstanding repercussions. Gretzky, Mio and Peter Driscoll were traded by the Indianapolis Racers to the Edmonton Oilers for cash and future considerations.

For Gretzky, it was the beginning of a fabulous career. For Mio, it was the first stop in an NHL career which later took him to the New York Rangers and, finally, the Detroit Red Wings.

In December 1981, Mio was traded to New York by Edmonton for Lance Nethery. Although he played only two seasons on Broadway, Mio quickly became a fan favorite and starred for the Blueshirts in both the 1982 and 1983 playoffs.

At a reunion with Ranger teammates at Mickey Mantle's restaurant in Manhattan during the 1992-93 season, Mio, who lives in Detroit and is president of the Red Wings' Alumni Association, sat down with Stan Fischler to reminisce about the Rangers.

I didn't play in New York all that long, but during the time I was there I had a hell of a good time. When I joined the Rangers in 1981-82, the club had three goalies: myself, Steve Weeks and Steve

Baker, plus John Davidson who played a game and so did John Vanbiesbrouck, who was a kid at the time.

The Islanders were a powerhouse that year. They had won the Stanley Cup the previous two seasons [1980, 1981] and finished first in the Patrick Division with a terrific record [54-16-10] while we were in second [39-27-14]. The Flyers were right behind us [38-31-11].

Herb Brooks was our coach and we had a nice team with a lot of little speedy forwards. Our leading scorer was a center named Mike Rogers who finished with 103 points, and we had another wee guy, Mark Pavelich, who had played for Brooks on the 1980 American Olympic team. Boy, could he ever motor. Mark was our second-leading scorer along with Ron Duguay who was the matinee idol of the team.

We had another little guy on defense — Reijo Ruotsalainen from Finland — who had a good shot and could skate like the wind. He usually teamed up with our big defenseman, Barry Beck.

In the first round of the playoffs we wound up playing the Flyers. We had a better team than they did that season although not by much, but we lost the opener 4-1 at home, and then rebounded to take the next three in what was a best-of-five series. We won the last two games in Philly, 4-3 and 7-5.

That sent us into the division finals against the Islanders who were heavily favored to beat us. They had All-Stars like Mike Bossy, Bryan Trottier, Clark Gillies and Denis Potvin. I mean they were loaded, and we started the series at Nassau Coliseum.

A year earlier the Islanders had beaten the Rangers four straight in the playoffs, so there wasn't exactly a great deal of hope that we'd beat them this time around. Anyhow, we skated on to their home rink and slapped a 5-4 defeat on them in Game One.

Even though they beat us 7-2 in the second game at Nassau, we were feeling pretty good about ourselves when the series moved to Madison Square Garden for games Three and Four. We figured that if we could take Game Three, the series would be up for grabs.

Man, that was a terrific game. We were tied 3-3 at the end of regulation time which meant it would be settled in sudden-death. I figured that if we could keep Trottier, Bossy and Gillies quiet, we had a chance. So, now it's overtime and I'm a little nervous.

For the first couple of minutes, we played them even. Then, all of a sudden they had the puck in our end. People like to romanticize about sudden-death goals being beautiful but, lots of times, games end on the flukiest of shots. Ask me, 'cause I was the victim.

Bossy, Trottier and Gillies were all out there buzzing around our net. They were trying to set something up when, finally, the puck went to Trottier who was way over to my left side just out from the corner of the rink. Hockey writers like to describe the kind of shot

Trots took as being from "an impossible angle" and I guess to a certain extent it was.

I'm sure that if he had taken that same shot during regulation time, it wouldn't have gone in, but this time it hit one of our players and somehow found an opening on the short side between my body and the goal post — and it was in, at exactly three minutes of the first sudden-death period.

It was a very innocent play, but the damage to us was terrific. That loss was the turning-point of the series; that one bad play, game over! Not to take anything away from Trottier — he fought for the puck, got it and took the shot, which is all that mattered.

We didn't die then and there, but we did lose the next game at home to go down three-games-to-one. The fifth game was at Nassau and everyone figured we'd just lie down and die, but we fooled them. We beat the Islanders 4-2 and came home figuring that we could take them and tie the series; after that, all bets are off.

Game Six at the Garden was another doozy. We had them even until late in the third period when their big, hitting defensive defenseman, Dave Langevin, came down the left side and scored on a long shot.

That was the difference. They had three good lines and lots of defensemen and we were one line short. We had two-and-a-half lines and just couldn't match the Isles. They went on to win their third straight Stanley Cup, which says plenty about how strong they were.

Yet, in 1982-83, a year later, they slipped a bit during the regular season while the Flyers came on strong. Bob McCammon, a pretty funny guy, was coaching them and got Philly into first [49-23-8] while the Islanders were second, the Capitals third and we ended up fourth with a .500 record [35-35-10]. I handled most of the goaltending, but for backup we also had Glen Hanlon and Steve Weeks. John Davidson played two games and Stevie Baker just one.

In the opening round, which was a best-of-five deal again, we had to play the Flyers, starting with two games at the Spectrum. Philly was riding high and McCammon, after seeing all the little guys on our roster, made a wisecrack to the effect, "We won't have any problems with these guys. We'll get rid of them in three straight because THEY'RE SMURFS!"

You can debate this 'til the cows come home; that is, how much of an effect calling us "Smurfs" had on our team in the motivational sense. But this much I can tell you; it helped get our team together in that we were saying to each other, "Hey, those Flyers think we're just a bunch of Smurfs, so let's show them just what we can do. We've got nothing to lose, so get out there and beat them." McCammon may have done more for the camaraderie of our club than anybody in the Rangers front office could have done.

After hearing that Smurf stuff, I began caring more about the guy sitting next to me in the dressing room than I had before. It brought us together in the room and, later, out on the ice.

That was just what Herbie Brooks needed as a motivational tool and we went to Philadelphia and beat them in two straight — 5-3 and 4-3. The third game was in New York at the Garden and we gave them the real Smurf treatment; like a 9-3 win for us. That last win was my most memorable experience as a Ranger, and happiest memory.

That series served as a good lesson. We may not have had as many quality players as the Flyers did, but we had more determination. Once you get into the playoffs, a club can do a lot if it plays as a team.

Herb Brooks saw to that. I remember before the series even started, Herb took us to a resort called Downingtown, owned by the actor Mickey Rooney. It was a resort hotel a ways away from Philly. We were away from the hubub of the city and were able to concentrate. I remember Brooks saying, "Listen, we're not supposed to be in this series, so just be humble. Praise the Flyers."

So, all people read in the Philly papers were how they were going to kick our butt. They kept saying, "New York can't compete" and "We'll intimidate the Rangers", but we proved otherwise. The moral is, if you play together as a team and you get a few bounces, anything can happen. And it did!

Brooks was the best coach I ever played for, although I know a lot of people disagree with me. The only thing Herb didn't have in his favor was how to relate to professional hockey players; that is, how to be their friend and not just their boss and their coach.

But when it came to adapting to the dressing room, giving motivational talks, it was a joy to play for Herb. If we were losing, Brooks knew exactly what was beating us and why we were doing wrong and how to change it. He was a master at taking a team that didn't have a lot of talent and making it into a winner.

After that big playoff win over Philly, we got beaten by the Islanders in another really exciting series. They won the first two games pretty easily [4-1, 5-0], but we came right back and beat them at the Garden. Our first win was a wild and crazy game — 7-6 for us — but the Islanders came darn close to tying it at the end. Next we beat them 3-1, tying the series. But they won the next two, 7-2 and 5-2, which put them in the finals where they beat Edmonton in four straight. So, we had nothing to be ashamed of when you look at what kind of team they had.

Less than two months after we packed our bags I discovered that I had been traded to the Red Wings. Myself, Ronnie Duguay and little forward Eddie Johnstone went to Detroit in exchange for Willie Huber, Mark Osborne and Mike Blaisdell.

This put me closer to home, but I didn't get to play as much as I had in New York. Besides, I loved playing in Manhattan, so moving to Michigan was not an easy thing for me and I struggled in my first year with the Wings.

I may not have done as well with the Red Wings as I did with the Rangers, but I can say that I made the best save of my career in Detroit. I remember it well because that save had something to do with ending my hockey career.

We were playing the Flyers, a team I loved to beat. Bobby Clarke, their captain, was on the ice and he took a pass in the slot. He took his patented wrist shot and the puck was sailing right to the top of the net. I managed to get a glimpse of the rubber and did the splits, making a glove save. But at the precise moment that the puck went into my mitt, my hamstring popped — in not one but *three* places! And that just about ended my goaltending days.

The funny thing is that Clarke also figured in my second-best save which came in my first year with the Rangers. We were winning, 4-3, in this particular game when the Flyers were swarming all over us. There was about a minute left in the second period when he shot at the open net. It looked like a sure goal because I was sprawled outside the crease. In desperation, I lifted my stick and — guess what? — it was a once-in-a-lifetime thing; the puck hit my stick and went sailing into the stands. I can still see Clarke slamming his stick on the ice.

My NHL career ended after the 1985-86 season and, in retrospect, I would have to say that the best thing that happened to me as a hockey player was simply getting a chance to play at the top level. I was an average goaltender who had an opportunity to play with the likes of Wayne Gretzky and to meet a lot of great people who I'm still friendly with even though I'm not directly connected with the league any more.

Because of my past connection with the Rangers, I'm occasionally asked why it has been more than 53 years since they last won a Stanley Cup. It's a tough question. I don't think it has anything to do with the organization or the city. I know people say that New York City is a tough place to play in, but I loved playing there and I still say it's one of the great cities in which to be a professional hockey player.

Why can't the Rangers win the Stanley Cup? I can't pinpoint anything. It's not the talent; they've had some awfully good teams down through the years when they didn't win it. And it's not the division.

It's hard to explain. But hey, look at the Red Wings. They've had really good clubs and they haven't won the Stanley Cup since 1955. And the Blackhawks haven't won since 1961. That sure is a difficult thing to explain.

Bob Nystrom   **(Hockey Hall of Fame)**

Chapter 15

BOB NYSTROM

Few players accomplished more with a minimum of talent than Swedish-born Bob Nystrom. An original New York Islander, "Ny" arrived at Nassau Coliseum in 1972 when the club made its National Hockey League debut, and has remained with the organization through the 1990s, most recently as a radio analyst and front-office figure.

As a player, Nystrom's trademark was "Swedish Steam," (hard work) and he quickly came to epitomize the battling, blue-collar Islander. A poor skater as a rookie, Nystrom took power-skating lessons from guru Laura Stamm and became a speedster. A two-fisted fighter in his early years, Nystrom practiced his scoring skills and emerged as one of the best clutch scorers of his era. His most famous goal of all — and the Isles' trademark score — was the sudden-death game-winner in May, 1980 which delivered the first of four straight Stanley Cups to Nassau Coliseum.

A thumping right wing, Nystrom toiled in the shadow of the more prolific Mike Bossy throughout his career. Nevertheless, it was Nystrom who became — along with Bryan Trottier — the most familiar player on Long Island and one who is most closely associated with the team.

Nystrom's clutch-ability was most evident during the playoffs. In the Isles' 1980 run for the Cup, he tallied nine goals and nine assists for 18 points in 20 games. When New York won its fourth Cup in 1983, Nystrom was good for seven goals and six assists for 13 points in 20 games.

For a portion of his career, Ny played on a unit with John Tonelli at left wing and Wayne Merrick at center. The trio was known as "The Banana Line," although an injured Merrick was replaced by Lorne Henning when

Nystrom deflected his playoff-winner past Pete Peeters of the Flyers in 1980.

Nystrom was accidentally clipped in the eye by teammate Gerald Diduck in 1986 and was unable to regain enough sight to return on a full-time basis. He worked briefly as an assistant coach before moving into the front office and behind a microphone. The following is a compilation of interviews with Nystrom by Stan Fischler, who covered Ny's career from its inception, including one by Ashley Scharge during the 1993 playoffs.

Looking back at my career, I make a distinction between the regular season and the playoffs. It's interesting, because every so often you read something in the papers about how the NHL really has two seasons: the regular one and the playoffs. It's true; different things are done in each part of the year.

In my case, the playoffs were a little bit more important and I was a little bit more successful. Which is not to say that I didn't have some good years during the regular season. In 1977-78, when the Islanders were just beginning to flex their muscles, I scored 30 goals and had 29 assists. That was the season we played a seven-game series with the Maple Leafs and got beaten in the last game at Nassau Coliseum.

That was a very physical series — tough. Borje Salming, who was Toronto's best defenseman, went out early with an injury and we took the first two games at home. Then they came back and won a pair at Maple Leaf Gardens. So it went, back and forth, until we got to the last game at Nassau. We went ahead 1-0, but they came back and tied it and then it went into overtime and Lanny McDonald scored the winner, which was a big disappointment since we had such high hopes that year.

One of the toughest players on Toronto was defenseman Brian Glennie, who really liked to hit. In general I was having some serious problems with Glennie but, on this particular night, I beat him one-on-one — faked through the outside and went in through the middle — and beat Mike Palmateer for an overtime goal. That was my first in sudden-death and, naturally, a big thrill except that we went on to lose the series, so all the kick went out of it.

A year later I got another OT goal, only this time against the Rangers. That was the bitter 1979 playoffs after we had finished with the best regular season record in the league. We were favored in that series, but I could tell right at the start that the Rangers were going to give us trouble. They won the opener 4-1 at Nassau Coliseum, and we just squeaked back to tie the series in overtime, 4-3.

After that, the series switched to Madison Square Garden where they beat us 3-1. Game Four was tied 2-2 at the end of regulation and we went into sudden-death again. With almost four minutes gone, their goalie John Davidson came out to field the puck. Actually, it was a breakaway between myself and J.D. I was racing for the puck and he realized that he was about the same distance from it that I was. We seemed to decide, "Okay, it's going to be a footrace to see who gets there first." It goes to show you how slow I was, right?

We got there at the same time and John got to the puck with his stick. I got to the puck with mine and it deflected up in the air and went toward their net. It seemed to fly up in an arc behind John so I continued to skate and just follow the puck as it came down. The only trouble was that it seemed to take an hour for it to finally land on the ice, fluttering as it was.

Finally, it landed in front of the net and I was able to bat it in before one of their defensemen, Mike McEwen, could get back in time. It was a great goal — coming as it did in Madison Square Garden against the crosstown rival.

Unfortunately, we wound up losing the next two and were out in the cold again.

One of my favorite goals was in a series we won. That was in 1980 against Buffalo. The series opened at The Aud and we beat them 4-1. We knew that if we could take the second game we could practically wrap it all up and, as it happened, it was 1-1 going into overtime. Nobody scored in the first 20-minute sudden-death period, so we got ready for the second one.

Any time you get into that type of situation it gets tense, but I felt comfortable because I always worked a little bit harder in my conditioning and I felt it would pay off come playoff time because the NHL season is so grueling. The play on the winning goal started with the puck circling around the net and going back to the point. Butch Goring actually put it back to the point and our defenseman, Bobby Lorimer, just let the shot go. As Lorimer wound up, I was getting myself in position in front of the net. Bobby's shot rebounded off the goaltender, and I pretty much had the whole wide-open net. The time was 1:20 of the second overtime and we went on to beat them four games to two, then went up against Philly and won the Cup.

I've always told people that the great thing about scoring in overtime is that you don't have to worry about any more goals. The game is over, you go to the locker room and you can rest.

Mind you, I didn't always have the overtime luck. I had a real problem in 1975, which was the first year that we made the playoffs on the Island. I had been the club's leading scorer in 1974-75 with 27 goals and 28 assists and I really wanted to do well in the playoffs. As it turned out, we made it through three rounds — beating the Rangers and Penguins, then losing to Philly in seven — but I did terribly. In 17 games I only scored a goal and three assists. It was just brutal and a bitter disappointment for me personally. I had a tough summer dealing with it.

Shortly thereafter, I happened to come across a *Peanuts* cartoon. The symbol in it was the fact that he had "choked." Peanuts was playing tennis and double-faulted under match point. I vowed from that point on that I would approach the playoff games and give it my best effort. I knew that I couldn't stop myself from being nervous, but I went out with the attitude that I'd do my best and if I could look at myself in the mirror afterwards and say, "Hey, that's the best I could do," then, fine. After that everything turned out so well for me — which goes to show you how simple it is — thanks to *Peanuts*!

I was fortunate. A lot of good things happened to me but, of course, nothing tops the 1980 Stanley Cup-winning goal. That was my favorite; no question about it. To win a game is fine, but to win the Stanley Cup on your goal is a dream come true. It was the icing on the cake; the storybook ending; the culmination of so many good things that happened to me throughout my career.

Chapter 16

JOHN DAVIDSON

If John Davidson had been as successful a major-league goaltender as he was to become a hockey broadcaster, he would surely have won the Vezina Trophy. It is the height of hockey irony that the tall, moustachioed Rangers TV analyst entered the NHL in 1973 as an enormously promising goalie, but never fulfilled his potential. However, "J.D." — as he came to be known — entered the TV realm with virtually no expectations and has become one of the best in the business.

A native of Ottawa, Davidson played junior hockey for the Calgary Centennials. He was so impressive that the St. Louis Blues made him their first choice in the 1973 draft, and he became the first goalie to jump directly from junior hockey to the NHL.

However, Davidson was somewhat of a disappointment in his two seasons at St. Louis ['73-'74 and '74-'75].

On June 18, 1975, he was traded to the New York Rangers with Bill Collins for Jerry Butler, Ted Irvine and Bert Wilson. Davidson showed considerable promise for the Rangers, peaking in 1978-79 when he led the Broadway Blueshirts to an upset playoff triumph over the New York Islanders, taking the Rangers to the Stanley Cup finals, where they ultimately were beaten by the Montreal Canadiens.

A series of injuries bedeviled Davidson's career, forcing a premature retirement in 1983.

Davidson's career in hockey broadcasting started modestly, but grew rapidly after he was signed by Madison Square Garden Network to be analyst for Rangers games. Personable and eloquent, Davidson has become a leading hockey spokesman. He was interviewed by Stan Fischler in July, 1992 at his Madison Square Garden office in midtown Manhattan. Davidson is remarkably candid and insightful while discussing his rise to broadcasting eminence after a modest major-league career.

John Davidson   **(Hockey Hall of Fame)**

SF: You were interviewed by the Whalers. What about your pursuit of a general manager's job?

JD: I'm more qualified than some people realize. I worked with [former Rangers GM] Craig Patrick as a member of management not long after I retired in 1983. With Neil Smith, although I don't work with him, we discuss a lot of things. I would be able to do a decent job if I ever took that position and I know I would hire the right people, but I would only do a GM job if the situation was right and ideal. The thing about being GM is you have an absolute commitment to your job, and it is almost above your commitment to your family because of the competition and hours. It's a tough, tough job.

SF: Sources say you never were serious about taking the Whalers job; that you just interviewed for it as a lark.

JD: First of all, they called me, I didn't call them, looking for a job. We had a couple of lengthy phone conversations and they said you better come in and have a serious talk. I went in and spent four and a half hours and it was wonderful.

SF: But you weren't really serious about it?

JD: I went there for the experience. I didn't want the job because I have a better job right now. That's the point: I'm dealing from a strength position, working for the MSG Network.

SF: How strong are you at MSG?

JD: I was told it was a lifetime job and it is if I take care of it and work at it. Financially, it is very rewarding. When I take out the ledger and add pros and cons and think of my family, time off in the summer, longevity and money, without sounding like too much of a jerk, this is the best job in hockey.

SF: If you were the absolute god of hockey what things would you do, in order of importance, to make the game better?

JD: Far and away the number one issue would be a better level of communications between the league, the media and the public. Right now the perception of hockey is flat-out wrong and we have to find a way to change it. The league has to change its public relations. Why, here in New York they didn't have a full-time public relations department until Gary Bettman took over.

SF: Compare the public perception of hockey with that of any other sport that comes to mind.

JD: Take the Indianapolis 500. The race puts at least five or six people in the hospital and in the trials there were some drivers who got killed. Yet it's thought of as one of the great American spectacles and a good portion of the country watches it.

To the media, it's a wonderful thing, yet young people die. And here we have hockey where it's perceived as the most violent sport ever. Every time there's a fight, it's shown. We haven't had two brawls in one night of hockey in I don't know how long. Yet, if we did, they'd want to cover their kids' eyes and never let them see another hockey game. So, we have to get the average American to understand the greatness of the sport. Sure it's violent, yet we can still open people up to the violence of the sport. Football has done it. Hockey should be able to sell itself in a smarter fashion, not to coerce, but make people understand.

SF: What rule changes would you make?

JD: One would be to speed up the game by eliminating most of the clutching, grabbing, interference and pushing people off-side. It's too much. We have to find a way to make the game faster. Speed makes mistakes and mistakes lead to scoring chances and more good plays. The more speed you have, the more your skill level can be a part of the game. People pay to watch the stars.

SF: How do you get rid of those restraining fouls?

JD: We could use another official on the ice. Experiment. We have 26 teams. Each team plays about 10 exhibition games. That's a lot of games in which to try things. And the general managers have to be forceful about this change, otherwise it won't have any spine.

SF: Let's examine one aspect of hockey that has been criticized; the All-Star Game.

JD: The All-Star Game is awful and does not represent the game. I don't know if we should have the Stanley Cup champ play a bunch of All-Stars, but it would provide a better contest. The way it has been, some players, like Wayne Gretzky, don't want to play in it and I can understand that.

SF: What are the keys to John Davidson's success?

JD: Hard work and committed hours of study to the job. And the realization that, as a player I didn't do that. I was never in great shape as a player and once I got hurt I used that as an excuse. I had natural talent up the ying-yang and I always was a decent team player, but I never played the game to my potential. I'm convinced that with my talent as a 19-year-old coming into the league, I should have finished my career in a Hall-of-Fame situation. I played 300-plus games and never gave a commitment to the game as a player, and I'm the first to admit it.

SF: How do you explain this failure?

JD: I thought it would last forever. I wasn't disciplined on the ice and off the ice. I had strong intentions that I didn't follow up with strong working habits. My work habits have changed since I realized this could be a change in my game and, if I wanted to stay involved with hockey and provide the lifestyle I always had, I had to improve my working habits. Lucky for me, when I started with MSG-TV I had a producer, Pete Silverman, who would sit down with me game after game and critique the hell out of my work. Boy, I needed help then; why I didn't even say, "Philadelphia" right! Later Don Wallace, who was in charge of "Hockey Night in Canada," brought me up there.

SF: Who did the most for you?

JD: I hooked up with John Shannon, whom I consider the best producer in the game. He took a real interest in me for two years in Canada and we worked 115 to 120 games a year. With Shannon, you didn't go on the air, do the job and leave. We would talk and he'd have me improve things things like looking at the camera, not saying three different things at once and what to do when you're stuck with dead air. What I learned was that if you're in a new position, you'd better listen and ask for advice because it will only make you better.

SF: Associates say you work as hard on an off-day as you do when there's a game. Give me a typical off-day.

JD: I go to the Rangers' practice in the morning because a lot of times they'll work during practice what they're going to do during the next game. So, I pick things up and at the same time I talk to the players and might learn, for instance, that Mark Messier wears glasses or whatever. The night before the game is when I do most of my work. I like to tape the previous game of the next opponent and watch it. If the announcers are doing the job, they provide information. If it's in Detroit, I'd find out Bob Probert has a bad back or this guy is wearing new skates; this is info to give the viewer. I make calls.

SF: What's your best news source?

JD: The best way to gather information is to call the coaches themselves. Some are very good but others don't talk too much, so I weed them out. The other source is beat reporters or the actual radio and TV announcers. If it's Detroit I call Keith Gave. I file everything the day before because I have a terrible memory, so I write it all down.

SF: What's your weakness on the air?

JD: I talk too much. I get so excited that I step on my partner [Sam Rosen]. This is terrible on TV. Sometimes I'll jump in without using my hand and that gets our rhythm out of whack. In TV you should talk only when you have something to say. Sometimes I get caught up in wanting to say it the way it is and that's a complex situation when you work for a team.

SF: How does that get you in trouble?

JD: When I first started doing Ranger games [on TV], I said it the way it was and Phil Esposito disagreed with me on certain points. Phil and I had been roommates on the road for seven years when we played for the club. We still don't have a good relationship like we had; we don't talk stuff anymore. This happened when he was GM and he thought I was trying to get his job, while the absolute opposite was the case. All I was trying to do was say things the way they were.

SF: Was there a specific episode?

JD: The Rangers were playing against the Flyers in the playoffs and we were asked to predict the outcome. Sam said the Rangers would win in a close, hard-fought series. I said Philly would win in six games because the Rangers had given up 56 goals in their last 10 games and I couldn't see them winning.

SF: What happened?

JD: The Rangers lost in six, but what I said ruffled a lot of feathers. People were upset the Ranger announcer on the Rangers' network went on TV and said Philly would beat them in the first round. I mean you don't have to be a homer, but you have to give the homer's point of view since the fans listening on MSG are basically all Ranger fans. I spoke to Phil later that off-season and very candidly he said he would have picked Philly, too.

SF: If you had to do the same incident over again this year, would you have done it the same way?

JD: Yes, I would. I may have been forceful then. Now I would be lighter about it.

SF: You got into hot water when Esposito fired Michel Bergeron, the Rangers coach, didn't you?

JD: I was in a position to say what I felt, and we were very aggressive with it. We had Bergeron on crying and that didn't look good from a management's side; at least not the way it was run. Phil has not had the same feelings for the people [on MSG Network] and the network since then. But I saw Phil at the playoffs a couple of years ago, and we talked. Phil is a loyal guy and loyal to his people.

SF: Did what you people said help get Esposito fired in New York?

JD: It didn't help. But the results afterward [Rangers eliminated from the playoffs in four straight] helped.

SF: You've been critcized by Don Cherry for anti-Islander comments made after Pat LaFontaine was hurt in the 1990 playoffs and the Islanders [Mick Vukota and Ken Baumgartner] instigated a fight in the last seconds.

JD: We had words after the thing. Cherry had gone on the air and criticized me for my criticism of Al Arbour. I phoned Don in St. Louis and said, "You didn't even watch the [Ranger-Islander] game." He admitted, no, he didn't, but said, "A lot of friends told me about it." I confronted Don, we had it out and now we are good friends although we've had differences along the way. Now I talk to him on the phone quite a bit to get information.

SF: What do you think of Cherry's anti-European, pro-fighting act?

JD: If he was in the U.S., he'd have a much harder time pulling it off because of what happened to Jimmy the Greek. It's different in Canada which is low-key and nobody says off-the-wall stuff. When somebody like Cherry does, everybody listens and appreciates it and has fun with Don. But he was criticized more in the 1982 playoffs by critics than ever before for getting on Pavel Buré's case and I really think that affected him to the extent that he was sensitive to the criticism. Although it doesn't come over on TV, Don is a nice and sensitive guy and he didn't really enjoy the criticism too much. If I had a difference of opinion with Don, it's that we all have to change somewhat as we move along. I'm talking about the Swedes and Soviets taking jobs but, damn, these guys are talented and Don should appreciate that fact.

SF: Examining the broadcasting field, who would you say is the best TV analyst?

JD: [Former Flyers' and current ESPN analyst] Bill Clement and Harry Neale [HNIC, Maple Leafs] are good, hard workers. Mickey Redmond *could* be the best; he's a great communicator but Mickey has another job. He runs a travel agency and he's a very busy guy, whereas I have only one job and I have time to go to the arena the day of the game and get info. Most of the others don't have time. But if I was doing the hiring, it would be Neale or Clement in a tie.

SF: Who are your favorite play-by-play announcers?

JD: The most underrated in the game today is Sam Rosen [MSG] who is a terrific talent, Jiggs McDonald [Islanders] is a Hall-of-Fame broadcaster, has enthusiasm, a passion for the game, and great work habits. Mike Emrick gives you an indescribable feeling of eloquence. He gives hockey a great identity and is a great writer. The Canadian play-by-play guy I would pick is Bob Cole; he is the guy with the voice. He projects the most excitement. Also Don Whitman; he gets great information. I strongly feel that hockey is the toughest sport to describe, play-by-play-wise. If you get to the NHL, man, you're good.

SF: You've been accused of saying one thing during a Rangers broadcast and then going on radio the next day and contradicting what you had originally said.

JD: Time gives you a chance to rethink things, aside from being spontaneous.

SF: You were also blasted for the heavy-handed way you came down on the Islanders during and after Game One of the 1990 playoff which erupted in a brawl at the end.

JD: If there is one thing I regret more than anything else it's what I said about the Islanders' situation — and how I said it. I don't think I was overly wrong, but I used the word "garbage" [in reference to Al Arbour] and I should never have used the word "garbage." The Islanders have always been a class organization and have been very good to me. "Garbage" came out, but it was a situation where my emotions got going and the word came out. When it happens again, I will have more control over it — and it won't happen again.

SF: What was your gripe?

JD: I couldn't believe what I saw; players lining up at the blue line ready to fight. It was so much premeditation. Even the meanest, dirtiest Flyers' teams weren't as blatant as that in terms of being premeditated. It was wrong. Al Arbour was wrong [having enforcers Vukota and Baumgartner out at the end] and the league thought he was wrong with the suspensions and fines. But at the same time, I didn't have to use the word "garbage" because they aren't garbage.

SF: Would you have used the term "garbage" in reference to the Rangers?

JD: No, probably not. At the next home game Al came by before the game and there happened to be a sweeper cleaning up at the time. Al said, "There's some garbage." I said, "Al, I didn't mean to say that." He said, "Yeah, I know," and smiled and went by. I felt so much better. I have a lot of respect for Al and Kenny Baumgartner and for players. I should not have used the term "garbage."

SF: What's your definition of a "homer?"

JD: A guy who goes into the broadcast and has no concern for the opposition; no concern about background information and their style of play. It's someone who goes through three hours of broadcasting concerned with his own team. On the other hand, a home team analyst can give his own team's point of view.

SF: Aren't you being a "homer" when you do that?

JD: No. When I'm doing the Ranger games, I'm not doing them for NBC, I'm doing it for MSG and Rangers' fans. But I'll always do my homework and visit with the other team's players. A "homer" does not do any research into the opposition.

SF: As a home team broadcaster, you have a tilt, 60 per cent in favor of your club and 40 per cent for the other club. Right or wrong?

JD: That's not unfair to say.

SF: If you were working NBC doing hockey, then it's 50-50, but if you are the home announcer then it's 60-40?

JD: That's fair. I do it 60-40 from the Rangers' point of view, no doubt about it. I mean when I did the Olympics, it was probably 70-30 for the USA. The basic thing absolutely is the emotion. I know these guys personally.

SF: With that in mind, it seemed outrageous for you to say — after Mario Lemieux was clubbed down by Adam Graves and then Pittsburgh knocked off the Rangers in the 1992 playoffs — that the Rangers missed playing against Mario. Come on, John!

JD: I have a difficult time trying to fault Graves because I know him so well. There is not a better man in the game today and if the Rangers had gotten Lindros, Eric would have lived with Graves. Someday Adam will be a captain in this league. But the point is, what I said was taken out of whack and I don't know why it was written that way.

SF: What did you mean?

JD: The Penguins played a lot of games without Mario in the lineup and knew what it took to win without him. The Rangers had to play without Graves for the first time all year. [Mark] Messier had to do all his own work in the corners every game [because Graves was suspended]. Graves is not a Lemieux or a Messier or a [Ray] Bourque, but if you ask players who play with him or against him, they put him in that category for what he does game in and game out and what he means. He punishes and grinds and puts the shoulder into you. He's a great player and time will tell in that situation. All I tried to say is that Graves is a great player and him not being in the Rangers lineup hurt that team.

SF: Some critics believe Graves should have been much more severely suspended. After all, he chopped down the crown jewel of hockey.

JD: Jewels are jewels but there are a lot of rocks that are important, too. Does that mean you could hack Tie Domi and get two games, but you hack Mario and get 22? I understand the business about hockey's image, but there are so many circumstances involved. Yes, we have to do different things to create a better image, but we can't do it all over one incident.

SF: What would you have done to Graves if you were commissioner?

JD: Probably a very similar sentence. The negative press we got was about the worst you could ever get in hockey. Thomas Boswell [*Washington Post*] and some great writers ripped the shit out of hockey. What we have to do as a league is to get Thomas Boswell to understand what the game is about. He ripped the shit out of [then-coach] Roger Neilson in that article and that whole thing was taken out of context. Roger didn't say he was glad Lemieux was out. In retrospect, the Rangers should have done a better job, media-wise, in protecting their own. I'm talking about Roger and Adam.

SF: Roger Neilson has been described as a goon coach for incidents like Graves-Lemieux and the uprising after Game Six of the Devil-Ranger playoff.

JD: All season long and especially on the road, Roger put them [his hitters] out in the last minute. I was there every game and this is what he did. This Game Six thing was flaming up for a long time. It was bad and exploded and this is something Roger did all year. I'm not defending it. It added a black mark, and especially when you're in New York with the Rangers, it magnifies it even more. But it's hard for me to sit here and discredit Roger. I don't work with him, but I worked alongside him for a couple of years. I know what kind of person he is. It was like a father-and-son relationship between Roger and many players. The only thing negative I'd say about Roger is the playoff coaching in 1992. The team, in retrospect, did not play their own game and they went out of their way to run people too much and to be too physical.

SF: Did you endorse Neilson's tough style?

JD: I've been in New York 20 years and the 1991-92 team, while not necessarily a goon team, was the toughest team that was ever here. All those years we got beat up on the Island and in Philadelphia, and I mean got beat up. In Philly, it was a lot more obvious, the beat-up part, because the Flyers were a much meaner team. The Islanders were not as mean, but they beat the shit out of you politely. When we left the Island, we were just bruised up and beat up and cut up. Bryan Trottier, as good as he was, was the best at this. In those days the Rangers were criticized and we, as players, wanted to be much tougher but we never were. Nick Fotiu wanted to help us and he was great at it, but we didn't have a team that was capable of grinding it out with everybody. Now we do and everybody started criticizing us. Well, too bad. It's about time this team got bigger and tougher and greedier. I don't think that the way the rules are now that you go out looking for it.

SF: There's a lot of hate in hockey, isn't there?

JD: I don't think hatred should be there. A lot of fans have the hatred because they live with their team. But we don't need to have the hatred. We pull for our own teams and want them to win, but hatred shouldn't be part of it.

SF: Did you ever go on the air and deplore the hatred of Ranger fans who tried to turn over the ambulance containing Pat LaFontaine when he was removed from the Garden after Game One of the 1990 playoffs?

JD: I certainly did. Absolutely. That was sick! For them to push the ambulance outside the Garden, that was awful.

SF: How do you explain hatred like that?

JD: Maybe it's New York's society. In my mind people in New York are more emotional than those in Toronto or Calgary and more emotional than in Hartford. Maybe it's the way they live their lives everyday, or maybe it's frustration over years and years of not winning. But there is no room for any excuses here whatsoever. Patty LaFontaine is a gentleman and he got run over and was injured badly, and for people to do what they did, they should have no excuse.

SF: What was the most embarrassing thing that ever happened to you in broadcasting?

JD: I had the wrong team on the power play once, because of a lack of concentration. It's kind of the way I used to play goal!

SF: Did anyone besides Al Arbour get really mad at you?

JD: Yeah. The year Philly and Edmonton went seven games [1987 playoffs], the seventh game was in Edmonton. I get a tap on the shoulder from Reg Higgs who left the Rangers to go to Philly [I was working for "Hockey Night in Canada"]. He takes me into a little room with Mike Keenan and Mike says, "I think you're painting Dave Brown as a goon on television throughout Canada." I said, "Mike, you're using him as a goon." He says something and I say something. We both had our say and heard each other out and I admitted I was wrong during the last game in Philly, because Philly had the last change and they were only putting their big boys on the ice because Edmonton had their boys out there. I got anti-Flyer because of that and I was wrong, because Mike should have had his boys out there if the other team does that. I was wrong and I admitted that to him. We had battled for a few minutes, screaming at each other, but we got it out and now we are good friends.

SF: What is your policy in terms of criticizing players?

JD: If I ever say something negative about a player during a game, I go to them the next day and say that I said this. I believe that if you are honest with them and you tell them to their face whether they disagree or not, and you tell them why you said it, they appreciate the gesture.

SF: What advice would you give hockey broadcasters?

JD: I'd like to see every announcer spend more time preparing for games, and be well-informed about the opposition. It's funny for me to say that because I get letters from fans who don't like that I talk about the opposition. I'll tell them about Pierre Turgeon with his skates and wide feet, and I'll tell about Ray Ferraro and his Little League stuff. Some fans get offended because they don't want to hear about the other team; they want to hear about their team. They're just being blind, yet others appreciate it.

SF: As a player you were involved with Nick Fotiu in some classic off-ice pranks. Tell me about your favorite.

JD: We're in Toronto, got a midnight curfew. We're staying at the Harbour Castle Hotel and Nicky and I came in about five to twelve. We had a couple of beers over dinner and stuff, felt pretty good, walked into the lobby and sure enough, we're by the entrance to the hotel's restaurant. It's midnight. It was a lobster pub. So we go over and I open my topcoat; Nicky looks around, grabs a lobster and throws it in my coat and off we go to the room. He was rooming with Bill Goldsworthy. We snuck into the room, real quiet, and Goldsworthy was sleeping on top of the bed, not a stitch of clothes on, arms out, legs over the end, snoring away. We took the elastic off the lobster's claws, and sat it down on his chest, but the thing slid off. We can hardly stand it, we're killing ourselves. We pick the lobster back up, put it right down on him. All of a sudden the lobster starts moving and Bill wakes up. If you could have heard the scream! He reaches up, grabs the lobster and throws it against the wall. Nick and I are standing at the door bent over laughing. Goldsworthy shouts, "You sons of bitches" and starts after us. We open the door, and we're down the hall. Meanwhile, the door to his room slams shut, and he doesn't have one stitch of clothes on! Meanwhile, we ran down the fire escape, and we were flat-out gone.

SF: You were involved in a notorious Christmas Eve toilet-papering incident. Would you please explain?

JD: It all started earlier. We were in a restaurant in Long Beach, and we're finishing up dinner, and there's a whole group of us, and I get paged to go to the front of the restaurant, which I did, and they said my truck was being towed away. I go outside, and holy Jesus, I look and I can't see it. It's underneath all of this stuff. So I go, "Jesus!" And all of a sudden you hear — honk, honk, honk — there's Nick Fotiu waving with his wife and they were laughing, and I was going, "You sons of bitches." I've got a suit on and everything else. So about an hour later after hauling all this stuff off, we get back into the truck, and go over to another restaurant and have some wine and things. All of a sudden, it's about four in the morning and we say, well, it's time to get Nick.

SF: Who's we?

JD: It was Walter Tkaczuk, myself, our wives, a couple of other players, but Walter Tkaczuk was there for sure. And we got toilet paper and we got all this stuff, parked a block away from Nicky's house, and we started to put toilet paper over the roof, back and around the trees, and around all the supports of the house, and the garage. I think almost the whole thing looked white when we were done. And then we rang the doorbell. It's got to be five in the morning now, and out he comes. He's got his pajamas on, and he looks, and he stops, and he can't believe it. So you know what he did? He goes in and phones the cops in Long Beach. "Somebody's vandalized my house." So now, all of a sudden, we start to leave. We're getting out of town, right? Cop cars are coming from all over the place. Cops are getting out. They started to laugh. But a couple of them, though, didn't like it because once they're called, they're supposed to do something. So they were going to arrest us. But later on it rained. The toilet paper stuck to the tree branches. It took weeks to get it off. Weeks. We had fun in those days. Everybody. . . . The team was a good team.

SF: Where are you on the fighting issue?

JD: On the fence. Actually I'm leaning towards getting it out of the game because I think vision is important. Developing the game's important, expansion properly, perception, and I just don't think we can continue having fighting in the game, and try to sell the game to all markets, including some of the markets we're already in. And finally, the best reason why: I'm sitting there watching a game this winter, and my daughter came in, she's seven years old. She sits beside me on the recliner, we're watching, and all of a sudden a fight starts. She says, "Dad, why are they fighting?" I couldn't answer. I could not give her an answer that made sense as to why they were fighting. And that's when it hit me. I said, gee, I'm from Canada, I grew up with it in Canada, it's part of the game. I mean, 90 per cent of the hockey fans in Canada think fighting's just a part of the game. That's hockey. They say, "Boy, did you see that one last night with Probert and Domi?", or, "Did you see George McPhee or those guys going at it?" It's just a part of life, and it's accepted as a part of life. But I don't think we need fighting.

SF: What went wrong?

JD: Visors and shields and helmets. I understand visors and shields and helmets, but at the same time we've been remiss in not taking care of the sticks themselves. There's a false sense of security for the men who play the sport. Kids this big, once they put a helmet and a visor on, they'll go skate into the boards as fast as they can go, thinking that they can't get hurt because they've got these on. Now, sticks are used as a weapon on players' arms and hands way too much.

SF: Sometimes you'll sound almost gleeful on the air when a guy gets away with a foul. In a sense, you condone breaking the law with your joy.

JD: It's a matter of emotions more than being gleeful. You try to get an edge. You think guys on the line in football aren't grabbing each other and hoping the referee doesn't see them? That's sports. That's pro sports. What are you going to do? That's the way it goes. Sandpaper in the gloves by a pitcher; that's breaking the rules. Now that's cheating. That's kind of an unethical edge, moreso than clutching and grabbing. Spearing and stuff like that, no. Sorry. I don't get gleeful. I think I get emotional probably more than anything else.

SF: How much braintrusting do you do with [Ranger GM] Neil Smith?

JD: Quite a bit. I enjoy talking hockey with Neil. We always talk. We talked a lot about Messier before he came here. We talk quite a bit. I think anybody in his position, when you've got people who have been around the game somewhat, ask them questions. Ask, ask, ask. Scotty Bowman, I think, one of the great minds in hockey, whenever he does things, he always calls and asks people. I remember Scotty called Dave Maloney before he traded for Dave Maloney. You know what he did for Dave Maloney when Dave Maloney landed in Buffalo? When Dave went up there it was going to be tough because he'd always been here in New York City, his family has been here. Bowman took him to his house. You know the first thing you see when you walk into Scotty's house? Replicas of five Stanley Cups. Dave said that hit him right between the horns. Never seen anything like it. You learn things when you deal with Scotty Bowman over the years, or people like Scotty. They ask questions, they ask everybody.

SF: But is it your job to give somebody like Neil advice?

JD: If they ask. I don't go giving them advice. Not ever. If they asked me, I'd be happy to give my opinion. Sometimes I do it and a lot of times I don't.

SF: What's the toughest part of your job?

JD: You catch yourself trying to make everybody happy and you can't do that. You learn that after a while. You simply say it's a big market, you've got to work hard at doing your job to live with yourself, to inform the viewer, and to represent your firm. But, at times you say to yourself, you've got to be more honest, you've got to be more forceful. You just can't say things diplomatically all of the time, and sometimes I catch myself trying to do that.

SF: Where are you weak in hockey knowledge?

JD: I don't know the history of the game like I should. I try to read, but I have a bad memory.

SF: What do you want to do with your life, your personal life, that you haven't yet done? What do you want to accomplish?

JD: Well the Olympics certainly had a lot to do with it. What I'd like to see, honestly, I'd love to see hockey make it on a network, and be part of that. I'd like to see hockey played on a certain night of the week or a certain afternoon of the week, on television, where a large portion of the United States watches. It's okay if it's like "Hockey Night in Canada," every Saturday night in Canada. Every Saturday night in Canada is hockey night in Canada.

SF: What makes you think hockey can be sold on the networks?

JD: We have to find a way to make people understand the beauty of the game. And beauty, there's a lot of beast involved with beauty, but that's part of sports; it gets the adrenalin flowing. That's part of it. You've got to have an adrenalin flow to get people going, to get them hyper. How does it work in the Olympics? Women sat down and watched that stuff to pull for the country. Maybe Gil Stein was right. Maybe we need to put it in the Olympics so people can identify with it. Brian Leetch scored the winning goal to beat the Czechoslovakians for the gold medal. He's an American kid from just outside of Hartford. Plays for the Rangers. Or maybe it was Pat LaFontaine or maybe it was Jeremy Roenick. We're here right now. To get to here, I think we have to dismantle. Not everything, but we need to drop it back down and start over. We have no choice because we're not going to be able to go another level. We just can't. We've pissed too many people off. We haven't promoted ourselves properly. We've been narrow-minded and closed-eyed involving and regarding the awful communications with the media. It's absolutely terrible.

SF: What was the best NHL game you've ever handled?

JD: Game Seven of Edmonton-Philadelphia. I worked it for Global, in Canada, head-to-head with "Hockey Night." I had a lot of fun with that one. It was fun not only because it was the seventh game, but because we were head-to-head with another network. They did half the series, We did half the series. If it went seven, we were both doing it, Global and "Hockey Night."

SF: Last question. Just give me your personal All-Time, All-Star team.

JD: I've got to go with Ken Dryden in goal. He was a control goaltender. He was terrific. On defense, Bobby Orr and Denis Potvin. Up front, Wayne Gretzky, Bobby Hull and there's almost a tie between Guy Lafleur and Mike Bossy. I played against them both. Lafleur was probably better carrying the puck up the ice with speed and brought people out of their seats, but Bossy was more dangerous when he didn't have the puck. They both had great shots, both could find corners, both were wonderfully competitive and it's a great difficulty to distinguish between the two.

Reg Fleming   **(Hockey Hall of Fame)**

Chapter 17

REG FLEMING

Nobody is quite certain about the identity of the original National Hockey League ice cop, enforcer or policeman, if you will. It has been suggested that the role originated with John Ferguson when he was signed by the Montreal Canadiens in 1963 to protect captain Jean Beliveau.

In fact, Reginald Stephen "Reggie" Fleming was doing everything that Ferguson had done even four years earlier as a member of that same Montreal team. And when Fleming was dealt to the Chicago Blackhawks in 1960, his role as protector of Bobby "The Golden Jet" Hull became even more pronounced.

But Fleming was more than a hitter. He could score goals and in the final game of the 1961 playoff between the Blackhawks and Red Wings at Detroit's Olympia Stadium, it was Fleming who delivered the key goal that sped Chicago to its first Stanley Cup championship since 1938.

Nevertheless, Reggie is remembered more for his fists than his wrist shot. He first achieved notoriety during the 1960-61 season when he punched out New York Rangers goaltender Jack McCartan at center ice at Madison Square Garden. McCartan had been the 1960 U.S. Olympic hero who arrived in Manhattan with great fanfare. Fleming was unimpressed, as his right cross indicated.

In addition to his run with the Blackhawks, Reggie played for the Bruins and then was traded to New York where he, ironically, became a hero. Interestingly, one of his most successful bouts was with John Ferguson, whom he bloodied on Garden ice. He later played for the Philadelphia Flyers and Buffalo Sabres before concluding his pro career with the World Hockey Association's Chicago Cougars.

He then entered the business world, eventually forming his own company, R.F. Industries, dealing in promotional items. Fleming, who calls the Windy City home, was interviewed by Chicago reporter Rick Sorci from which the following narrative was drawn.

There were so many positive memories from my hockey career, such as making the playoffs my first year. But, most of all, winning the Stanley Cup with the Chicago Blackhawks in 1961. Funny thing was that we finished third in 1960-61 behind the Maple Leafs and Canadiens. Montreal had a dynasty then. They had won five straight Stanley Cups and were going for a sixth. Toronto had a good team, too. The Leafs wound up second, only two points behind the Habs. Detroit was fourth, well behind us.

But you know how things go in the playoffs; it's a whole new ball game and Detroit knocked off Toronto, four games to one, while we were playing Montreal. It was a tough series, but we knocked them off in six games, ending their string of championships and putting us in the finals against Detroit. This was the first time the Blackhawks had gotten to the finals in a long, long time, so you can imagine the frenzy over hockey in Chicago at that time.

We wound up leading them three games to two and the sixth game was at their rink. Detroit went ahead by a goal in the first period. I was out there killing a penalty when they scored, but I made up for that early in the second when I tied the score. I was fortunate to get the puck and blast it past Hank Bassen who was in goal for them. I was going from left to right and pulled him. As he was falling, there was an opening on the right side and I just flipped it in.

That must have given our guys a lift because we scored four straight goals after that and won the game 5-1. I still have the puck that I scored with in the second period. I got it mounted and everything.

I'm not remembered for my goals as much as I am for my fighting. The night I fought John Ferguson at Madison Square Garden was a pretty good one. It was near the end of the game and the puck ended up between my legs. I looked around for it and all of a sudden Fergie came along and hit me with his stick. He suckered me. I knew that everybody said that he was a tough guy, but that didn't matter to me. I came back and gave him a couple of good shots and I did well. That was the last time we tangled.

It was a different NHL than it is now, by a lot. There were only six teams in the late 1950s and early 1960s. If you wanted to make it to the top, chances were you had to pay your dues in the minors, which is what I did. I played four years in the minors before I got my break. The Canadiens had a huge farm system and I was a part of it, playing for some good coaches like Roger Leger, who had been a Montreal defenseman, and Fred Shero, who had played for the Rangers.

I played for Fred in Shawinigan Falls, Quebec, when they had a good hockey team there. I learned a great deal from Fred and I found that everyone he touched came away with a better understanding of the game. In those days I wasn't much of a sleeper; I used to get up early nearly every morning and walk the streets. Then I'd meet Fred in a restaurant and we'd have breakfast. Afterward, we'd go over to the rink and work out together. That's where I picked up a lot of tips from Fred. He used to tell me, "Reggie, I may be the coach, but you're a coach, too. Anytime you can help another player out, you're helping me do my job."

He gave me hints on how to improve my skating, how to have better balance on my skates, what I could do to strengthen my wrists. Fred was far ahead of his time and serious about having his players teaching each other. For instance, I had played football as a kid, so Fred had me teach the defensemen how to use their shoulders when they threw a check.

I finally got a tryout with the Canadiens at the end of the 1959-60 season. My first game was against the Bruins and I went into the corner after the puck on my first shift. I got to the puck, looked up and Fernie Flaman, who was known for being a pretty rough customer, was charging down on me at top speed. If I hadn't stepped out of the way, Fernie would have run me through the boards. He was a veteran and I was a rookie, so he had to come at me, to test me out. He said to me, "Hey, man, you're in the big leagues now, and here I come." That's how it was: either you could take it or you couldn't.

Even though I finally made it to the Canadiens, I knew it would be very tough to stay with Montreal, because they had so much talent at the end of the '50s. There were the two Richards, Maurice and Henri, Dickie Moore, Jean Beliveau and Boom Boom Geoffrion. They were loaded. Getting traded to Chicago was a break for me.

It was funny, because when I was still playing minor league hockey our games would be at the Forum on a Sunday afternoon after the Canadiens had played on Saturday night. Well, this time we came a day early and I went to the Canadiens game with Fred Shero. The Blackhawks were in town that night and Freddie knew Glenn Hall, the Chicago goalie.

After the game, Shero took me down to the Blackhawks' dressing room and introduced me to Hall. "This guy is going to be playing for you next year, shooting his mouth off and all that," Shero told Glenn. A year later I was playing right alongside Hall.

I knew I could make it in the big league if I worked hard. I came to training camp and worked my butt off and made the team. But even before that, during the summer, I knew if I wanted it bad enough, I could have it. With the Blackhawks, my job wasn't just to go out there and beat up on people. I had to play hockey to survive in the NHL. But when trouble started, I didn't back down. Ever.

I had never been much of a scorer and I didn't become one in Chicago. But I did learn a lot about defensive hockey. Checking, forechecking and backchecking. I checked all the great scorers. When we played against Detroit, I went against Gordie Howe. When we saw Toronto, I checked Frank Mahovlich. If we played New York, I would be assigned to shadow Andy Bathgate. Some of my biggest thrills came after I'd gone to the Rangers and we played the Blackhawks. Then I got to check Bobby Hull. For me it was more important that I keep the other guy from scoring than scoring a goal myself.

Chicago had a great bunch of guys — Bobby Hull, Stan Mikita, Pierre Pilote, Moose Vasko, Billy Hay and Murray Balfour. We were a club on the rise. We turned it all around right after Christmas. We went into Detroit and beat the Red Wings. Instead of taking off right after the game, we had to wait because the train didn't leave Detroit until about three or four in the morning. Billy Hay, Murray Belfour and I tried to find some place where we could get a drink, but it was so late that the bars were closed. The only place we could find was a Greek tavern which wasn't very crowded. We got friendly with some of the Greek people and they invited us over to their house, where they fed us a bit. We drank and ate, then took off. From that point on, for some reason, we became the hottest team in the league until we met Montreal in the first round of the playoffs.

The Canadiens were favored because they had won all those Cups, but their captain, Maurice Richard, had retired in the spring of 1960. They weren't exactly the same team they had been before. Besides, a lot of our guys were super-motivated because they had played for the Canadiens before. Dollard St. Laurent had played defense for some of Montreal's Cup-winners and he was with us now. Murray Balfour, Billy Hay, Ab McDonald and Eddie Litzenberger — all were ex-Canadiens now with Chicago.

Even though we were underdogs we felt we could beat the Canadiens — and we did! After that, we knew we could beat Detroit. What helped was the fact that Rudy Pilous wasn't afraid to play Bobby Hull opposite Gordie Howe. Bobby was young then and very strong, and he skated over Gordie. Gordie couldn't hold on to him. That was a big factor in our favor.

The night we beat them there was a big snowstorm in Detroit so we couldn't fly out to Chicago where our owner, Bill Wirtz, had planned a big party. Instead, they rented a suite in the old Detroit Leland Hotel, where we stayed then, and had a party there.

It was a great feeling to be a part of a Cup-winner; killing penalties and scoring goals. Not that it made me a lot of money. When I went to negotiate my next contract, management didn't care whether we won the Cup or not. I told them I contributed to the championship and their answer was, "Yeah, you got paid for it!" I was the type of person who was happy to be in the National Hockey League, playing and all that, but I still thought we should have gotten more of a reward. Who knows, maybe that's why Chicago never has won the Stanley Cup since.

I made $8,000 then, plus the $3,000 we got for winning the Cup. So, it came to $11,000 altogether. Next thing I know I get a contract that was less than they had offered me the year before. No bonuses — nothing. I thought, Jesus, after winning the Cup they should have come up with at least two or three thousand.

What do you do? You try to forget it. But I believed that if management took care of its team, and satisfied them, that we'd have given a little more. But you have to remember that times were different then with a six-team league and jobs being so scarce — not like it is today with 26 NHL clubs and more expansion on the way.

Not that it dulled my intensity. Any fights they wanted me to fight, I'd fight. I set a penalty record for 37 minutes in one game against the Rangers one night in New York. It was the night Stan Mikita got beat up by Andy Bathgate and then John Hanna of New York tried to get into it and I grabbed Hanna. I got a couple of minors, then I got into a fight with Dean Prentice and another one with Eddie Shack.

When I went with Shack, I first chased him with the stick but, when I got to him, I dropped it and just gave him a shot. But Eddie wasn't a fighter. Matter of fact, I haven't seen him drop the gloves yet. While I was chasing Shack, their goalie, Jack McCartan, threw his big stick and hit me, so after Shack and I were broken up, McCartan went to pick his stick up. As he skated by me, I didn't bother wondering whether he had hit me deliberately or not with his stick. I just remembered that he had hit me, so I jammed him one in the face and decked him.

Our coach, Rudy Pilous, was a jovial guy and I liked him. Rudy coached us through the 1962-63 season when we finished second behind the Leafs. When Detroit beat us four games to two in the opening playoff round, there was a lot of disappointment in Chicago. Management thought, geez, we should have won. That's when they replaced Rudy with Billy Reay. Unfortunately, they never won another Stanley Cup, although the Blackhawks had some awfully good players.

One of my favorites was our goalie, Glenn Hall, who in my opinion was the greatest goalie to play the game. They can say what they want about Terry Sawchuk and Jacques Plante, but as far as I'm concerned, they couldn't put on Hall's jockstrap. Hall was a great guy who mostly stuck to himself. He was a team man who just came to play.

People like to talk about how nervous he was between periods and how he would throw up before games because of his nerves. Well, let me tell you this; if it wasn't for Glenn, nerves and all, we never would have won the Stanley Cup. That's how good he was. The saves he made were unbelievable.

Hall played more than 500 straight games without a mask, which tells you a lot about him. I can't single out any one particular outstanding game he played because they were all great. That's the thing with Glenn; he always played top-notch as long as I was with them. He didn't get the nickname "Mister Goalie" for nothing.

Glenn was quiet in the locker room whereas a fellow like Bobby Hull was kidding around all the time. He was funny, and even though he was a superstar, Bobby had a common touch about him. Remember, he was a big star, working a regular shift and the power play, whereas I was just a penalty-killer who didn't get much ice time. One day he came over to me and said, "Just remember, Reggie, that your job is just as important to this team as mine." That really made me feel good.

Our other offensive superstar was Stan Mikita who was a very cocky kid. He could skate and he was smooth. I saw him put moves on guys. He would come in on a defenseman, "give" the defenseman the puck, take it back, put it between his legs and get by the guy all by himself. Stan did amazing things with his stick and he also got into a lot of fights in his early years, but then he settled down and realized that he wasn't a fighter. He used to fight Henri Richard quite a bit, and even though Henri was small, he could fight. After a while, Stan decided to play hockey rather than be physical, and it paid off for him in the end.

Bobby Hull was the most dynamic player I've seen. When he wound up behind the net with the puck and started going down the wing, picking up speed, the people in the seats used to stand up just so they wouldn't miss it.

One night we were playing in New York and the Rangers assigned Johnny Wilson to check Bobby. Now Johnny was one of the fastest skaters in the league and one of the best checkers. At this particular time, the Rangers had a penalty and Bobby was out on our power play. Wilson was assigned to guard him.

Bobby got the puck behind our net and started motoring toward the other end. Wilson tried to cut in front of him to angle him off. By the time they got to the other side of the boards, Bobby was gone. Wilson couldn't even catch up! Remember, when you're carrying the puck, you're supposed to be a step or two slower but, still, he was way ahead of Wilson who didn't have the puck.

I always liked visiting New York. In those days we used to stay at the Roosevelt Hotel on Madison Avenue near Grand Central Terminal. To get to the Garden, which was just across town, we'd cab over.

Billy Hay was our cab captain, so any time we took a cab, we had to meet in the hotel lobby with Billy.

We did a lot of walking in New York. Sometimes we'd come in the night before a game and just walk around Times Square past all the theaters and look for the stars. Usually Billy would have some kind of funny remark about them. But one time we had the laugh on Billy. We were walking along when he suddenly says we have to find a piece of cardboard. Nobody could figure out why until he showed us that he had a big hole in the sole of his shoe. Since it was raining at the time, he had to plug his leaky sole!

Little did I know, standing in the rain on Broadway with Billy Hay and his leaky sole, that some day I'd play with the Broadway Blueshirts — the New York Rangers.

Rocket Richard   **(Imperial Oil-Turofsky/Hockey Hall of Fame)**

Chapter 18

MAURICE RICHARD

Few observers who had the good fortune of seeing Maurice Richard in action will question his title as the most electrifying performer of the post-1940 pre-expansion era. And there are many who will unqualifyingly assert that Richard was the most exciting player of all time.

The Rocket's galvanic qualities stemmed from several elements, not the least of which was his hyper-intensity, which was most evident with his piercing eyes. Hall-of-Fame goaltender Glenn Hall, who faced Richard many times during the 1950s, once said that when the Rocket bore down on him, it was like no other feeling in the world. "His eyes," said Hall, "were like searchlights."

But it was more than Richard's intensity that created such high voltage. He was a powerful skater who frequently would defy defensemen to stop him simply by skating right at, and sometimes over, them. "I remember once he carried two defensemen on his back and still managed to score on me, recalled former Chicago Blackhawks and New York Rangers goalie, Emile "The Cat" Francis.

Richard's weaponry included an excellent forehand wrist shot, but since he was a left-handed shot playing right wing, the Rocket frequently used his backhand, which became the most deadly in hockey history.

Before becoming a full-fledged star, Richard had to overcome innumerable obstacles including a spate of injuries early in his career that had some newsmen branding him a brittle athlete. But by the 1943-44 season, the Rocket had clearly established himself as a power forward on one of the most feared lines of all time. Teaming up with center Elmer Lach and left wing Hector "Toe" Blake, the trio was nicknamed the "Punch Line," and they terrorized goalies through the mid-1940s under coach Dick Irvin.

Despite his success, Richard was branded a war-time wonder, and some doubted his ability to perform at a high level once NHL stars returned from the armed forces. But the Rocket seemed to get even better as the post-war competition increased and, even after the retirement of Blake and Lach, Richard was among the scoring leaders. He also was one of the most abused — by enemy checkers — and one of the most temperamental. His most legendary outburst occurred at Boston Garden in March, 1955.

When linesman Cliff Thompson grabbed Richard during an altercation with Boston defenseman Hal Laycoe, the Rocket leveled Thompson and was brought before NHL president Clarence Campbell for a hearing. At the time, Richard, who had never won a scoring championship, was the NHL's point leader with a week remaining in the season. Then, it happened!

In an unprecedented decision, Campbell suspended the Rocket for the remaining regular season games as well as the playoffs. This brought down the wrath of the Montreal populace. Shortly after a critical Red Wings-Canadiens game on March 17, 1955, Campbell was attacked in the arena and a teargas bomb was set off, emptying the Forum. A night of rioting followed, until Richard appeared on radio and television appealing for calm. The din eventually subsided, but only after enormous damage to downtown Montreal. To the chagrin of Montreal fans, Richard lost the scoring title to teammate Bernie Geoffrion, while the Canadiens lost first place to the Red Wings.

In the aftermath, Irvin was replaced as coach by Toe Blake, who had a calming influence on Richard. The Rocket never won a scoring title, but captained the Canadiens to five straight Stanley Cups between 1956 and 1960, after which he retired.

The interviews with Richard were conducted on tape by Stan Fischler during meetings at Montreal's Mt. Royal Hotel after his retirement. The Rocket has remained an active figure in Montreal, authoring a weekly column in the newspaper La Presse.

Oh, we had some great Canadien teams in those years before expansion. I know everybody thinks the one in the late 1950s was the best, with Doug Harvey on the point of the power play with Boomer Geoffrion, Dickie Moore and my kid brother, but I'll take the 1943-44 team any day. That year we had Murph Chamberlain, Bill Durnan,

Ray Getliffe, Toe Blake, Elmer Lach, Butch Bouchard and Mike McMahon. We also had Phil Watson on loan from the Rangers, and wound up losing only five out of 50 games.

Maybe I like that team because we had more fun together; there was a kind of brotherhood that disappeared later. We always traveled by train and we only played 50 games then which gave us a lot more time to socialize. This meant a whole different way of living — we were just one big happy family. It stayed that way until 1950 when the changes started taking place. Bill Durnan finally quit, some of the other oldtimers threw in the towel, and a lot of new kids came along.

But I still had a lot of hockey left in me until that crazy thing happened in November 1957. There was a pile-up in front of the Toronto net and I fell. Then Marc Reaume, the Leafs defenseman, landed right on top of me.

He tried to get up while I was lying on the ice, and damned if his skate blade didn't jam in behind my tendon guard, getting caught in the tape that held everything together. Well, his blade was so sharp it cut right through my tendon as he got up and just about ruined me. I had been leading the league in scoring, and even though I was getting older this looked like a great year until Reaume came along.

I was out for three months with my foot in a cast. I never thought I'd play again that season. However, they took the cast off late in the year and I asked Dick Irvin, the coach, if I could play. "Might as well try it," he said, "and see how it's gonna go." First game I scored two goals; second game, I got two more. In the playoffs I had a total of 11 goals. The way I got those goals gave me confidence and I kept playing. But the tendon was stiff and hurting me; every year it would get harder. I stopped scoring so many goals and I played just like anybody else on the ice.

The last five years that I played I was over 200 pounds and just wasn't the same guy I was 10 years before. I could've gone on a diet for a month or two and even tried it a couple of times. I'd lose eight or nine pounds, but I wasn't feeling very good and started to get weak. What I should have done was to go on a diet for the whole summer, then start eating when the season began. I probably would have felt a lot stronger.

I quit in September 1960. I could have stayed on another year if I had wanted, but management was dropping hints for me to take a front office job. Besides, I felt the fun had gone out of it. The great days, the great teams, were all behind.

What was the sense of going on if I could do only some of the things the fans paid to see me do? Like that night against the Bruins in 1952. We were at the Forum in the seventh game of the semifinals. I was going around the defensemen or between them and Leo

Labine of the Bruins hit me just as I was falling to the ice. While I was down he hit me on the head with his knee. I was cut open and knocked out cold.

They took me to the Forum clinic and woke me up, and I came back to the bench. I actually didn't know where I was or what team I was playing. They probably could have sent me to the hospital, but I wanted to finish the game. Then I went out on the ice and was dizzy; I didn't know which end was which. But don't you think I wound up scoring the winning goal? I hit the puck, didn't know what happened, and only found out afterwards because I saw a movie of it. But when it actually went in I wasn't too sure. My father came into the dressing room after the game and everybody said it was my best goal. I scored some as good as that one, I think, but it was the winner in the playoffs.

If Labine didn't hit me that way, who knows what would have happened? But that wasn't the first time a guy took a run at me and it certainly wasn't the last. They started doing it from the year I scored 50 goals in 50 games [1944-45]. I'd be put into the boards or tripped, and I used to get mad and retaliate. Most of the time when I fought back, I'd wind up getting the penalty alone. The first guy never got it.

When we played the Maple Leafs in the 1947 playoffs, they really laid on the wood. Between Vic Lynn and Bill Ezinicki, I had my hands full. Lynn started off giving me a bad check and I tried to get at him. I was running after him and when he spotted me he lifted his stick in the air; when I saw that I swung my stick and hit him, too. I hit him first, on the head. He was bleeding a little bit and I got five minutes. Then, I became tangled with Ezinicki. We both had our sticks up in the air and I clobbered him, too. Before he hit me I struck him and I was in trouble. More penalties.

After the game I went out to eat and had a bad meal. Then I found out I was suspended for one game because of Lynn and Ezinicki, and we ended up losing the series to Toronto.

We were fighting the Rangers a lot in those days, too. One night we were at Madison Square Garden and there was what you'd *really* call a first-class brawl; everybody was in on it.

I must've fought with three different Rangers over a span of 15 minutes since the referee just couldn't break everything up in time. There was a lot of stick-swinging; this happened mostly because we were close to the Rangers' bench and the fans were also giving us trouble. I remember one of the Rangers swung his stick at me and I came back, hit him a couple of times, and knocked him down on the ice. Then, I lifted my stick up and had the intention of hitting him again with it. But he was on the ice and so when I brought the stick down I hit the ice instead of him. You know I was so mad I really wanted to get him, but I changed my mind.

I played against a lot of tough but clean players. Milt Schmidt of the Bruins was a gentleman. Oh, there were a few times when we had little arguments because I probably hit him against the boards, and a couple of times would throw him a dirty check. He used to tell me, "Rocket, don't you do that again or I'll get at you." But Milt was a nice guy. Syl Apps, the Toronto captain, was another one like that. Never, absolutely never, would he say anything on the ice. His left wing, Harry Watson, also was the same — a strong, clean hockey player and a good skater. They fitted in well in Toronto since the fans there were the best in the whole circuit. Whenever a team played good hockey and the Leafs were bad they'd give you, the visitors, a hand and cheer you.

In Montreal the fans were more rabid and they favored French players. They gave Bill Durnan trouble at the Forum, even though he was one of the greatest goalies in history. In 1949-50 he was doing all right but after a bad game the fans got on him and he started to worry a little, then worry some more.

It really hurt because Durnan was a wonderful, nice guy who smiled at everybody and never said a bad word against a soul. He took the blame every time there was a goal scored, never mentioning the defensemen. But that year they got on him, and I remember after one game he came into the dressing room after it was over and he was crying. He couldn't take the punishment; that's the reason he quit. But Durnan was in a class by himself as a goaltender. He was the best I've ever seen.

He was the kind of goalie who never went down to block a shot and was always using *both* hands. Like a switch-hitter, he'd wait for the forward to make the first move, then he'd switch that stick if he had to. That's why he was so hard to beat on the breakaway. The only place where he was weak was on the screened shot — he used to hate somebody standing in front of him. After Durnan, I liked Frankie Brimsek of the Bruins; he was a good one but couldn't switch hands the way Bill did.

I talk about my own team because I knew it best and the one guy I knew as well as anyone was my center in those early days of the '40s, Elmer Lach. He was one of the toughest men in the business but he also took a lot because of that.

One year — I think it was April 1944 — we were up against the Blackhawks in the Stanley Cup finals. We were leading Chicago 3-2 on their ice and it was late in the game when Elmer started a rush from behind our net. The Blackhawks had a big, bald defenseman named Earl Seibert, and he had been running at Elmer all night. That was pretty tough on Lach since Seibert was about 40 pounds heavier. Well, a strange thing happened as Elmer crossed our blue line; he collapsed and slid right across the face-off circle at center ice. Nobody had touched him.

Poor Elmer must have taken so much punishment he just couldn't stand up anymore, and there he was on the ice with his eyes closed, not moving a muscle. When Seibert took a look at him he shouted, "Holy Moses, I've killed him!"

Lach wasn't dead. He was carted off to the dressing room and recovered okay. Meantime, we went on to beat Chicago in four straight games and won the Cup. Elmer came back to play a few more years of great hockey with me and Toe Blake. In those days we were known as the "Punch Line."

Elmer wasn't the kind of guy you wanted to skate against. I remember Durnan once saying, "Elmer can be mean and grouchy. The way he plays just has to antagonize people." Because with him the most important thing was getting the puck, and the means weren't important. And more often than not, he got it; so he not only annoyed players, he showed them up, too.

The opposition cursed him a lot. There was a guy on Detroit called Flash Hollett who said some pretty hard things about Elmer. "He had a trick of coming in under your arms when you were carrying the puck," Hollett once commented. "Then, he'd hoist you up off your feet. He cross-checked at your face and head all the time, too. I don't have any sympathy for him."

One year we played Toronto, and before the playoffs one of the Metz brothers — I think it was Don — ran into Elmer and broke his jaw. Dick Irvin was coaching us at the time and he said that God would prove it was a dirty play by letting us win the Stanley Cup. But the Leafs beat us.

Jack Adams, who managed the Red Wings, used to say: "My guys are lambs compared to him. Lach is the nastiest, meanest, shrewdest so-and-so in the league and there's nobody in hockey I'd rather have on my club."

Elmer's reply was okay, too. "Hockey is no game for little gentlemen," was the way he put it. "Those guys take the bread and butter out of my mouth when they beat me. Injuries are part of hockey. If you don't want to get hurt, you'd better not play."

We had other guys who could get the team excited. In his earlier days Doug Harvey was one of them; he had a terrific sense of humor and he'd relax us with a good gag whenever we were tense. But later on he got too direct and instead of making guys laugh he'd get them mad at him. By that time Boomer [Geoffrion] was with us, and he took over where Doug left off. The Boomer loved to sing and pretend he was an opera star, and he'd get us laughing.

I think one of the things that changed Doug's attitude was the way the league treated him when he tried to organize a players' association. Doug was the organizer in Montreal and Ted Lindsay, the guy who'd get me so mad, did the work in Detroit. Both guys wound up getting into trouble after that with their teams. Finally, Detroit traded Lindsay to Chicago and, while he was still good, Doug was traded to New York. Now they've got a good players' union, but Doug and Lindsay were the guys who did the real work although they didn't have the right luck then.

I was in a funny position. Unions for athletes weren't common in those days, and I was sure that if I became involved with the hockey players' association I'd get into trouble with the Canadiens, and with Selke in particular. He was always nice to me and I didn't want to hurt him or get into an argument with him. I thought the general plan for the union was perfect but felt they had some wild ideas. One thing they were asking was that after so many years in the league a player would be allowed to go anywhere. I knew they'd never get that.

Maybe my attitude wasn't the best and perhaps some of the players didn't like me for it. Who knows? There were lots of guys who did things their own way and didn't care what people thought. Look at Jacques Plante. He was some goaltender — and some character. After Durnan there was Gerry McNeil, then Plante. McNeil came in when Durnan got fed up in the 1950 playoffs and stayed in goal after that for a few seasons. McNeil was just fair, never a natural; he had to work for his job. You knew that because he couldn't play any other sport except hockey. Most of the players were good at golf and tennis and other things, but not McNeil — he played hockey and that's all.

Plante came up part-time in the early '50s and then got the job, full-time, in the mid-'50s. After Durnan and Brimsek, Jacques was the best. And you had to give him credit for his nerve in trying that new style of going behind the net to get the puck. That made him different from others right off the bat.

Jacques was a funny guy in more ways than one. He used to knit his own tuques and I think he even wore them during games in the lower leagues before he came to the Canadiens. When he first joined us he was a lot of fun, especially in practice. Really different from Durnan. You could never get Bill to bear down in practice. Never. Jacques was different. We'd make a little bet with him — $1 or $2 — on whether he could win the practice game and he'd be impossible to beat. He'd stop everything, that guy.

After a while, though, he'd get on people's nerves. Not that he talked too much, but he'd never take the blame for anything. It wasn't only with us; it was the management, with coaches, with Dick Irvin, with Toe Blake. Then later, when he was traded to New York, he couldn't get along with them down there, either. Nobody liked him because he never took anything from anybody. But as a goalkeeper he was hard to beat and he knew what he was doing because he stayed in the league so long.

Another thing you had to give him credit for was introducing the mask. Now nearly every goalkeeper wears one, but Jacques popularized it. He put it on one night in New York after he got hit hard by a shot from Andy Bathgate. That was something. His whole face was a bloody mess and he went into the dressing room and told the coach, Toe Blake, he wouldn't play any more if he couldn't wear the mask.

That was really some scene because Blake didn't like the idea of goalies wearing masks; it just wasn't done in those days. But there was nothing Blake could do and he let Jacques finish the game with that big thing over his face. From then on he wore the mask and, pretty soon, other guys picked up on it — Terry Sawchuk, Charlie Hodge, Gerry Cheevers. The oldtimers stayed away from it at first. Johnny Bower didn't want to put it on and Glenn Hall was another who wouldn't touch it. But before they quit they started to wear the mask.

The thing that turned hockey all around was the curved blade. I don't know the first guy to try it, but I was still playing when it came into the league. Some people think it was Andy Bathgate of the Rangers, but then Bobby Hull and Stan Mikita of Chicago began using the curve, and soon almost everybody was shooting with it and the whole style of the game changed. Look at today's hockey. There aren't too many guys who go into the offensive zone and try to make a play. As soon as they get the puck on that curved stick, all the young guys take a slapshot. Most of the time they miss, so then they run into the corners for the puck. You don't see hockey like you used to, 10, 15, 20 years ago — because of the curved blade.

They say expansion is the cause of the change in play, that it's not as strong as it was before. I don't agree; I believe it's the curved blade. Everybody wants to shoot the puck from the center zone, trying to score from the blue line or the red line. How can you see good passes and plays? Everybody shoots — and runs. Sure, it's a faster game now; they're running into the zone faster, but you don't see the good play. You see one good game every 10 or 15 games at the most. When we play oldtimers' games we go in the zone and try to make passes. You see better plays then, with guys who are 50 and older, than you see in the NHL today.

But I can't complain. Hockey was good to me in a lot of ways. I'll never forget my trips to Europe. By that time — I went in 1957 and 1960 when I was still a player — hockey was really popular over there but what really surprised me was that the Europeans knew the NHL players — all of them, especially the stars. In fact, they even knew the lineups of each team. When I walked into the rink in Prague people got up and started to cheer. What a feeling. It was the same thing in Russia. They knew that the NHL was the strongest league in hockey, but they themselves were growing fast.

Maybe I shouldn't be so outspoken. In the past I used to get in trouble by saying what was on my mind. Once, in the mid-'50s, I had an article ghostwritten under my name for a French-language paper in Montreal called *Samedi-Dimanche*. They had me doing a weekly column called "Le Tour du Chapeau" (The Hat Trick), and in one I got mad at Clarence Campbell for the heavy penalty he gave Geoffrion in a fight with the Rangers.

The whole tone of the article was that Campbell was prejudiced against French-Canadian players in particular and the Canadiens as a team. I wrote: "He smiles and openly displays his joy when opponents score against us."

It got me in trouble and I had to give up the column, but I went back to it again once I retired. I didn't mind that much because it let me concentrate on hockey again. In Montreal hockey is all business. It's the national game and it has to be taken seriously by the players because the fans are so crazy. Maybe things are more relaxed now with expansion, but when we had only six teams in the league there was no room for fooling around. When Dick Irvin was coach you couldn't even smoke in the Canadiens' dressing room, and there were no exceptions. I remember Durnan used to like to take a few puffs between periods of a tough game, but he couldn't do it in the dressing room; he had to stay in a small room nearby, away from the other players.

Between Irvin and Selke, the players were encouraged to play hard all the time. We used to have sayings hanging on little signs all over the dressing room in both languages; there was also one in Latin that Selke posted: *"Celeritas-Auctoritas-Aeternaque"* — "Speed, Authority, Eternally."

Irvin used to add his own sayings. Dick had a theory he'd always be repeating to us. "I've coached for more than 25 years," he'd say, "and have come up with three key points in hockey: (1) Don't let the other man get the puck; (2) If he gets it, take it away from him; and (3) Keep shooting and you'll score."

Dick wasn't tough on us when we were winning. The one thing that he wanted was for the players to be on time, especially for the 11 a.m. clubhouse meeting. If you missed that on the day of the game, you'd get fined $25.

It's too bad that Irvin couldn't finish his career with the Canadiens. The year I was suspended [March-April, 1955] was the beginning of the end for Dick. That's when I got into trouble in Boston and Campbell suspended me for the end of the season plus the playoffs and I lost the scoring championship. Some people said Dick had encouraged me to lose my temper. Actually, I think the reason he left to coach Chicago was because of the management at the Forum. He didn't get along with them, and when he left it had nothing to do with the players.

I was sorry he went and so was everybody among the players. The management we shouldn't talk about. What they didn't know was that Dick was already a very sick man suffering from bone cancer. We, the players, knew it. The next question was who would be his replacement.

Many names were mentioned, but we knew that it had to be Toe Blake. There just was no other guy for the job because we all liked him as a person and respected him as a player. Toe got the job and we had a lot of great years together. We came up with a terrific power play with Doug and Boomer on the points and me, Bert Olmstead, and Jean Beliveau up front. Jacques Plante was in goal. It was a good team, but I'd still take that team in the mid-'40s with Durnan in the nets any day.

It could be that I was getting too old and stuck up for the team I played for when I was younger. Anyway, in 1960 I came to training camp and worked out, but my weight was too high and management wasn't forcing me to play. So I retired before the season began and took a job with the Canadiens' front office. It was something — 18 seasons, 1,111 games, from 1942 to 1960.

You don't just leave hockey after that. The job with the Canadiens didn't work out, but I still kept close to hockey.

I coached young boys and continued playing — with the NHL Oldtimers Team in Montreal. You'd be surprised what crowds come out to see us. One night in 1971 we played against the Toronto Oldtimers at Maple Leaf Gardens and drew more than 15,000 fans. One trouble is that the fans still expect me to be the Rocket I was in 1945, but I can't go the way I used to. Besides, we play for fun now, although some of the guys do get carried away. One night Dickie Moore and Ted Lindsay started to go at each other with their sticks, just like old times. We had to stop games with the Detroit Oldtimers for a while. And Kenny Reardon used to go running around hitting guys just like he did in the NHL; we had to tell him to get off the team!

Mostly, though, we play for fun. No slapshots, no body checks and silly penalties. In that Toronto game the referee gave me a 20-second penalty for "missing an open net." That's funny. I did miss the open net, but I also scored. That's the way it is; sometimes I feel like a rookie, other times I skate like an old man.

I look at the papers to see how they're scoring these days. When I scored 50 goals in 50 games it was really something, a goal-a-game. Now, 50 goals isn't so important; there are weak teams, a longer schedule. Do you know that in all their years in the NHL Jean Beliveau and Gordie Howe never scored 50 goals in a season?

Chapter 19

BILL CHADWICK

A case can be made for Bill Chadwick being the most amazing referee to skate on a big-league hockey rink.

Throughout his 16-year National Hockey League career, the New York native operated at the highest level, though blind in one eye! Chadwick, interestingly enough, never mentioned his affliction to anyone during his officiating stint. "During my refereeing career I didn't think it would be smart to think about it, because I might not have been as effective," he said.

The NHL showed its faith in Bill by placing him in charge of some of the most important games ever played; among them, the seventh games of the Stanley Cup finals between Detroit and Toronto in 1942 and 1945. Game Seven (April 22) of the 1945 final was tied 1-1 late in the third period at Olympia Stadium in Detroit. It was then that Chadwick fearessly called a penalty against the home team. On the ensuing power play, Babe Pratt scored the Cup-winning goal for Toronto.

Chadwick, himself, would have been a professional had he not suffered two freak eye injuries which abruptly ended his playing aspirations. It was March, 1935 and he was going to play in an All-Star game at Madison Square Garden. As Chadwick stepped on the ice to start the game, he was hit in the eye by a puck accidentally fired by an opponent. After hospitalization, Chadwick was informed he now had only one good eye.

Amazingly, he returned to play the following season with the Rangers' farm club, the New York Rovers, and this time was hit in the good eye. At that point he quit playing, although he recovered full vision in his left eye.

A few weeks later he was pressed into emergency service as an Eastern League referee, when the regular official was snowbound. He soon became a regular arbiter, then an NHL linesman, and finally an NHL referee.

Bill Chadwick   **(Imperial Oil-Turofsky/Hockey Hall of Fame)**

Chadwick not only was an efficient whistle-blower; he was also responsible for officiating innovations including the system of signals now taken for granted by players and fans alike.

After retiring, "The Big Whistle" remained on top of the hockey scene as a television analyst for Ranger telecasts. Stan Fischler, who remembers watching Chadwick in his earliest days as an Eastern Hockey League referee, interviewed "The Big Whistle" several times over the course of their journalistic relationship. The narrative follows.

I was different from most of the people involved with the NHL because I grew up in New York City and learned my hockey there. That was in the '30s when there weren't many indoor rinks around, and the weather was seldom cold enough for outdoor ice.

Luckily, I went to Jamaica High School in Queens, one of the few city schools with an ice hockey team. I had always loved to skate and my father had bought me a pair of long, racing skates. When they had tryouts for the team, I showed up with the racers and they told me to beat it; I borrowed a pair of hockey skates and then made the team.

We used to play a lot of games at the Brooklyn Ice Palace, an old rink near the railroad tracks in the Bedford-Stuyvesant section. Manual Training High School, Brooklyn Tech and Brooklyn Prep were some of the other clubs. We won the championship and I went on to play for the Floral Park Maroons, a pretty good amateur team. In those days amateur hockey was really big in New York and the top teams were in the Metropolitan League. They played their games on Sunday afternoons at Madison Square Garden before the New York Rover games. It was quite common to draw crowds of from 12,000 to 15,000 fans on any given Sunday and, naturally, it was a great thrill to play there.

One Met League team was called the Stock Exchange Brokers. It was backed by some sports enthusiasts on Wall Street, and guys who played for the club usually got jobs on the Exchange. Somebody on Wall Street offered me a job as well as the chance to play hockey and baseball; that's how I got into organized hockey and eventually to the NHL.

I was 10 years old when I started skating. We'd go to Central Park when it froze over or to the Brooklyn Ice Palace for the regular sessions. So I had done quite a bit of skating in my early days, and even before I got the job on the Exchange, I was so enthused about hockey I used to play for a couple of teams while I still was going to high school. One of them was Fordham University's team. I played for Jamaica under the name of O'Donoghue and as Flanigan with Fordham.

But when I got the job on Wall Street, I played for the Exchange Brokers under my own name and began to play quite well. All during my high school days I had been a Ranger fan and used to sit in the gallery rooting for the Cook brothers, hoping that maybe, someday, I might make it to the NHL. But the accident changed my career.

I was 19 at the time — it was March 1935 — and I was selected to play on the Metropolitan League's All-Star Team which was playing similar teams from other East Coast cities. One afternoon our opponent was Boston and that's when I got hurt.

The Boston team was out warming up when we left our dressing room. Just as I stepped on to the ice, somebody on Boston shot the puck and it hit me smack in the right eye.

When I regained consciousness, they took me out of Madison Square Garden to the hospital. After two weeks, several doctors decided there was no way of restoring the sight in my right eye. Eventually, they released me from the hospital and I went right back to playing hockey the next fall. It was odd because I had tried to play baseball after the accident and found that I'd misjudge the ball after it bounced and really couldn't play the game any more the way I used to. However, I felt I could still make the same judgments in hockey as before.

I couldn't have been too bad because in 1936 I was picked to play for the New York Rovers, the Rangers' farm team in the fast Eastern League. This was really something because many players went from the Rovers to high pro leagues, and some even went to the NHL where they became stars.

I played center for the Rovers in 1936, and was back with them at the start of 1937 when the second accident happened. This time it was in a Rovers game and I got hit by a puck or a stick — I can't remember which — in the left eye. The blood started trickling into my eye and soon my vision was gone. Fortunately, it cleared up and I was able to see out of the eye again, but decided that I'd had enough as a hockey player.

Tommy Lockhart, who was president of the Amateur Hockey Association of the United States, also ran the Rovers at that time and, of course, he knew I had sight in only one eye. As a matter of fact, until the second accident I was the only player in the league wearing a helmet; I wore it far down on my forehead, trying to protect my good eye.

Well, after the accidents I still came regularly to the Sunday afternoon Rover games at Madison Square Garden. One afternoon, in March 1937, I was at the Garden when somebody mentioned that the referee wasn't going to appear because of a snowstorm that was blowing outside. Lockhart spotted me in the stands and said, "Bill, will you fill in?" I was glad to, and Tom must have liked what he saw because he then asked me to become a regular referee in the Metropolitan League. He also said he wanted me to be a linesman for the Eastern League games.

At the time all the players in the league knew I had only one good eye, but nobody gave me any trouble about it. In fact, right from the start I thought I had a psychological advantage and consequently was a better official. You see, because I was using only one eye, that fact was always on my mind and it made me work harder than the other fellows. I skated harder and was closer to the play; in most cases I was on top of it. Pretty soon Lockhart asked me to referee in the Eastern League which led to my being picked as a linesman for the NHL. Actually, I almost quit before making it to the NHL — if I had, I would never have been named to the Hockey Hall of Fame.

What caused me to think of quitting was a game at a rink in Rivervale, New Jersey, about an hour or so from New York City. There was a team there called the Rivervale Skeeters and its manager, Art Chapman, really gave me the business that Saturday night for the way I was officiating. I was so mad after it was over I went to Lockhart and said, "I'm finished! I'm never going to referee again."

Remember, this was on a Saturday night. The following Wednesday I got a wire from Frank Calder, president of the NHL, appointing me a big-league linesman. This was quite a shock, but I was told that Red Dutton, who ran the New York Americans, and Lockhart were behind it all.

Officiating was different at that time. It was customary to have "home-town linesmen"; that is, linesmen from each city would handle games for teams in their city. This meant there were linesmen who worked only the Rangers games and those who'd handle the Americans games. I was the linesman for the Americans.

It wasn't very long before I was in trouble. In one of my first games the Americans were playing the Montreal Canadiens at Madison Square Garden. At the time the NHL used one referee and one linesman. Bill Stewart, who was such a great baseball umpire, was the referee then. During the game the Canadiens manager, Cecil Hart, gave us a real hard time; and here I was, a kid of 22, and this was all new to me. As soon as the game ended, Stewart said, "Follow me!" So I followed him and he walked right into the Canadiens' dressing room to challenge Hart. I knew then what refereeing was all about. Of course, nothing really came of it. Hart just brushed him off because Stewart was a bit of a hothead who felt nobody should criticize what he was doing.

Whether Stewart eventually retired on his own or not I don't know, but in 1941 I was appointed a referee in the NHL. Calder made the official appointment, but he was fronting for the governors. In those days somebody else made the bullets and he fired them.

Whatever the case, everybody on the board of governors knew I only had one eye, but never said anything about it. I decided to ignore the matter and everything moved smoothly until I crossed the Detroit Red Wings.

It was really strange because up until then I had been the fair-haired boy in Detroit. Jack Adams was the Detroit manager and he was a roly-poly tough little guy. The Red Wings were a powerful organization and the feeling was that if you called one wrong against Adams in Detroit — or one that he thought wrong — you were a goner because each club owner carried so much power. Apparently, if you didn't satisfy them they'd get rid of you. If you check the records, you'll see that few officials lasted very long then.

In my case, the thing that annoyed Adams was a call I made in the seventh game of the Stanley Cup finals between Detroit and Toronto. A few years earlier they had played in the finals and Detroit had won the first three games. Then, Toronto bounced back to win the next four — the only time that ever happened. Well, this time it looked like the reverse. Toronto won the first three; so there we were in the seventh game at Olympia Stadium in Detroit and I'm the referee.

My problems started when I called a big penalty against Syd Howe of the Red Wings. He had cross-checked Gus Bodnar with a few minutes left in the game and the score tied 1-1. While Howe was in the penalty box, Babe Pratt of Toronto scored the winning goal and Toronto got the Stanley Cup.

That infuriated Adams and Norris, the Red Wings' owner. From that time on, every year I'd be sent for an eye examination and in my opinion it was at Norris' instigation.

Actually, the fact that Norris and Adams weren't fond of me was the greatest thing that ever happened because it meant that the other five governors were for me. But don't think I wasn't still under a lot of pressure. We all were, except that officials felt it differently than they do today.

One big difference was that the dressing room of the referee and linesman stood practically open to the coaches and managers. As a result they'd almost wait in line outside just to get in and intimidate us. There was no such thing as keeping your door closed. After every period somebody would come in, complaining or bitching and trying to intimidate. Nowadays, though, the referees have all the protection in the world.

Meanwhile, I was going along and doing my best. Ironically, every so often some fan in the balcony would yell down at me, "Chadwick, you blind bastard," and I'd chuckle to myself, because I knew they were half right.

My condition didn't hamper me. I had 20-20 vision in my good left eye and was on top of the play even more than they are now. I was never away from the net when there was a play on goal and I didn't have much trouble from the players, except for a few.

Maurice Richard of the Canadiens and Ted Lindsay of the Red Wings gave me the toughest time, although I never thought they were picking just on me. I believe it was because of their personal make-up and their character — they would have done it to anybody.

Richard was possibly the fiercest competitor I've ever seen in any sport. If you weren't playing on the same team with Maurice Richard, you were his enemy; and that applied if you were a referee giving him penalties. I remember being at a Lester Patrick Trophy dinner once, on the dais with some of the all-time great hockey players including Richard and Milt Schmidt. I tried to get an autograph for my son from everybody there. I asked Schmidt for his and, naturally, he gave it to me. Richard was sitting beside Schmidt, so I asked him next. "I give you no autograph; you only give me penalties!" he replied. He was serious; it wasn't any joke with Richard and I wound up without his autograph.

Because of the way Richard and Lindsay were on the ice, I had a special thing I'd do with them at the start of every season. To this day I'm not sure whether I did it purposely or not. In the first three or four games of every season, I'd give Richard and Lindsay misconduct penalties. I'd do it right away, because if I didn't they might think I wasn't the boss. I had to assert myself early and it was easier to do it then instead of later on in the middle of the season or at the end.

I'm pretty damn sure Richard and Lindsay knew I had only one good eye, especially with guys like Jack Adams in Detroit and Frank Selke in Montreal. And there *was* one time when the fact actually busted out in print. It was in a Detroit paper when I was asking for a two-week draft deferment to allow me to clear up the Stanley Cup playoffs before being drafted into World War Two. The headline in the paper read, "ONE-EYED REFEREE ASKS FOR DRAFT DEFERMENT." But nobody else ever picked it up, not even the New York papers.

As it turned out I wasn't drafted and continued refereeing, liking it more and more. Lots of fascinating things happened, like the 1946-47 season when Richard lost the Stanley Cup for the Canadiens all by himself. Montreal was playing Toronto in the Cup finals and I was refereeing. In one of the early games Richard cut Vic Lynn of Toronto and I gave him a five-minute major penalty. Later in the game he got into a fight with Bill Ezinicki of the Leafs. In those days it was the referees who separated fighting players, not the linesman, and so I went in between them, but Richard reached over my shoulder and cut Ezinicki in the middle of the head. That meant a 20-minute match penalty, whereby the team had to play short-handed for 20 minutes. Toronto won that game and league president

Clarence Campbell suspended Richard for the next game — and Toronto went on to capture the Stanley Cup.

During the mid and late '40s there was an occasional suggestion that I leaned over to give the Rangers a hard time. On the one hand I was accused of being a "homer" with the Rangers because I lived in New York; otherwise I wasn't one and was out to prove it by calling them hard on the Rangers. One thing I know for sure: I wasn't a homer anywhere I worked; I would have quit refereeing if I was considered such. I can't say I was extra-hard on New York, especially if you consider that in the days I refereed in the NHL the Rangers didn't have much of a hockey club. And it wasn't my fault.

Surprisingly, I never had a tough time in Montreal. I'm smug enough to think that I did well there because the fans know the game. Likewise, I was always well-received in Toronto; but the toughest place was Chicago and I don't know why. I just never felt comfortable in that big Chicago Stadium.

Don't get the impression I never made a mistake. I'm a great believer in God Almightly and I think He's the only one who never makes a mistake. I made plenty. One of them made me a better official in the eyes of the NHL people. It happened during a playoff game between Boston and Montreal. At the time Lynn Patrick was coaching the Bruins and we had a delayed penalty ruling. This means the referee holds off blowing the whistle if the offended team has the puck. What happened was that Doug Mohns of Boston was fouled just as he shot the puck and, instead of delaying my whistle, I blew it immediately thus halting play. Mohns' shot went into the net, but the goal was disallowed since I had mistakenly blown the whistle.

If the goal had counted it would have tied the game and given Boston a good chance at winning, and of course Lynn Patrick raised cain about it from the bench. Finally, I skated alongside him and said, "Lynn, I made a mistake."

After the game Patrick came into the officials' dressing room and said he'd never criticize me again since I was big enough to admit my error. But mistakes are part of the game and it really was a great life. I refereed for six months and had the other six off. That's why I remained for 16 years in the NHL as a referee.

I decided to quit in 1955 at the age of 39, because I believe an athlete, whether a participant or an official, should stop while he's on top. Five years after I retired I was elected to the Hockey Hall of Fame.

If I had stayed on as a referee — I think I was capable of five more years — possibly I'd have been asked to leave and been given a cushion job someplace, but I'm not the type who can take that. I didn't want anybody to give me anything; I wanted to earn it. In retrospect I think it all worked out well and have no regrets about my officiating. I learned a lot over those years. In order for a referee to be good he must have the respect of the players, and even though Richard and Lindsay gave me a rough time, I'm sure they respected me.

The trick was to gain the regard of the older players on each team — the leaders. It couldn't be done in a year or two; it took four, five years and more. When I refereed I think I got away with more on the ice than any of my colleagues because I had the players' esteem. I could make a call that a new guy, who didn't have the players' respect, couldn't get away with, without getting the business.

Remember, I refereed for three NHL presidents: Frank Calder, Red Dutton and Clarence Campbell. Calder was a gentleman, whereas Dutton was one of the rabble-rousers of the NHL. In fact, when he was a manager he would lead the parades to our dressing room to protest decisions, but as president he was all for the referees — except once.

Around 1944, during a game between the Blackhawks and Canadiens in Chicago, the score was tied 2-2 when Chicago's George Allen felt that Elmer Lach of the Canadiens was holding him. Instead of waiting for a whistle to see whether I thought so or not, Allen started arguing with me and Elmer put the puck in the Chicago net. The Blackhawk fans went wild, tossing debris all over the ice. It must have been 20 minutes before they stopped throwing things at us.

I had Ed Mepham and Jim Primeau as my linesmen and we stood in the center of the ice to avoid the litter. Finally, I sent Primeau over to the bench saying, "Get Dutton in the corner there and ask him what the hell I should do."

Primeau came back to me about five minutes later. He reported Red's answer: "You got yourself into it, now get yourself out of it!" That didn't help me very much and from then on I had to have a police escort into as well as out of the Chicago rink.

Still, in all those years only one fan actually hit me; that was in Boston during a Stanley Cup series between the Bruins and the Toronto Maple Leafs. I had refereed in Montreal the night before and had to come down through New York in order to get to Boston the next day. When I arrived at the train station in New York, I picked up a paper and noticed front-page pictures of the Boston players with cuts and bruises all over their faces. That made up my mind as to how I was going to referee the next game in Boston.

There was only one thing to do: crack down early in the game with penalties. As it turned out I called 17 penalties in the first period alone, five of them against Wild Bill Ezinicki. After his fifth penalty Ezinicki said to me, "Bill, what are you doin'? What the hell are you doing?"

"What would you do if you were in my position?" I asked.

"I'd do the same thing," he said.

But in the second period the rough stuff continued, although not as bad. During one play there was a scramble along the side of the ice and I tried to avoid the action by hoisting myself up on the sideboards. Just as I did, some fan who'd rolled up his newspaper like a club hit me over the head with it. He hit me so hard I was knocked out cold.

Then, a funny thing happened. Earlier in the game I had given Jimmy Thomson, the Toronto defenseman, a misconduct penalty which carried an automatic fine. Thomson had come back on the ice just before I got hit on the head, and when I regained my senses he skated over to me and pointed toward the seats. "Bill," he said, "there's the guy who hit you." I had the guy thrown out of the rink and the incident proved what I knew all along: players may disagree with the referee, but they don't want fans interfering with their game. As for the fan, I got a letter from him a week later apologizing.

I was never hit by a player. The closest I ever came to that was in a game between the Leafs and Red Wings at Detroit. I had my finger pointed at Tod Sloan of the Leafs, ready to give him a delayed penalty. Before I blew the whistle he skated by and called me something other than my proper name. I said, "That's it — misconduct!" After I blew the whistle I called "Ten and two." I had added the 10 after he had skated into the penalty box, and when he heard that he came storming out with his hand raised as if to strike me. I gave him a misconduct penalty, but he never did hit me.

That was small potatoes, however, compared to some of the trouble I saw. Once I was handling a game between the Red Wings and Canadiens at the Forum in the early '40s. That was when Detroit had a pretty good club with guys like Don Grosso, Sid Abel, Eddie Wares, and Jimmy Orlando and Jack Stewart on defense. Orlando was a Montreal boy and his family always came out to see Detroit play the Canadiens.

We were in the second period of the game when a fight broke out in the stands. Orlando looked up and realized that his father was in the middle of it. So he climbs over the boards and starts up the steps in the stands with skates, stick and all — and the rest of the Detroit team follows him before I could stop them. The last guy I could get to was Eddie Wares who was going up there with his stick in his hand. I yelled, "Eddie, drop your stick! Drop your stick!" He dropped it all right, but somebody hit him right on top of the head with a bottle and cut him wide open. I was sorry I had told him to drop the stick, and to make matters worse had to ride down to New York that night on the same bus with the Red Wings. It was murder.

At least an incident like that stopped the action on the ice and gave me a little rest. There were some games where I was really exhausted at the end. In fact, I refereed the longest game ever handled with one official. It went into sudden-death overtime and didn't end until one-thirty in the morning. When it was over my legs were so swollen I could hardly take my skates off and my ankles remained puffed up for several days after. But it didn't stop me from officiating my next turn. As a matter of fact, I never missed an assignment in my 16 years in the NHL.

The longer I refereed the easier it became. When I started refereeing I traveled all alone, and when I'd come to a city I'd work with a hometown linesman — and, as much as I don't like to use the word homer, there was such a thing in those days. Then Campbell came along and changed things. Hometown linesmen were eliminated and replaced by linesmen who traveled around the league just like referees. But that wasn't all he did to make a referee's life more pleasant. Previously, when a referee called a penalty, he was sure to have 10 people around him arguing; Campbell changed that so only the captain or alternate captain could discuss the penalty. Then the circle was added around the penalty timekeeper's area to prevent players from interfering with the referee when he announces his penalty.

I was the one responsible for developing all the arm signals now used in the NHL. I started using them from almost the first day I was in the league, but they were only made official the year after I retired.

This was all because I studied the game; before each one I'd examine the recent history of the two teams so I knew what to expect from them. Sometimes I'd phone the referee who had handled the teams a day or two earlier to get his impressions. If I felt my game was going to be especially rough, I'd get the two centers out for the opening face-off and caution them, "This is going to be a tough one. Be careful."

Of course, silly things happen. Once during a game between the Blackhawks and Americans, Red Dutton, manager of the Americans, complained that Chicago's goalie, Sam LoPresti, was wearing pads that were too wide. The rule book says the pads cannot be wider than 10 inches. "I want you to measure LoPresti's pads," said Dutton.

So, I went out and measured his pads and they were 10-and-a-quarter inches wide. Dutton yelled, "See, see, I told you he was over the limit. We're goin' to protest!"

Then Paul Thomson, the Blackhawks coach, said, very lethargically, "Bill, measure Robinson's pads." Robinson was the Americans goalie; his pads were 10-and-a-half inches wide.

Another funny thing took place in Chicago when Johnny Mariucci was on defense for the Blackhawks. In the early '40s, in Chicago Stadium, the gallery gods had a habit of playing cards before the game started. Once the action began these fans would wrap up their deck of cards with a rubber band and keep them handy just in case they didn't like the referee's decision.

Midway in the game I gave Mariucci a misconduct penalty, and suddenly all those damn cards flew out of the balcony onto the ice. Meanwhile, Mariucci kept giving me the business from the penalty box.

I leaned over, picked up a bunch of cards, skated to the penalty box, and handed them to Mariucci. "John," I said, "you're gonna be here a while. You might as well play."

Jack Adams of Detroit gave me the toughest time of anybody. He'd constantly put pressure on the referees and try to intimidate them by continual needling. I don't know if it really worked; I imagine it might have with some of the guys.

On the other hand, there were the milder, pleasant types like Frank Boucher who managed and coached the Rangers for so long. Frank Selke, the manager of the Canadiens, was also like that.

If there was one thing I really objected to over the years, it was the idea introduced by Toronto of taking films of the game and then, a day or two later, asking the league to look at them to pick out the referee's mistakes. It's very easy to referee on Sunday a game played on Saturday.

Detroit also gave me trouble; when the Red Wings had that powerhouse hockey club in the early '50s, they'd needle me like crazy. They had the best team in the league for five or six years and they'd let you know it in more ways than one. But if I said anything back to them it was apt to wind up in the NHL office.

When I look back on all those years in the NHL, I know I'd do it all over again the same way. Hockey's been great to me and I hope I've contributed as much to it. That's an old phrase, but it's true.

I still love the game. In fact, I enjoyed the game more as a broadcaster than when I officiated. Sometimes I find myself in a rooting capacity and enjoy that; after all, it's only been in the last few years that I've been able to sit back and really watch a hockey game.

Why, I even find myself yelling at the referees sometimes — I'm not very proud of it. But I've never called the referee a "blind bat," because I might be half right saying it!

Chapter 20

ULF NILSSON

When the World Hockey Association challenged the National Hockey League for ice supremacy early in the 1970s, the new organization sought as many ways as possible to catch up to its established rival.

One technique successfully explored by the WHA was the exploitation of the vast European market which heretofore had largely been ignored by the NHL.

After an All-Star group of NHLers was almost beaten by a select squad from the Soviet Union in 1972, it had become apparent that the Europeans were nearly as skilled as the North Americans and, in some cases, even more talented.

The Winnipeg Jets under John Ferguson was one of the first WHA clubs to go the European route. In 1974 Ferguson signed a pair of speedy Swedish forwards, Ulf Nilsson and Anders Hedberg, and paired them with Hall-of-Famer Bobby Hull, who was a fugitive from the Chicago Blackhawks. Nilsson was the center and Hedberg the right wing.

"I played some of the best hockey of my life with those guys," says Hull. "They were genuine artists. I led the WHA in goals [77] that first season with them and we put on quite a show."

In 78 games as a WHA rookie, Nilsson produced 26 goals and 94 assists for 120 points. (Hedberg was 53-47-100.) A year later, he went 38-76-114, but more importantly, played magnificently in the playoffs (7-19-26) as Winnipeg won the Avco World Trophy, emblematic of the WHA championship.

Nilsson led the WHA in assists in the following two seasons after which Ferguson had moved to New York where he had become general manager of the Rangers. Fergie persuaded Ranger president Bill Jennings that the Broadway Blueshirts would do well to sign the two

Ulf Nilsson   (Hockey Hall of Fame)

Swedes, and New York obtained them as free agents on June 5, 1978.

In their maiden NHL season Nilsson and Hedberg demonstrated that they were equal to the major-league standard. Playing under head coach Fred Shero, they galvanized the New Yorkers and won fans for their dazzling play. Nilsson played in 59 games during the 1978-79 season and produced 27 goals and 39 assists.

One can only fantasize about the grand NHL career Nilsson might have enjoyed had he not been riddled with injuries. During his first two seasons in New York, Ulf was leading the Rangers in scoring before being sidelined. By far the most controversial incident involved a collision with New York Islander defenseman Denis Potvin on February 25, 1979. The resultant leg injury sidelined Nilsson through the end of the regular season and into the Stanley Cup finals when he was able to make only two token appearances.

The injuries forced Ulf into a premature retirement after the 1982-83 season. Although the Rangers made the playoffs both in 1982 and 1983, Nilsson was not able to return to the lineup.

After hanging up his blades, Nilsson remained in the New York area as a businessman, staying close to the hockey scene. He is an active member of the Rangers' Alumni Association and has been involved with the growing "Hockey In Harlem" program.

During a visit to the Lester Patrick Award luncheon at New York's Plaza Hotel in February 1993, Nilsson spent a few moments reviewing his career with reporter David Margolit. The following narrative is based on that interview.

I was enjoying my hockey life in Sweden at the start of the 1970s and could have had a nice career there, but North American teams had begun taking a closer look at players in my homeland. The Toronto Maple Leafs had their eyes on Borje Salming who would become one of the best defensemen of that era and other NHL clubs were looking at us.

The Buffalo Sabres had me on their list while Toronto had Anders Hedberg, and Minnesota wanted Lars-Erik Sjoberg, who was a small but excellent defenseman.

All of us wanted to come to North America and play professionally over here, but what we really wanted in addition was to play together, if that was possible. It couldn't have happened if we went to the NHL, because each of us would have wound up on a different team. But we discovered that if we came to the World Hockey Association, all three of us could play on the Winnipeg Jets.

That turned out to be quite a break because the Jets had a nifty team that was just coming together. On top of that, Bobby Hull was on the club and he was still able to do a lot of the things that had made him a great player with the Chicago Blackhawks. For Anders and I to play on a line with The Golden Jet was, well, just as lucky as you can get; a truly great experience.

We had been warned before we came over that the North American game was different from ours. It wasn't just the fact that the rinks were bigger in Europe and that the Swedish game stressed more passing and playmaking, but also that the WHA would be physically rough and that we Swedes would be in for some heavy treatment.

When all was said and done, we found the game in North America not much different than what we experienced in Europe. It was a job and one that we thought we could handle. We were fortunate that a superstar like Bobby Hull was willing to take time and teach us the things we should know. He made it a lot easier for us in every way, in that he taught us what it was like.

The bottom line was that we all enjoyed hockey so much that we were willing to make the sacrifices that were necessary to be a pro on this side of the Atlantic. We were well aware that there were Canadian players who resented us, and there was a lot of talk then about how we were taking potential jobs away from those Canadians who might have had them. But we soon got accepted because the other players and the public appreciates talent.

Because the WHA rinks were smaller than what we had been used to in Sweden, there was a lot more body contact. That's where we took abuse because we were among the first Europeans to come over. In our favor was the fact that there were three of us, because if I were alone, it would have been a lot more difficult to put up with that nonsense. Anders, Erik and I helped each other and supported each other when things were tough.

It's ironic that the one fellow who was such a big help to us, John Ferguson, was a true-blue Canadian and one of the toughest players ever to skate in the NHL. Fergie was terrific in Winnipeg and then, when he came to New York, he had his eye on us.

Leaving Winnipeg was not easy. We had put together a good team, won a championship and got a lot of recognition, even though the WHA still was not considered exactly on a par with the NHL. Still, there was a lot of good talent in the WHA. Gordie Howe was starring for Houston, along with his sons, Marty and Mark; Rejean Houle was in Quebec; Frank Mahovlich with the Toronto Toros and Gerry Cheevers with Cleveland.

The coaching was good, too. We had Bobby Kromm in Winnipeg; Calgary had Joe Crozier; Indianapolis had Jacques Demers, who won a Stanley Cup for the Canadiens in 1993; Bill Dineen was in Houston and Harry Neale in Minnesota, to name a few.

Every year there was a rumor that the WHA was going to fold, but it kept on rolling along and we stayed with Winnipeg through the 1977-78 season. By that time there were eight teams in the league — us, New England, Houston, Quebec, Edmonton, Birmingham, Cincinnati and Indianapolis. We finished first with New England second and Houston third.

In the playoffs that year, we beat Birmingham, four games to one, in the semi-final round and then played New England in the finals. We beat them four straight — 4-1, 5-2, 10-2, 5-3 — to win The Avco World Cup. Anders and I finished off our Winnipeg careers very nicely. He scored the last playoff goal and I got an assist.

By this time we had become pretty well known throughout the NHL and there were rumors that the Rangers were after us. John Ferguson had moved to New York and there was a lot of behind-the-scenes maneuvering to get us.

Meanwhile, Anders and I had become free agents as far as the NHL was concerned, so we had a chance in 1978 to go to any NHL team without compensation. Our lawyer was Don Baizley, who is based in Winnipeg. He and our wives traveled around to a lot of NHL teams who were interested in our services. We also had in mind that we wanted to play for a club that we thought had a chance to win the Stanley Cup or a club that we thought we could help to that goal. Eventually, the list was narrowed down to three teams, then two and, finally, we ended up with the Rangers.

At the time, a fellow named Sonny Werblin was running Madison Square Garden and the Rangers. He was a very flamboyant sports promoter who had once signed Joe Namath to be quarterback of the New York Jets before they won the Super Bowl. Werblin was determined to turn the Rangers into a winner and he was willing to spend money. Werblin was a terrific guy who really knew how to make people feel a part of the organization. When Anders and I came to New York, he gave us the royal treatment and created a great family atmosphere.

The whole Rangers' organization made the transition easier for Anders and me. It also didn't hurt that Fergie had put together a pretty good team in New York. Young guys like Pat Hickey, Don Maloney, Ronnie Greschner and Ron Duguay were coming into their own and we had some good goaltending with John Davidson and Wayne Thomas doing most of the work with Doug Soetaert in there, too.

Competition was very keen in my first NHL year. The Islanders, who had been getting better every season since they first made the playoffs in 1975, had finished first in our [Patrick] Division with 116 points and led every team in goal scoring. Mike Bossy led in goals [69], Bryan Trottier in assists [87] and Trottier also won the overall scoring championship [134].

The Flyers had a pretty good club as well — they finished second in the Patrick — and ended with a few more points than we did. Still, our record was good [40-29-11] and we were playing for a very creative coach in Fred Shero.

I was having a real good season until the Potvin incident and the injury. The way I look at it, with the four years in Winnipeg and all the physical abuse that I had taken, my body had started to deteriorate, hockey-wise. At that time I had had four knee operations.

Every so often I'm asked if I feel bitter toward Denis Potvin because of what happened that night. Not really. After all these years I have not seen the episode on a replay. Some people who have seen it have told me that it was a hard check but, then again, those things happen all the time on the ice. To this day, I have a lot of respect for Denis Potvin. He was a great player.

Sure, the Rangers' fans have been abusive toward him. I've said over and over again that I think the Rangers' fans are frustrated over the fact that Potvin has four Stanley Cup rings and we haven't won one on the Ranger side since 1940. That hurts a lot and it hurts even more to me because we had a chance to win it that year I got hurt, in 1979.

Everything came together for us just right in the playoffs. We beat Philadelphia, four games to one, and then went up against the Islanders. They were big favorites, but Shero's strategy was the same as it had been in 1974 when he coached the Flyers against Bobby Orr and the Bruins. He wanted to force Boston to have Orr carry the puck all the time and wear him down. That was what they did against Potvin and the Islanders.

We beat them 4-1 in the first game of the series at Nassau Coliseum and had them off-balance from that point on, even though they rebounded to win the second game in overtime, 4-3. We beat them at the Garden, 3-1 in Game Three and then they won another OT game on our rink to tie the series.

The big one was Game Five. We beat them on their ice and wrapped it up at home, 2-1. It was a terrific upset and then we took on the Canadiens in the finals. We got the jump on them in the first game but they took over from there, and that was that.

The injury had kept me out of all but two playoff games. From that point on it became more and more difficult for me to play. My heart told me I should play and I wanted badly to play, but by the early 1980s my body couldn't take the physical contact any more. It was hard to accept because I so badly wanted to play. But my body had the final say.